SOCIAL WORK THEORY & PRACTICE

SOCIAL WORK THEORY & PRACTICE

LESLEY DEACON & STEPHEN J. MACDONALD

MASTERING Social Work Practice

Learning Matters
An imprint of SAGE Publications Ltd
1 Oliver's Yard
55 City Road
London EC1Y 1SP

SAGE Publications Inc.
2455 Teller Road
Thousand Oaks, California 91320

SAGE Publications India Pvt Ltd
B 1/I 1 Mohan Cooperative Industrial Area
Mathura Road
New Delhi 110 044

SAGE Publications Asia-Pacific Pte Ltd
3 Church Street
#10-04 Samsung Hub
Singapore 049483

Editor: Kate Wharton
Development editor: Lauren Simpson
Production controller: Chris Marke
Project management: Deer Park Productions
Marketing manager: Camille Richmond
Cover design: Wendy Scott
Typeset by: C&M Digitals (P) Ltd, Chennai, India
Printed by CPI Group (UK) Ltd, Croydon, CR0 4YY

Library of Congress Control Number: 2016954952

British Library Cataloguing in Publication Data

A catalogue record for this book is available from
the British Library

ISBN 978-1-4739-5869-2
ISBN 978-1-4739-5870-8 (pbk)

Contents

About the authors

Dr Lesley Deacon is a Senior Lecturer in Applied Social Studies and Social Work, and Faculty Disability Tutor at the University of Sunderland (which she joined in 2011). Prior to this she was a practising social worker within safeguarding children with a particular interest in parents with learning disabilities. She teaches theory, research and practice across the BA and MA Social Work programmes and the BSc Health and Social Care. She is also programme leader for the Foundation Degree in Health and Social Care. Her research is primarily focused on how generic health and social care services respond to people who have more specialised needs. In her current research she is co-researcher with Dr Stephen J Macdonald researching the relationship between dyslexia, homelessness and substance use; as well as missed opportunities for intervention. The final part of the research will focus on health and social care practitioners in order to understand how they respond to adult service users who may have particular needs in relation to their dyslexia.

Dr Stephen J Macdonald is a Reader in Social Science. He joined the University of Sunderland in 2005 and is now the strand leader for the Centre for Applied Social Sciences. He teaches undergraduates and postgraduates in sociology, criminology, education, social work and social care. Stephen has published broadly in the areas of dyslexia and social exclusion, including issues concerning diagnosis, educational disengagement, digital inclusion, crime, victimisation and homelessness. His work is underpinned by the social model of disability. Stephen is also the associate editor for *Insights on Learning Disabilities (ILD),* an international journal. He is also a Fellow of the Higher Education Academy. In his present research, he is investigating the relationship between dyslexia and homelessness and disability and hate crime.

Professor Catherine Donovan is a Professor in Social Relations and Head of the Centre for Applied Social Sciences at the University of Sunderland. She is part of the Sociology programme team, teaching the sociology of family, gender and sexuality as well as the sociology of health and gendered violence. Catherine has spent nearly 30 years researching the intimate and family lives of lesbians, gay and, more recently, bisexual and trans-people. Her recent co-authored book, *Domestic Violence and Sexuality: What's love got to do with it?* reports on the first study comparing love and violence in heterosexual and same sex relationships with a focus on how love is implicated in violent and abusive relationships. Catherine led the Coral Project, an ESRC collaborative project focusing for the first time on the abusive behaviours of LGBT people in their intimate relationships. She is also involved with a collaborative project on hate incidents; a survey of victimisation and perpetration in student populations;

and is developing a Bystander Intervention Programme. Catherine is also working in collaboration with colleagues at Huddersfield, Sheffield Hallam and an independent research organisation to develop projects on child sexual exploitation and sex and relationship education for young LGB and/or T people.

Jane Tunmore is a Principal Lecturer and team leader of Applied Social Studies at the University of Sunderland. She is responsible for the BA (Hons) Social Work, MA Social Work and BA (Hons) Youth and Community Work. She has taught across all areas of the curriculum in Social Work with a particular interest in social policy, law, social work practice skills and sociological theory in social work practice. She is a qualified social worker with experience working in mental health and safeguarding children.

Alan Marshall is a Lecturer in Social Work at the University of Sunderland where he has been teaching for the past three years. His responsibilities include being the admissions tutor for the BA (Hons) Social Work, supporting learners, teaching and module development. He runs the mental health teaching and teaches around social work theories, social policy, law and ADP. He has experience in working with people with mental health difficulties, practice education and working with street homeless adults. As a social worker he worked in integrated CMHTs in central London for ten years and West Yorkshire for two years. Alan completed his initial degree at the University of Hull in 1991. Before formally becoming a social worker Alan had also worked in care homes supporting adults with mental health difficulties to manage the transition from long-stay hospital environments to community living. Alan is trained as an AMHP and a stage 2 Practice Educator. His academic interests are identity, anti-discriminatory practice, mental health and risk assessments.

Mark Bradley is a Social Work Practitioner currently practising in a front-line Child Protection Team in the North East of England. Coming from a military and law enforcement background, Mark became a qualified social worker in 2014 after gaining a first class award for his BA (Hons) Social Work at the University of Sunderland. Mark has a keen interest in research and recently began the pursuit of his PhD in 2015; he is particularly interested in researching the sexual abuse of children with learning disabilities. In practice, Mark is fascinated with the concept of the reflexive-practitioner (which, of course, he considers himself to be) and is taking his theoretical knowledge of this first-hand into social work practice.

Acknowledgements

Lesley Deacon would like to thank the following people at the University of Sunderland: Stephen J Maconald, her research mentor, for working with her on this project; all the authors who contributed to this book; and Jane Tunmore, her line manager, for supporting her. At SAGE, she is grateful to Kate Wharton for being so supportive of the proposal; and all the staff for their excellent work on the book. Finally, she would particularly like to Matt and Jake Deacon for their huge encouragement, support and unofficial work on this book! She would like to dedicate this book to David Staward.

Stephen J Macdonald would like to dedicate this book to Jude, Jamie and Claire Macdonald.

Introduction

Lesley Deacon

The intention of this book is to introduce students and social work practitioners to key theories in understanding individuals' experiences and behaviour in the course of social work practice today. The theories covered are not meant to be an exhaustive list but to give a flavour of some of the key areas of theory that students and practitioners alike need to consider in order to understand service users and carers that they encounter in practice. Chapter 1 sets out the theoretical paradigm applied to this book, which is also applied to the way in which social work theory is taught at the University of Sunderland, where all the authors and contributors teach and research.

It is important to note that the way in which this book is written is to try and explain the theories in clear language in order to remove some of the barriers students and social work practitioners feel exist between them, their practice – and their understanding of theory. Certain theoretical terminology is necessary but where this is used explanations are given. The intention of this is to equip the reader with the knowledge and understanding of theory in order for them to research further.

Each chapter sets out the key principles of the theory concerned and demonstrates to the reader how they may be applied to practice through debates, activities and case study examples. Throughout this book you are likely to encounter the phrase 'core social work values'. In order to explain exactly what this means would actually require another book(!) – however, what we refer to here is the ethics and values that underpin social work practice. According to BASW (2012) *Social work grew out of humanitarian and democratic ideals, and its values are based on respect for the equality, worth, and dignity of all people* (p5) and it is to these that we refer. What is significant about case study application is the use of a real situation through a Serious Case Review (SCR). The SCR concerned is from Manchester Safeguarding Children's Board, Child Z in September 2013 (www.manchesterscb.org.uk/prof-scr.asp). This is a public document which can be accessed online. Each chapter addresses an aspect of this case and demonstrates how the theoretical perspective considered can be applied in order to help understanding of the service users and carers concerned – either their behaviour or experiences. It is important to note that these applications are not meant to question or criticise the SCR or anyone involved but to raise questions to facilitate understanding. It is the authors' understanding that this is a unique idea in order to help students and practitioners understand applied theory in social work – by seeing the same case study (which is real) considered throughout the book.

The way in which the chapters are written are based on lectures given by the authors on both the BA and MA Social Work programmes at the University of Sunderland. The intention is, therefore, to explain the key principles of the theories and then illustrate understanding of them with examples and explanation. It is anticipated that this will make the theories (and theory in general) more accessible and understandable to students and social work practitioners.

The book is divided into five main theoretical realms: Psychological, Sociological, Ethics and Moral Philosophies, Political Theories and Ideologies, and Organisational Theories. Each Part consists of a brief introduction to the focus of that Part as well as a brief summary of each chapter within.

Focusing on psychological theories first (Part One) does not determine their theoretical authority in social work practice but simply the theoretical origins of the profession. The Casework principle of the first social work professionals was based in psychological thinking so it is not possible to consider essential social work theoretical perspectives today without considering their foundations. Stephen J Macdonald sets out the key schools of thought: Psychoanalysis, Behaviourist, Cognitive and Humanist – these are all key ways of thinking in order to understand human behaviour in different ways. Attachment theory is often a key theory referred to in social work practice. However, while it is relevant it is by no means the only psychological theory that can help to understand people and their relationships to others. This section is completed by Lesley Deacon who summarises key theories in Human Growth and Development, specifically the work of Erik Erikson which is relevant and helpful to social work practice today.

Part Two focuses in on some sociological theories that have influenced theoretical understanding in social work practice from their origins around the mid-twentieth century onwards. Jane Tunmore sets out Social Constructionism in order to help the reader begin to think sociologically. She then addresses the General Systems and Ecological Theories, which are often the go-to theories used in social work practice as they are evident in the assessment model. This chapter specifically focuses on the underpinning theories as students and practitioners often go to the framework first, i.e. the model *that set{s} out a clear sequence of actions to take when we are faced with a particular situation* (Payne, 2014, p8). In considering and applying theory into practice it is imperative that the underpinning theory is understood in order to understand how and in what way people and their behaviours and experiences are being viewed. Catherine Donovan introduces students and social work practitioners to the key developments in feminist theories and how these are applied to social work practice. She raises questions regarding the assumptions made concerning gender identity which happen in social work practice and specifically focuses on the issue of domestic violence from the SCR. Finally, in this part, Mark Bradley who is a practising social worker considers the sociological theory of Reflexivity – framing the concept of Reflection in Action into a theoretical basis.

Part Three introduces Ethics and Moral Philosophies – each of the chapters in this section is written by Lesley Deacon. A problem in ethical thinking in social work practice today is that there is too much focus on rule-following (i.e. legislation, policy and organisational procedures) and not enough time spent on the fundamental principles that underpin social work practice (i.e. the concern for other people). Lesley Deacon therefore focuses on the Moral Philosophies of Deontology, Utilitarianism, Virtue Ethics, Ethics of Care and Radical Ethics in order to stimulate a different way of thinking about the relationship between the service user and the social work practitioner.

Part Four concerns some key developments in political theory that are intrinsic to social work practice today. Lesley Deacon sets out the historical development of Radical Social Work and its increasing relevance to social work practice today. Stephen J Macdonald then highlights the key models to understand disability of which, he argues, there are five. Although these identifications may not be acknowledged by others, this can be helpful for student social workers and practitioners in order to understand more fully the key principles of the different perspectives. Finally, Alan Marshall presents an understanding of the theoretical basis of Anti-Discriminatory and Anti-Oppressive Practice using the concept of racism to present applied understanding. At the time of writing this book the issue of racism has become more prominent again due to the outcome of the Brexit vote (2016) and the demonstrations concerning #blackmatters (2016).

Finally, Part Five covers Organisational Theories, written by Lesley Deacon. Readers may initially wonder at the relevance of this Part to social work practice. While the theories set out do not specifically concern the behaviour and/or experiences of service users and carers, they do concern the experiences of students and social work practitioners in practice environments; and therefore have an indirect impact on the experiences of service users and carers. Lesley Deacon sets out these chapters initially considering management theory and then organisational theory. Management theories are relevant not just to managers but also to those who are managed and how they work with their manager and colleagues. Charles Handy's work *Organisational Culture* is used as the basis for Chapter 20 as it is still as relevant today as it was at the time of writing.

To conclude, Lesley Deacon and Stephen J Macdonald draw the book together at the end with some concluding remarks about social work theory and practice and its future development.

Chapter 1

Introduction to social work theory

Lesley Deacon

Achieving a Social Work Degree

This chapter will help you meet the following capabilities, to the appropriate level, from the Professional Capabilities Framework:

PCF 5 Knowledge

- Demonstrate an initial understanding of the application of research, theory and knowledge from sociology, social policy, psychology, health and human growth; and demonstrate an initial understanding of the range of theories and models for social work intervention;

PCF 8 Context and Organisations

- Demonstrate awareness of the impact of organisational context on social work practice.

What is social work theory?

While there may be different ways to describe and understand the concept of a theory, according to Payne (2014) *a theory is a generalised set of ideas that describes and explains our knowledge of the world around us in an organized way* (p5). So, taking this to a social work perspective, it can be suggested that social work theory is 'a generalised set of ideas that describes and explains' people and how they can be understood. Rather than considering two separate issues of social work *and* theory, it is important for social workers to have a theoretical perspective that is compatible with both the ethos of the practice itself and of the theoretical understanding of people and their behaviour and experiences. This chapter will therefore set out how social work theory has developed as an entity in its own right, and how it can be understood in practice. It therefore begins with an overview of the theoretical perspectives of social work practice from the origins of the Charity Organisation Society (COS) and considers other key historical events that influence social work's theoretical paradigms to the present day. Following this, the reader is introduced to the concept of the Theory Circle by Collingwood et al. (2008), which is presented not just as a tool or model but as a theoretical framework for understanding the concept of social work theory.

Overview of social work and thinking about theory

To understand social work theory, first social work as a profession needs to be understood as well as its intentions in terms of working with, and understanding, people and their experiences. Knowledge about social work *is in a constant state of flux and might best be described as a continuing activity that is formed and reformed over time* (Gray and Webb, 2013, p2). There is no doubt that this is influenced by and, it could be argued, beholden to the political climate in which it is practised. When considering the historical context in which the first official social work organisation, the Charity Organisation Society (COS), emerged we must first consider the repercussions of the Industrial Revolution, and the significant historical time period of industrialisation (1700–1850) that led to a need for a society to address issues concerning the *social impact of the factory system* (King and Timmins, 2001, p10).

The ramification of this period of time was the large-scale movement of people from rural communities to urban towns and cities. Where communities had previously been able to support some residents when in need, this became problematic in urban environments. It could be argued that this was in part related to the speed in which these urban areas grew (King and Timmins, 2001), presenting the practical problem of adjusting to these numbers. Therefore, an inability to work became a key factor in terms of views regarding morality. There were strong views in society that idleness was part of a morally deficient character and so philanthropy should not be encouraged for fear that this in itself encouraged idleness. And it was in this context that the COS emerged in 1869 with its initial intention to prevent philanthropy (where the rich willingly shared some of their wealth) as it was perceived that it encouraged the poor to remain so. Charles Stewart Loch was the first secretary of the COS between 1875 and 1913 and the ethos of this organisation was that poverty was caused by the moral failing of the individual and so assessments by the COS concerned the worthiness of individuals. When considering the concept of assessment in social work practice, we must consider its historical conception as a tool for assessing worthiness – whether an individual should be given support or not. These were the origins of the concept of casework – to find the problem in the individual (Glasby, 2007; Howe, 2009). When considering the theoretical basis of this understanding of people we can see different theoretical perspectives emerge: those of moral reasoning regarding worthiness; and a psychological focus on the inadequate adaptation by the individual. This focus meant that the theoretical paradigm of initial social work practice was on the need for the individual to be changed in order to fit in. Society was not to blame for poverty and instead there was a need to teach people to manage their weaknesses.

These events were closely followed by a very different focus to social problems, i.e. social enquiry. This was the work of Canon Samuel Augustus Barnett (1844–1913) who was the founder of the Settlement movement. Although visits to people's homes had become common, the intention of Barnett and his colleagues was to live among the poor in order to understand them. This was considered, working 'in the field' and they found themselves welcomed for example in workhouses (Beauman, 1996, p xxiii). Through this work they were able to identify that the problems being experienced were caused, not by the people themselves, but by the structures in society. The theoretical basis for this work was therefore a sociological one, which was also, it could be argued, the initial origins of a more radical focus for social work. The emphasis of this movement was that of social change and action, led predominantly by those who had been university educated (Beauman, 1996; Glasby, 2007).

The radical concept of social work developed further following the Second World War (1939–1945), which led to the development of the Welfare State (the National Assistance Act in 1948). The separation of social welfare and social care technically removed the concept of *poverty* from social work provision (Glasby, 2007). However, it was evident that this was still a contributing factor in people's lives and when this was not resolved the influence of university education on social work practice was further developed, from the 1960s onwards. Here we see the significant influence of radical social work theory with an emphasis on social action by Brake and Bailey in their seminal work *Radical Social Work and Practice* (1975). This and further politically driven theoretical perspectives such as the Social Model of Disability and Anti-Discriminatory and Anti-Oppressive Practice are significant political theories which have influenced the theoretical basis of social work. This was also a significant period of time for the influence of feminist theories in social work practice, the origins of which can be seen in the settlement movement in the 1800s (Beauman, 1996).

Political changes during the 1980s under Margaret Thatcher's Conservative government have had a lasting impact on the way in which today's social work is practised and its theoretical basis. At that time, public services were seen as inefficient and a new political movement attempted to move away from what was viewed as the *paternalism* of the Welfare State (Aldgate et al., 2007). The origins of a management-focused driver for social work can be seen in the application of management theories and concepts such as New Public Management (NPM) from this period onwards, which were further re-enforced by the Third Way Agenda of the Labour Party from

1997 onwards leading to an individualist neo-liberalist-focused society. This is felt more so today than ever due to imposed austerity measures by the Coalition (2010) and then Conservative government (2015). There is no one accepted definition of NPM but it must entail application of private business ideas to public institutions with a focus on outcomes and targets rather than processes; and the power moved from the professionals (social workers) to the managers to drive change (Aldgate et al., 2007). A significant change in terms of service users was the shift to service user involvement in the design and delivery of services rather than as 'passive recipients' (DoH, 2010) and this continued with New Labour in the form of public and patient involvement (DoH, 1999; DoH, 2000a; DoH, 2000b). While significant changes happened during the Coalition government (up to 2015) the management and neo-liberalist theoretical basis for social work remains.

So, what is social work theory?

What should be evident from this brief historical overview of key events in social work as a profession is its eclectic nature with theoretical influences from: psychological; to sociological; to radical; to organisational; to neo-liberalist individualism. What we can see in this section is how these different theoretical perspectives have been applied to social work practice depending on the historical and social context. This goes someway to helping students understand why social work theory does not follow one particular theoretical discipline. Therefore, social work theory is eclectic and cannot be any other way. It reflects the changes in the views of society regarding people in need. Today, that mixture is seen depending on the political party in power and their agenda for sanctions or intervention.

The Theory Circle: theoretical framework

The Theory Circle by Collingwood et al. (2008) sets out a framework for social work students and practitioners to help make sense of social work theory. As the authors themselves note:

> *Social Workers have grappled for many years now with the tension between theory and practice. The struggle may be to bridge a perceived gap between the academic knowledge base of social work and the complex realities of practice.*

> (Collingwood et al., 2008, p70)

As Teater (2010, p1) acknowledges, *[t]heory is an essential ingredient in practice that guides the way in which social workers view and approach individuals, groups, communities and society.* While not always commented upon by practitioners themselves, there is no doubt that theory underpins their understanding of, and interaction with, service users in practice. These are sometimes viewed as *assumptions and beliefs* that guide practice rather than recognition of the theories themselves (Teater, 2010, p1). However, this does not acknowledge the significance of theoretical perspectives which guide social work practitioners to help them understand themselves, others, society and their own practice. There often appears to be an apathy, or sometimes even fear, by social workers to consciously recognise theory as being significant for social work practice. The intention of using the Theory Circle as a theoretical framework is an attempt to contextualise theory into practice in a clearer way for social work students and practitioners (Collingwood et al., 2008).

The Theory Circle was devised by Collingwood et al. (2008) in recognition of the need to identify the *formal knowledge base for {social work} practice* and for theory to be integrated in practice (pp71–2). They refer to this 'formal knowledge base' being guided by academic disciplines such as those listed in this chapter (i.e. psychological, sociological, ideological) which, according to the authors, is what 'equips' social work students and practitioners with the tools to help understand a service user's behaviour and (or) their experience/s.

Before an appropriate theoretical perspective can be considered, however, the student or practitioner is required to investigate the service user's life: their experiences and their behaviour, etc. This forms the Service User Profile (KIT). Each piece of information is then analysed and considered against an understanding of relevant theoretical perspectives (Collingwood et al., 2008). The *theory to inform* concerns identifying appropriate theories to underpin understanding of the key elements concerning the person's experiences and/or behaviour. The *theory to intervene* involves developing a strategy based on theoretical understanding for intervening in the service user's life, in order to change behaviour and improve outcomes. In essence, what Collingwood et al. (2008) have identified here is what constitutes social work theory. This is presented to students and practitioners as a simple formula:

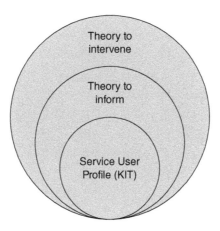

Figure 1.1   Diagram based on Collingwood et al.'s (2008) Theory Circle

Because of their practice-based focus, social work theories are not sufficient if all they do is help the social worker to understand a person's behaviour or experiences.

As a social worker, they also need to be able to intervene in a person's life and this intervention should also be underpinned by theory. This book therefore addresses the first part of Collingwood et al.'s (2008) Theory Circle: *theories to inform* in order to establish the foundation of understanding a service user's life.

Chapter Summary

This chapter has set out the context and influence of different theoretical paradigms in social work practice. It has suggested that social work theory is underpinned by Collingwood et al.'s (2008) Theory Circle, which provides students and practitioners with a theoretical framework for understanding service users and social work intervention.

Further Reading

Collingwood, P, Emond, R and Woodward, R (2008) The Theory Circle: A tool for learning and practice. *Social Work Education*, 27(1): 70–83.

Gray, M and Webb, SA (eds) (2013) *Social Work Theories and Methods* (2nd edition). London: SAGE Publications.

Healy, K (2005) *Social Work Theories in Context: Creating Frameworks for Practice*. Basingstoke: Palgrave Macmillan.

Howe, D (2009) *A Brief Introduction to Social Work Theory*. Basingstoke: Palgrave Macmillan.

Payne, M (2014) *Modern Social Work Theory* (4th edition). Basingstoke: Palgrave Macmillan.

Teater, B (2010) *An Introduction to Applying Social Work Theories and Methods*. Maidenhead: Open University Press.

Introduction to Part One – Psychological Theories

Initial thinking about psychology can occur when our thoughts turn to questions regarding *why people do what they do or how their personalities differ* (Nevid, 2012, p2). This means we are questioning the individual psychology of others and how this compares to ourselves and what we know. Psychologists are primarily focused on the study of behaviour, be that in humans or in animal life, and in doing so to understand the mind. The five chapters in this section of the book initially address the four main schools of psychological thought: Psychoanalysis; Behaviourist; Cognitive and Humanist. Each of these chapters is written by Stephen J Macdonald to assist social work students and practitioners to understand the psychological basis of social work (as set out in Chapter 1).

It is imperative that in order to understand and be able to apply psychological-based theories in practice, that social work students and practitioners must first have knowledge of these key schools of psychological thought. It is also imperative that on reading these, that social work practitioners are concerned ethically with the way psychological experiments were conducted as well as the challenges that applying psychological theories can lead to in social work practice – for example, the focus on individual pathology being in some way *maladaptive,* i.e. the individual's inability to adapt themselves to their environment.

This section finishes with a chapter introducing the idea of Human Growth and Development across the lifespan, which is common to understanding people in social work practice. This chapter, written by Lesley Deacon, primarily focuses on the work of Erik Erikson (psychosocial theorist) in order to begin to see the emergence of an additional sociological focus, blended with the psychological one.

Chapter 2

Psychoanalysis, psychodynamics and social work practice: the conflicted 'self'

Stephen J Macdonald

Achieving a Social Work Degree

This chapter will help you meet the following capabilities, to the appropriate level, from the Professional Capabilities Framework:

PCF 1 Professionalism

- Describe the role of a social worker and the importance of personal and professional boundaries and behaviour, demonstrate ability to learn using a range of approaches;

PCF 2 Values and Ethics

- Understand the professional's ethical principles and their relevance to practice, and demonstrate awareness of own personal values and how these can impact on practice;

PCF 3 Diversity

- Recognise the importance of diversity in human identity and experience, and the application of anti-discriminatory and anti-oppressive principles in social work practice;

PCF 4 Rights, Justice and Economic Wellbeing

- Understand the principles of rights, justice and economic wellbeing, and their significance for social work practice;

PCF 5 Knowledge

- Demonstrate an initial understanding of the application of research, theory and knowledge from sociology, social policy, psychology, health and human growth and development to social work;

PCF 6 Critical Reflection and Analysis

- Understand the need to construct hypotheses in social work practice;

PCF 7 Intervention and Skills

- Demonstrate an awareness of a range of frameworks to assess and plan intervention and demonstrate initial awareness of risk and safeguarding;

PCF 8 Context and Organisations

- Demonstrate awareness of the impact of organisational context on social work practice.

Introduction

When working in the field of social work, it is important to recognise the complex nature of negative, destructive and dangerous behaviours, and it is imperative to try to understand these behaviours from different perspectives. So, rather than accepting behaviour and social interactions at face value it is vital to attempt to comprehend how and why these behaviours manifest themselves in particular spaces and at particular points in individuals' lives. From a psychoanalytical perspective, behaviour is a result of unconscious responses to certain situations, which are in turn influenced by early life experiences that affect emotional development.

In order to understand issues that social workers are confronted with on a daily basis, such as domestic violence, substance and alcohol use/addiction, child neglect, etc., practitioners must consider, in a non-judgemental way, *why* individuals, partners, parents/guardians, families and communities may be displaying these negative and destructive behaviours. Therefore, this chapter will explore the key ideas that underpin *psychodynamics* as a school of thought within psychology and social work practice. It will begin with a look at how it developed as a means of trying to understand the complexities of behaviours and human development by considering how *early* experiences can affect the emotional development of adult service users.

The chapter commences by examining key ideas that arose out of the work of Sigmund Freud, where we see an early representation of the mind which forms the bases of psychoanalysis, and this representation leads to the development of certain key principles of psychodynamics as applied to social work practice. Although Freud's research develops the foundation of psychoanalysis, this chapter also briefly examines how the works of Carl Jung, Melanie Klein, Jacques Lacan and Erik Erikson develop beyond Freud's initial ideas in order to understand how psychoanalysis evolved into psychodynamic theory. After the introduction to psychodynamics, the chapter will apply key ideas from this theoretical framework to the Serious Case Review (2013) of Child Z, therefore concluding by illustrating how psychodynamics can be useful in the social workers' toolkit in contemporary practice.

The history of psychodynamics

In order to understand psychodynamics, we need to explore a brief history of psychoanalytical theory. Psychoanalytical theory was developed from the work of Sigmund Freud, an Austrian medical doctor and neurologist. After working within the asylum system in Austria, he rejected some of the key ideas of his contemporaries which conceptualised behaviour/mental illness as being entrenched within a person's biology and neurology. For Freud (1916), the onset of mental distress was not due to biological dysfunction, but as a result of early childhood experiences, so instead Freud developed a theory which looked towards *nurture*, rather than nature. He identified a new form of therapy based on his unique representation of the mind, which was grounded in analysing adults' past experiences. This was because it is these experiences (Freud argued) that result in individuals behaving in particular ways in adult life. He suggested that scientific methods could help us to understand the formation of the mind by constructing a *model* of the mind, which could then be applied to interpret people's behaviours. For Freud, childhood experiences affect and construct our emotional development and determine our perceptions and personalities in adulthood. So stages of development become central to how the mind develops from birth to adulthood – this new way of thinking about emotional development and behaviour was *radical* at the time, as Freud went beyond the concept of consciousness, i.e. what we are aware of. He stated that consciousness is but a window into the mind and cannot on its own explain why adults behave in particular ways (1916).

Instead, Freud understood behaviour through *unconscious* desires, not just through our conscious experiences, and those unconscious desires develop out of experiences in our childhood. Freud attempts to understand behaviour through the *pre-conscious* and *unconscious* mind, and it is this model that lays the foundation for contemporary psychodynamic theory. What makes Freud's psychoanalytical approach unique is that he did not accept people's interpretations of their own experiences at face value. He rejected people's own explanations of their own behaviour and developed key principles that allowed psychoanalysts to reinterpret conscious experiences, and in some cases dreams, to reveal hidden meanings to explain behaviours. This was achieved by seeking clues to an individual's past experiences, which determine unconscious processes, which in turn influence present behaviours. In essence, we tell stories, and in these stories there are key symbols, meanings and clues that reveal our 'true' feelings and emotions, which are embedded within the unconscious part of our minds.

Activity 2.1

Think about dreams you have had, for example, before a big event such as an exam or an important meeting or home visit. What do you think your unconscious mind is trying to tell you about how you *really* feel?

The conscious, pre-conscious and unconscious mind

The general principle of Freud's psychoanalytical theory conceptualises the mind at three different levels. The *conscious* level is the part we can access and observe. The *unconscious* is the dominant part of our mind and its function is to store our past memories and past experiences, but it is inaccessible and we are completely unaware of it during general social interaction. There is also the *pre-conscious* level, which regulates and communicates between the conscious and unconscious parts of the mind, and it is this level which, although we are generally unaware of it, can be accessed through therapy. Only through the pre-conscious level can we attempt to analyse and interpret the unconscious level of the mind.

It should be noted that psychoanalysts are specifically interested in interpreting the unconscious. According to Freud (1916, 1961) many of our past experiences, in particular maturing as an infant, are unpleasant, and a natural defence mechanism is to bury these past experiences in our unconscious mind through what he refers to as 'repression' and, although we are unaware of those experiences, they create our identities, our emotional responses and our perceptions of the social world around us. Hence, it is the unconscious level which constructs our aspirations and determines our behaviours. For social work practitioners, this allows an analysis and interpretation of service users' behaviour especially when that might appear to be illogical, destructive or damaging. By applying psychoanalytical theory practitioners can begin to explore the possibility that a service user's past experiences are defining their present-day lives.

The id, ego and superego

Freud added to his theory by defining how the mind matures emotionally at different stages of a person's development through the *id*, the *ego* and the *superego*.

Id

First, Freud suggests, we are born with the *id*, which is our basic instincts. The id is constantly seeking pleasure, but it can also be violent. The id is submerged within our unconscious, although we can observe the id in a new-born infant, where the id constantly seeks pleasure through food, warmth, sleep, etc., and this is the central driving force in a child's *and* an adult's emotional development. Freud calls this the 'pleasure principle'; we all seek pleasure from the day we are born, so this is one of humanity's basic instincts.

Ego

Yet, from an early stage in our development, our mind recognises that we cannot be pleasured without developing strategies (i.e. engaging with reality) to fulfil our 'pleasure principle'. We need to eat, but in order to do this we need access to food, and therefore we need to strategically engage with reality in order to achieve this. Freud refers to this as the 'reality principle', and this instinct develops early in a child's life in order to appease the id – an example of this is when a baby cries to get food, to get cleaned, to get warmth. The 'reality principle' is enabling the survival of the infant child (and later allowing the child to function within the family unit and, ultimately, society), and this leads to the development of what Freud refers to as the *ego*, the key role of which is to appease the id by engaging with reality and developing plans of action.

Superego

Freud defines the final part of our emotional development as the development of the *superego*. Like the ego, the superego also grows to regulate the id, but where the ego matures to *appease* the id, the superego develops to *discipline* the id. So, the superego is the part of our personality that emerges through discipline, and this grows out of interactions with parents and later other sources of authority (i.e. education, religion, police officers, social workers, health workers, and other agents of the state). Therefore, the superego evolves our *morality*. The emergence of the id, ego and superego also creates internal conflict – the superego is constantly looking to suppress the id, whereas the id is continually looking to pleasure our basic needs. As the ego develops out of the reality principle, the ego's role develops to regulate both the id *and* the superego, and this interaction and conflict results in the formation of our personalities from an early stage of our development.

Equilibrium

As we emotionally develop, we see (ideally) equilibrium develop between the id, ego and superego. What Freud was attempting to accomplish was an understanding of the crucial stages of childhood development, which construct different aspects of our personalities. Successful progression through those stages of development is essential in order for individuals to grow into healthy and well-adjusted adults. If a stage of development is disrupted, and a part of our personalities becomes over- or underdeveloped, then this can cause behavioural problems and/or the onset of neurosis or psychosis in adult life. A simplistic example of this could be that an adult with an underdeveloped superego may be more likely to take risks or engage in criminal behaviour. This illustrates how an understanding of the id, ego and superego is important in social work practice, as our personalities and behaviours in adulthood may have been affected by disruptions in our emotional development. These developmental disruptions could directly explain why some service users display harmful, destructive or anti-social behaviours, which negatively affect themselves and their family members, and which may cause them to come to the attention of social or even criminal justice services.

So, from a social work perspective, to understand service user behaviour we must therefore try to understand a person's emotional journey, which has led to the development of their id, ego and superego.

Five stages of sexual development

When applying a psychoanalytical approach, Freud (1916, 1953) suggests that there are five stages of sexual development which take place during childhood:

- Oral stage (0–1)

- Anal stage (1–3)

- Phallic stage (3–6)

- Latency stage (5–puberty)

- Genital stage (puberty–maturity)

It should be noted that Freud (1916, 1953) suggests that the first three of these stages are the most important periods in the development of our personality and our emotions. By progressing through these stages we should see the emergence of our ego and superego, but after the third (phallic) stage these memories are repressed into our unconscious mind – we are unaware that we have been through them. These stages are complex, but there is a brief description of them below (further reading is recommended):

Table 2.1 Five stages of development

Oral stage (0–1)

- Infants are preoccupied with oral sensitivity
- Relationship between mother and child is central
- Child develops early behaviours through experiences of basic discipline
- Child is confronted by the reality principle (see *Ego* above)
- Ego starts to develop and id is repressed into the unconscious
- Bonding between the child and mother begins to develop
- Child needs to interact in different ways to please the mother and to gain food, but also needs to obey rules.

Anal stage (1–3)

- Infant becomes aware of capacity to excrete and urinate
- Child can gain pleasure going to the toilet, but also becomes aware of their ability to *control* capacity to excrete or urinate
- Child becomes aware that they can not only be controlled, but can rebel and even control its parents

- Superego starts to develop
- Child begins to develop recognition of self and the capacity to control and have power over the external world, i.e. hold in excretion against parental instruction (rather than just being controlled themselves).

Phallic stage (3–6)

- Awareness now concentrated around genital areas (awareness of maleness and femaleness)
- Child becomes aware of its own genitalia and sexuality starts to develop
- Complex system of sexuality and relationships start to emerge between child and parents (different depending on sex of child)
- In the Oedipus phase, boys start to develop sexual desires for the mother; therefore the bond between the young boy and mother is strengthened through emergence of the young boy's sexuality
- Young boy becomes aware of the father – male child desires to have sex with the mother but fears the father because of castration; therefore learns he cannot have sex with the mother
- As maleness starts to develop he overcomes this conflict; child then starts to relate to the father
- The Electra Complex for females is reversed, as girls start to desire the mother, but recognise that they cannot penetrate her – females are already castrated; because of this recognition, the girl starts to desire the father resulting in the development of female sexuality
- It is at the end of this stage where the ego and superego have fully developed.

Latency stage (5–puberty)

- If we have successfully been through the first three stages we repress those memories in our unconscious mind; thus we are no longer aware of having been through those stages
- Sexual desires become secondary, sexuality is repressed, and gender roles and social identities begin to emerge
- Pleasure is not obtained through our basic instincts (oral, anal or phallic) – we get pleasure through developing relationships with peers, parents, teachers, etc.
- Gain pleasure by interacting and developing new skills.

Genital stage (puberty–maturity)

- Awareness of reproduction
- If we have successfully been through the earlier stages, our sexuality emerges, and the Oedipus/Electra Complex re-emerges, but our desires are no longer for our parents – we start developing our sexual desires for our peers
- This leads us to develop healthy relationships with other people
- By this stage we should have developed equilibrium between the ego, superego and id.

If any of these stages are disrupted, then this can have long-lasting effects in adulthood, and may result in neurosis which impacts on our personalities, e.g. phobias or obsessions; or psychosis which transforms our personalities, e.g. mental illnesses such as schizophrenia.

Psychoanalysis vs psychodynamics

Up until this point the terms 'psychoanalysis' and 'psychodynamics' have been used interchangeably. However, there is a distinct difference between the two concepts, which relates to Freud's five stages of sexual development. When Freud (1916, 1961) describes the development of our personalities and the emergence of the id, ego and superego he gives a very specific description of how they emerge based on the five stages of sexual development, as seen above. It is at this point we see the divergence between psychoanalysis and psychodynamics: applying a psychoanalytical approach follows a Freudian tradition that applies the five stages of sexual development, whereas in psychodynamics there is often a *rejection* of these. Furthermore, although in psychodynamics the id, ego and superego are still applied, they emerge in different ways depending on the theorist.

Windows into the unconscious

In both psychoanalysis and psychodynamics, it is through language where clues can reveal our unconscious desires. How we use language can often expose our hidden but true feelings on a matter. (Language is considered from a different perspective in Chapter 7, Social Constructionism.) In psychoanalysis the 'slip of the tongue' can often reveal true feelings, for example 'I really hate... I mean love your new haircut'. In this example our superego regulates what we think we should say, but a 'Freudian slip' reveals our true feelings. Furthermore, when listening to statements people make, there can often be contradictory meanings.

Example

'I'm not racist, but within Britain there's a problem with immigration which affects employment for British nationals.' From a psychoanalytical perspective, the phrase 'I'm not racist' reveals the opposite. Therefore, when analysing people's narratives, certain statements can reveal hidden meanings that are embedded within a person's unconscious emotional beliefs and desires.

Activity 2.2

Think of some examples in your own social work practice, work or personal experience where you have heard these 'Freudian slips'.

A psychoanalyst is looking for key symbols, for windows into the preconscious level of the mind, which might reveal the unconscious processes of repression. Although a social worker is not expected to be a therapist there are a number of tools they can use in an attempt to analyse an individual's repressed thoughts. As Ann Freud (1936) suggests, there are five primary defence mechanisms of repression. These are:

Denial

Denial allows justification of why a person might engage in destructive behaviours (such as drug abuse, alcoholism, or violence) by rejecting the consequences of their actions. So although people can have knowledge of the impact of their behaviours (e.g. the health implications of excessive alcohol consumption), they can deny the consequences within their own internal realities (e.g. but it will not happen to me).

Projection

Projection is central to exposing a person's 'true' feelings. Projection involves individuals rejecting and not accepting their own thoughts, feelings and motivations, instead 'projecting' their own feelings onto other people during interaction. They may dislike someone, but because the superego attempts to discipline the id, they reject their own feelings of dislike and interpret them as if it is in fact the other person who dislikes them.

Displacement

Displacement is when individuals cannot satisfy their own impulses due to their personal situation. For example, they might be extremely frustrated with their employer, and when they go home they will 'displace' these feelings of aggression. They cannot attack their boss – they would lose their job. Therefore, they might go home and act aggressively or violently towards their family.

Regression

Regression is where, in cases of extreme stress, individuals' defence mechanisms break down and they revert to an early child-like state. Examples might be crying, thumb-sucking, bed-wetting, refusing to leave the house, etc.

Sublimation

Sublimation refers to impulses which may otherwise cause regression, but because they are regulated through (or managed by) the superego they look to alternative activities. These often manifest themselves in extreme exercise, physical activities or sport obsessions. Individuals might not be satisfied in their sexual relationship, career or family life, for example, but their superego stops them developing aggressive or anti-social behaviour. Therefore, they take up excessive running, weight-lifting, snowboarding, etc.

It should be noted that the relationship between the social worker and service user is central in order for any analysis of an individual's behaviour to take place. Psychoanalysis/psychodynamics cultivates an understanding of social interaction by attempting to analyse service users' unconscious desires, and this gives a social worker a toolkit to look for alternative reasons which underpin particular behaviours during a case within professional practice. However, a note of caution needs to be raised here: first, social workers are not trained psychoanalysts, and interpreting stages of sexual development is complex; and second, psychodynamics is not the only way of understanding a person's behaviour (see Part Two – Sociological Theories).

> **Activity 2.3**
>
> If you are working with a family where there is evidence of domestic violence (e.g. through police reports) what examples of defence mechanisms might you see?

Psychodynamics and the evolution of Freud's ideas

Although the principles of psychodynamics developed out of the work of Freud, other theorists have used his definition of the mind to understand behaviour, but rejected some of his key stages of sexual development. A brief summary will follow and it is recommended that students and social workers research these in more depth.

Carl Jung

Jung (1921), although accepting of Freud's concept of the id, ego and superego, rejected the importance of his stages of sexual development. He elaborated on the concept of the id, ego and superego in an attempt to explain cultural phenomena (such as the phallic nature of tall buildings) and social development through history. From a psychological perspective, Jung's most significant advancement in psychodynamics is the development of *personality types* – it was Jung (1971) that defined the concept of the *introvert* (someone who is inward-looking, quiet, likes being alone) and *extrovert* (someone who is outward-looking and likes being the focus of attention).

Melanie Klein

Klein (1932), similar to Jung, dismisses many of Freud's claims about the stages of sexual development; however, she does view the oral stage as of particular significance in a person's emotional development. She suggests it is during this stage where 'attachment' is formed between a baby and parent. Studies by Klein laid the foundation of John Bowlby's (1965, 1969) *Attachment Theory*, and thus, because of Klein's research, 'attachment' is now a major area of scholarship in social work.

Jacques Lacan

Interestingly, unlike the other theorists referenced, Lacan (1992) accepted Freud's original writings, *including* the stages of sexual development. However, he does not accept these in the literal sense – he suggests that our mind, through conscious and unconscious processes, is constructed by symbolic meanings of language produced within our cultural environments, e.g. the symbolic nature of the 'mother' rather than the literal meaning of a 'mother'. Therefore, Lacan viewed the formation of our conscious and unconscious minds entirely within these linguistic terms, through the attainment of language and symbolic meaning. Within the stages of childhood development, our unconscious processes, our emotional self, our personality and our identities are formed through discourse which creates cultural narratives which creates symbolic knowledge, i.e. knowledge that we have that is based on cultural interpretations.

Erik Erikson

Erikson (1964) did not reject the importance of stages of human development, but he did reject Freud's stages of sexual development. Although Erikson did not think sexuality was a central part of our personality formation, his work did encompass aspects of Freud's five stages of childhood development into his own *eight* stages of human development. For Erikson these stages of development start at birth and finish at death, thus we are emotionally maturing throughout our lives (see Chapter 6, Human Growth and Development).

Case Study: Serious Case Review

It must be re-stated that a social work practitioner is not a psychoanalyst or psychotherapist. Social workers are not required to make judgements about how specific experiences have affected service users' lives and have impacted on their emotional development with reference to the id, ego or superego. Yet, having knowledge of these concepts can be a useful tool in order to comprehend how past experiences *may* have had an impact on present behaviours. When applying psychodynamics to the SCR concerning Child Z (2013), it should be noted that FZ (the father) and MZ (the mother) had both endured domestic violence during their childhoods. From a psychoanalytical approach, FZ's emotional development may have been affected during this period of his life, and this is one possible factor that might help identify why he engages in violent and unpredictable behaviour. MZ also grew up with violence within her family, which again we can accept may have affected her emotionally. From a psychoanalytical approach, this could be one explanation why FZ has been able to exercise power over MZ, normalising violence within the home. There may even be some evidence to suggest that MZ blames herself for FZ's violent behaviours due to her suicide attempt noted in the case study.

We can also observe evidence of FZ and MZ presenting defence mechanisms in the case review. If we accept that FZ's emotional development may have been affected by his past experiences, we can observe evidence of 'displacement'. FZ seems to find it difficult to control his emotions and 'displaces' his frustrations through violence towards his partner and children. FZ also shows evidence of 'denial' in relation to his harmful behaviours, with reference to violence, drug use and the death of Child Z. We see evidence of this in his statements: such as he does not appear to acknowledge the impact that his violent behaviour has on family life; he does not concede that having a cannabis farm within the house might cause the

(Continued)

(Continued)

children harm; there is also no clear acknowledgment that the decision to leave his children unsupervised in the bath resulted in the death of Child Z. For this reason the child's death is possibly internalised as an 'accident'. Therefore, from a psychoanalytical perspective, both parents exhibit problematic behaviours which have *potentially* been influenced by childhood experiences, *potentially* having caused further neglect, violence and mental health problems in adulthood.

Chapter Summary

To conclude, what defines psychodynamics as a school of thought is the notion of the unconscious, preconscious and conscious processes that determine behaviour and social interactions. What unites psychologists and social workers (who apply psychodynamics as a theoretical framework) are that conscious behaviours taken at face value cannot by themselves *explain* actions and interactions. Conscious behaviours can only reveal hidden *clues* to unconscious desires and preconscious regulation of those desires. Therefore, as a social worker applying a psychodynamic approach to practice, we can understand that adult service user behaviour can be determined by past experiences, which can impact on their emotional responses to social situations and social interactions. To understand that behaviour we must consider how people's identities and personalities may have been formed by their emotional experiences, and the ways in which those experiences may have developed the equilibrium of their minds through their id, ego and superego.

Further Reading

Freud, S (1962) *The Ego and the Id. The Standard Edition of the Complete Psychological Works of Sigmund Freud*. London: W. Norton & Company. (Original work published 1923)

Nicolson, P and Bayne, R (2014) *Psychology for Social Work Theory and Practice*. Basingstoke: Palgrave Macmillan.

Chapter 3

Behaviourism and the science of control

Stephen J Macdonald

Achieving a Social Work Degree

This chapter will help you meet the following capabilities, to the appropriate level, from the Professional Capabilities Framework:

PCF 1 Professionalism

- Describe the role of a social worker and the importance of personal and professional boundaries and behaviour, demonstrate ability to learn using a range of approaches;

PCF 2 Values and Ethics

- Understand the professional's ethical principles and their relevance to practice, and demonstrate awareness of own personal values and how these can impact on practice;

PCF 3 Diversity

- Recognise the importance of diversity in human identity and experience, and the application of anti-discriminatory and anti-oppressive principles in social work practice;

PCF 4 Rights, Justice and Economic Wellbeing

- Understand the principles of rights, justice and economic wellbeing, and their significance for social work practice;

PCF 5 Knowledge

- Demonstrate an initial understanding of the application of research, theory and knowledge from sociology, social policy, psychology, health and human growth and development to social work;

PCF 6 Critical Reflection and Analysis

- Understand the need to construct hypotheses in social work practice;

PCF 7 Intervention and Skills

- Demonstrate an awareness of a range of frameworks to assess and plan intervention and demonstrate initial awareness of risk and safeguarding;

PCF 8 Context and Organisations

- Demonstrate awareness of the impact of organisational context on social work practice.

Introduction

When working in social work practice it is important to recognise that there are multiple ways of understanding why service users behave and interact in particular ways. The previous chapter discussed how psychodynamics offers social work practitioners the tools to analyse service user behaviours through interpreting their unconscious processes and their unconscious desires. This chapter offers an alternative option grounded in the theory of *behaviourism*, where actions and social interactions are understood in mechanistic terms, i.e. unthinking. As the reader will discover, behaviourism contradicts Freud's core explanations of behaviour (which he suggests are formed by our emotional development and our unconscious desires), instead it conceptualises social interactions based on the notion of 'conditioning'. This chapter will give a brief account of behaviourism and examine the work of some of its major proponents: Ivan Pavlov, John Watson and B.F. Skinner. The chapter will introduce the concepts of classical and radical behaviourism, which focus on conditioning and positive and negative reinforcement and the argument that they determine both animal and human behaviours.

Watson and Skinner endeavoured to develop a new type of psychology using scientific principles to understand behaviour, rejecting previous forms of 'introspection psychology', the examination of feelings, emotions and conscious thought (i.e. the subjective mind), and focused solely on observable behaviours. By considering the key principles of behaviourism and applying them to social work practice, this chapter will allow social work practitioners a pragmatic interpretation of behaviour through studying the concept of 'behavioural reinforcement'. The chapter will conclude by examining the work of Albert Bandura and discuss how behaviourism progresses into what we now refer to as 'social learning theory', exploring the concepts of 'attention, retention, reproduction and motivation' in order to make sense of the social actions and behaviours of service users.

Classical behaviourism

Ivan Pavlov

In order to understand behaviourism, we need to first discuss the work of Ivan Pavlov (1902). Through Pavlov's studies on animals (i.e. dogs) he discovered that the behaviour of his experimental animals could be controlled by a system of *reinforcement*. By controlling the dogs' external environment, Pavlov could produce *conditioned responses* in the form of observable behaviours. He noticed that when his lab technicians went to feed the dogs, the animals produced an increase of saliva (an unconditioned response). Thus, whenever the lab technicians came into his laboratory the dogs reacted as if they were going to get fed, even if they were not. Pavlov (1902) wanted to see if he could change the unconditioned stimulus (food) and unconditioned responses (saliva) into a *conditioned* stimulus and a *conditioned* response.

In the first stage of his experiment, every time the dogs were to be fed he would ring a bell. After a period of weeks, the dogs would associate the bell ringing with being fed. Pavlov measured the amount of saliva produced when the dogs were fed and a bell was rung, and then began to reduce the food the dogs would get, until finally the dogs were not fed at all. However, he carried on ringing the bell and measuring the saliva, and Pavlov observed that the dogs would produce the same amount of saliva when they heard the bell, even when they were not fed at all. Therefore, Pavlov had successfully produced a conditioned response in his dogs – all Pavlov now had to do was ring a bell (conditioned stimulus) and the dogs would produce saliva (conditioned response). What he realised was that he had manipulated the natural responses of the dogs, and had therefore unintentionally accomplished the first behavioural experiment, which transformed psychology from a theoretical discipline to that of a measurable science through the notion of reinforcement and conditioned behaviours.

John Watson

Although Pavlov developed the key concepts that underpin behaviourism, it is John Watson who is described as the founder of this form of psychology. Watson developed the 'behaviourist manifesto' and suggested that there is no difference between animal and human behaviours. Watson (1913) believed that by measuring, observing and manipulating behaviours psychology could discover universal laws that underpin human behaviours. He suggested that it is possible to set up experimental labs to scientifically measure not just animal behaviours but also human behaviour. It follows that if we can *measure* behaviour we can also *change* it through the practice of reinforcement similar to what Pavlov's experiments had demonstrated. Behaviour for Watson is entirely learnt, and if it is entirely learnt then that suggests it can be unlearnt, changed or manipulated. For Watson (1913) the objective of behavioural psychology is not just to understand behaviour but to *control* it. Watson believed that behavioural psychology could help us to understand why we behave in particular ways, and help us to develop knowledge about how to control behaviour to make a better society.

To demonstrate how Pavlov's work could be transferred from animal to human subjects he established what is now referred to as the 'Little Albert Experiment', to discover if he could condition a young child to develop a phobia. He introduced the child (Albert) to a white lab rat, and observed that Albert played with and touched the animal and showed no fear towards the rat. Watson then hit a piece of metal with a hammer to make a loud noise while the animal was present, and on hearing the loud noise Albert would automatically start crying. Albert was repeatedly introduced to the animal at the same time as hearing the loud noise. Watson then used the same technique as Pavlov and gradually stopped making the noise when the rat was introduced, until finally the noise was stopped altogether. The experiment concluded with Albert automatically crying every time he was introduced to a rat. Thus, Albert had developed a fear of rats, and Watson had successfully manipulated the environment by introducing a conditioned stimulus (a loud noise) to produce a conditioned response (a fear of rats) in a human.

Activity 3.1

While this is an important experiment to prove reinforcement works on children, consider some of the ethical concerns and social work values regarding these methods.

This led Watson to claim that all human behaviour is the result of conditioned and unconditioned responses to external stimuli, and all behaviours are a product of *nurture* rather than nature; hence external factors are critical in producing behaviours. Watson (1924) suggested that to develop a scientific form of psychology, we can only use what we can observe and measure, and the only thing we can observe is how people behave and react to particular environments. We cannot observe how people think or feel (this is subjective), therefore we cannot scientifically define the mind or our emotions – to describe why and how we think is immeasurable and unscientific. Thus the concept of the 'mind' is rejected in behavioural psychology.

Operant behaviourism

Emerging from the principles of John Watson's classical behaviourism, we see the development of what is referred to as 'operant behaviourism', and this is defined within the work of Burrhus Frederic Skinner (1938) who concurred with Watson's notion that the mind was immeasurable and psychology should not seek to scientifically understand this subjective entity. Nevertheless, Skinner (1938) viewed classical behaviourism as over-simplistic and suggested that in that form it could not explain the complexities of human behaviours. So in his research he attempted to progress classical behaviourism by building on the concept of reinforcement. Skinner suggested that human consciousness could be understood by observing human actions and reactions to their environments. What Skinner adds to classical behaviourism is the concept of neutral, positive and negative reinforcement, suggesting that to understand why people act in particular ways we must seek to understand how their behaviour has been shaped by those reinforcements, and by examining those reinforcements further behaviour can also be manipulated.

Activity 3.2

Skinner uses gambling as an example of reinforcement in action. Can you think of some examples you might meet in social work practice settings where certain behaviours can become addictive? Some examples could be drug use, alcohol use, violence.

The key concepts that underpin Skinner's (1938) work are:

- *positive reinforcement:* behaviour has been rewarded, so the environmental factors *increase* the probability of that behaviour being repeated;

- *negative reinforcement*: behaviour has been punished, so the environmental factors *decrease* the probability of that behaviour being repeated;

- *neutral operant:* behaviours have not been reinforced in either way, so environmental factors do not increase or decrease the probability of that behaviour being repeated.

To test these concepts, drawing on the behaviourist assumption that animals' simplistic behaviour can be used to explore complex human actions, Skinner (1948) set up a series of experiments with pigeons and rats. He trained rats and pigeons to give the impression that they could solve complex problems and even read simple signs. Of course they were not actually reading or engaging in complex thought processes, but through positive and negative reinforcements Skinner produced a set of behaviours, which made the behaviours of these animals *appear* complex. Skinner (1948) concluded his research by suggesting that all behaviours are shaped through the notion of rewards, proposing that animals and humans will always act in a way that will result in a positive outcome for them, and try to avoid a negative outcome. Skinner states that, in complex human behaviour, we make choices based on what we think will lead to positive outcomes for ourselves, and we learn how to adapt our behaviour to achieve those outcomes through our reactions to external positive and negative reinforcement.

Activity 3.3

Can you think of some examples from your own life that demonstrate positive reinforcement? For example, what kind of rewards might encourage certain behaviours?

Are there any ethical concerns regarding this in a social work practice environment?

Human behaviour, although complex, can be explained through layers of positive and negative reinforcements, giving the *impression* that we are acting because of 'rational choice' and 'free-will' when in fact we are just responding to those past reinforcements. In a social work setting, in order to better understand how and why people act and interact we must try to comprehend how their behaviour may have been positively and negatively reinforced within a range of social environments; for example, learned parenting skills from one generation to the next. By examining how a child's behaviour is influenced by these reinforcements we can not only explain childhood and adulthood behaviour, but Skinner (1953) also emphasises Watson's assumption that behaviour can be *manipulated* by reinforcing certain behaviours, for instance in order to create a future doctor, artist, criminal, lawyer, accountant, etc. It should be noted that this theory is not just relevant to childhood development but also explains adult behaviour. Adult behaviours are not necessarily determined by past childhood experiences, but their behaviours are constantly changed by positive and negative reinforcements. Therefore, adults are products of their past, present and future environments. We can easily observe examples of these positive and negative reinforcement within society: on a simplistic level, people go to work in order to earn a wage (positive reinforcement), and people don't commit crime because they may go to prison (negative reinforcement). Thus people's lives are controlled through a series of rewards and punishments. What makes Skinner's (1985) form of behaviourism radical is that he suggests that all behaviour can be *entirely* explained through the concept of positive and negative reinforcements, therefore rejecting free will as a myth.

Activity 3.4

If free will is a myth then is anybody truly responsible for their actions? What are the implications for social work practice in this case?

By applying behaviourism, this develops a distinct methodology to understand universal laws of behaviour. Both Watson and Skinner suggest humans are born with no conditioned behaviours. Once we are born, relationships are formed with our parents and behaviours develop due to environmental stimulus as a result of social interactions throughout a child's life. As the child gets older, it has access to a number of different environments (family; peers; school; sports; employment, etc.), which, through conditioned and unconditioned responses to stimulus, reinforce social and cultural rules resulting in individualised behaviours. Therefore, behavioural psychology explains all forms of social interaction by means of positive and negative reinforcements and conditioned responses. It is these concepts that define the principles of behaviourism.

Social learning theory

As behaviourism became the main school of thought in psychology in the 1960s, Albert Bandura transformed the work of Watson and Skinner with a series of experiments exploring learnt behaviour and violence. Bandura's (1961) research used the principles of behaviourism in a number of studies referred to as the 'Bobo Doll experiments'. Bandura devised experiments with children in order to observe whether violent behaviour was a result of nature, i.e. genetic factors, or nurture, i.e. environmental factors. He presented the children with an inflatable doll resembling a clown (referred to as a Bobo Doll), but when the Bobo Doll was presented to the children, the adult researchers would kick, punch and act violently around the Bobo Doll. Bandura then placed the Bobo Doll in an empty room and let the children have access to the doll. Interestingly, as soon as the children saw the Bobo Doll they replicated the violent behaviour they had observed in the adults. Hence, they seemed to have learnt the behaviour of the adults, suggesting that violence was learnt within a social environment. Bandura also noted that once a child had viewed violent behaviour towards the doll they were more likely to engage in violent play, compared with the children who had not witnessed violent behaviour in his experiments. Bandura concluded, based on his findings, that if a child observed violence, for example in the home or in their neighbourhoods, this would increase the likelihood of them acting in a violent manner.

What Bandura (1977) revealed went beyond the positive and negative reinforcement theory presented by Skinner. He suggested that to accurately understand behaviour, we need to think about how humans model their own behaviour on what they observe. The children in Bandura's experiment did not just copy behaviour, but modelled their own behaviour on that of the adults they observed. This led Bandura to develop the concept of what is now referred to as the 'role-model'. He concluded that human behaviours are far more complex than previously proposed by behaviourists, because most of the previous studies were based on animal experiments used to explain human behaviours. He suggests that if all behaviour could be controlled by positive and negative reinforcements then all children would act in similar ways in controlled environments, which is not the case. If we take education as an example, children all act very differently in this environment – many engage with education, but many disengage or rebel, rejecting school rules, disrupting classes and not responding to positive or negative reinforcements. Although Bandura (1977) did accept the significance of positive and negative reinforcement, he suggested that his findings reveal that children create a model of behaviours which they either copy or reject, and he suggested that in order to understand why certain behaviours are copied and others are rejected we must acknowledge the concepts of 'attention, retention, reproduction and motivation'.

Attention

In order for positive or negative reinforcement to change behaviour, individuals must first become aware of a particular behaviour and its result. Thus, attention is essential for a person to be able to learn a new behaviour within a social environment. It should be noted that individuals are exposed to hundreds of interactions on a daily basis, but many of them are forgotten (neutral reinforcements).

Retention

Once we have got the attention of a person, he/she must be able to remember the specific details of a particular behaviour. For learning to take place the individual must actively remember the precise features of the interaction in order to reproduce that behaviour at a later date.

Reproduction

Without the ability to reproduce an action, behaviour change cannot be accomplished. Therefore, not only do individuals need to be able to observe and remember behaviours, they also need to reproduce them. However, what makes humans unique is their ability to improve on something that they have learnt – not only can a person replicate a model of behaviour, they have the capacity to improve upon it, and can thus progress the behaviours beyond the original observed performance.

Motivation

What underpins all three stages of learning is a person's motivation. In order for learning to take place an individual must be motivated; there must be a particular drive to reproduce and perfect a particular behaviour. This motivation is often based on an expected reward, but it can be equally an expected punishment. An individual has the ability to evaluate the consequences of their actions, and the observed behaviour, even if positively reinforced, may be rejected by the individual if they consider their actions will lead to negative consequences, but if they perceive that their behaviours will lead to a positive outcome this may motivate them to reproduce the action. Hence, motivation is central to behavioural modification.

What Bandura's research offers is a more complex version of behaviourism, demonstrating why certain individuals may be motivated to learn particular skills, develop resilience and accept or reject certain behaviours. In social work practice this can be evidenced in the observation of siblings who can respond differently to situations depending on the reinforcement received. Bandura also demonstrates the importance of understanding the effect of social and cultural environmental factors on shaping behaviours, particularly family environments, friends and peers, the media, and sociological influences such as deprivation. More importantly, Bandura (1977) highlights the importance of understanding how learning takes place through the notion of incentives. Bandura does not reject the importance of unconditioned and conditioned responses, or positive and negative reinforcement, but develops these concepts through those of attention, retention, reproduction and motivation, therefore offering a more complex toolkit for understanding how human behaviour is learnt and modified. But by doing this, Bandura (1977) goes beyond the limits of behavioural psychology, outlining the importance of cognitive abilities during the learning process, laying the foundations of what will later be referred to as 'cognitive psychology' (see Chapter 4).

Case Study: Serious Case Review

By applying behaviourism to understand service user actions, this allows social workers to conceptualise behaviours as conditioned responses to environmental factors. These conditioned responses may have been formed through previous reinforced life experiences, which have facilitated service users to act, interact and behave in particular ways. If a behaviourist approach is applied to the SCR concerning Child Z (2013), we can see how negative behaviours have been reinforced throughout FZ (father) and MZ's (mother) lives. Both have witnessed and been a victim of domestic violence and abuse as children. Both FZ and MZ have matured in households where neglect was a common feature. For MZ, growing up in a household where domestic violence, neglect and poor parenting were an observable behaviour, we can make an assumption that this behaviour has been reinforced throughout MZ's life, although we don't know if that reinforcement has been positive or negative. Although MZ would have certainly recognised the negative connotations of this lifestyle, her conditioned responses seem to be more accepting than someone from a different family background. FZ matured in similar family circumstances and there seems to be some evidence that his behaviour has been shaped by his experiences within that environment. However, as Bandura (1977) indicates, reinforcement can only be successful if it is underpinned by motivation. For FZ, engaging in violent and abusive behaviour it could be suggested, has certain benefits within his life, such as access to a sexual relationship, a criminal career and a carer for himself and his children. For FZ the motivation behind his conditioned responses could be that it gives him power over his family unit. We can also see evidence that suggests that FZ may not have had the experience of a caring family member within earlier life – evidence of this can be observed in his apparent decision to leave two infants in an unsupervised bath.

(Continued)

(Continued)

From a behaviourist perspective, the behaviours of FZ and MZ could have been – and still can be – modified through the practice of reinforcement, conditioning and learning, e.g. through child protection plans; although behaviour modification does raise ethical concerns in social practice regarding values. (This element of control is discussed further in Chapter 16, Radical Social Work.)

Conclusion

Behaviourism as a school of thought in social work provides practitioners with a pragmatic understanding of how behaviour can be influenced through positive and negative reinforcement (Skinner, 1980). It provides social workers with an understanding of how behaviour becomes diversified due to the concept of modelling (Bandura, 1961, 1977). Furthermore, behaviourism demonstrates how, because of reinforced routines, our behaviour can be shaped without us consciously realising how it has happened (Watson and Rayner, 1920, 'Little Albert Experiment'), raising significant ethical questions concerning social work values. Therefore, behaviourism offers an alternative to psychodynamics, as the focus is on how service users may have been conditioned to behave in a certain way due to their family, local or cultural environments, rather than that behaviour being determined purely by unconscious processes and desires.

Behaviourism and social work practice

To conclude, behaviourism offers social workers an important perspective when understanding service user behaviour through a system of conditioned reinforcements. Behaviourism is a scientific model of analysing human interaction, emphasising the concept that practitioners can begin to understand why individuals act in particular ways by observing their behaviours. Unlike other forms of psychology, behaviours are conceptualised as conscious processes created by conditioned reinforcements throughout a person's life. Practitioners can attempt to understand what motivates individuals and the key external incentives that shape their behaviours. Social workers can also consider how certain behaviours have been positively and negatively reinforced throughout their lives, allowing practitioners an insight into why individuals model particular behaviours based on their past experiences and their present environments. Although childhood experiences are often important in determining how and why a person has learned certain behaviours, these behaviours are not only determined by their past. Hence, if we can understand how people have learned certain behaviours in the past then it is possible for those behaviours to be modified, changed or unlearned in the present and the future. Therefore, we have the potential to produce new behaviours through a system of reinforcement to allow individuals to create new models which can transform how they interact within their local and social environments.

Chapter Summary

Although it can be argued that behaviourism over-simplifies human behaviour, it does offer a genuine scientific and measurable method for analysing behaviour and social interaction. However, it should be noted that just because behaviourism can provide a scientific approach to social work practice, this does not necessarily mean it leads to the most effective interventions, and (as with all social work theories) it must be applied critically.

Further Reading

Nicolson, P and Bayne, R (2014) *Psychology for Social Work Theory and Practice.* Basingstoke: Palgrave Macmillan.

Chapter 4

Cognitive psychology and social work: A brave new world

Stephen J Macdonald

Achieving a Social Work Degree

This chapter will help you meet the following capabilities, to the appropriate level, from the Professional Capabilities Framework:

PCF 1 Professionalism

- Describe the role of a social worker and the importance of personal and professional boundaries and behaviour, demonstrate ability to learn using a range of approaches;

PCF 2 Values and Ethics

- Understand the professional's ethical principles and their relevance to practice, and demonstrate awareness of own personal values and how these can impact on practice;

PCF 3 Diversity

- Recognise the importance of diversity in human identity and experience, and the application of anti-discriminatory and anti-oppressive principles in social work practice;

PCF 4 Rights, Justice and Economic Wellbeing

- Understand the principles of rights, justice and economic wellbeing, and their significance for social work practice;

- Demonstrate an initial understanding of the application of research, theory and knowledge from sociology, social policy, psychology, health and human growth and development to social work;

- Understand the need to construct hypotheses in social work practice;

- Demonstrate an awareness of a range of frameworks to assess and plan intervention and demonstrate initial awareness of risk and safeguarding;

- Demonstrate awareness of the impact of organisational context on social work practice.

Introduction

This chapter will examine cognitive theory as a school of thought in psychology and social work practice. Cognitive theory develops out of key ideas that emerge from behaviourist research in the 1950s and 1960s. As with behaviourism, cognitive theory endeavours to apply scientific principles to explain human behaviour. Equally, the key emphasis of this theory is on exploring the concept of conscious behaviours which drive our decision-making abilities; thus, there is a rejection of the psychodynamic notion of unconsciousness. Cognitive theory not only attempts to explain behaviour but endeavours to define the mind through *mental processes*. In contemporary psychology, cognitive theory has become one of the most influential schools of thought and has led to new practices within counselling and therapy, as well as in social work, youth justice and probation work. This chapter will examine the history of cognitive psychology, and although there is no single scholar that led to the emergence of this theory, we will examine research from Albert Bandura as a basis for this framework. Although Bandura is often defined as a behaviourist, it is possible to view his work as a significant theoretical component which led to the rise of cognitive psychology. As discussed in Chapter 3, he expanded behaviourism to integrate features of memory and personal abilities, which establishes the foundation for studies into mental processes.

This chapter explores how, in order to explain the concept of mental processes, psychology looked towards the emerging field of computer science to help shape ideas about brain functioning. This conceptualises the brain as an information processor and, through means of coding and retrieving information, a manifestation called *cognition* results in complex human behaviours. The chapter will then expand on the notion of cognition by referring to research conducted by Jean Piaget on childhood development. Piaget progresses the concept of cognition by presenting evidence on how it occurs within key stages of development, from childhood to adolescence through to adulthood, suggesting that these stages lead us to develop our sense of self, individuality and identity. The chapter will then conclude by applying cognitive theory to social work practice, illustrating how, in order to comprehend human behaviour, we must conceptualise it in terms of learning processes. Thus, to make sense of how and why service users interact, behave and make life choices, we must consider how learning processes are affected by stages of cognitive development, mental capabilities and environmental factors.

From behaviourism to cognitive theory

Although Bandura is defined as a behaviourist in the previous chapter, within his research he establishes the concept of 'social learning theory'. As previously discussed, Bandura (1977) emphasised the importance of understanding how people *learn* behaviours, which affects how they act and interact within social environments. From Bandura's perspective, in order to understand behaviour change there needs to be an acknowledgment of how 'motivation, attention, retention, and reproduction' affect people's ability to learn new information. For Bandura (1977), a person's ability to 'retain' and 'reproduce' information is essential for learning to occur, but within his 'social learning theory' we see a shift away from some of the core principles of behaviourism (i.e. the concept that the mind cannot be scientifically identified). Hence, what Bandura develops in his work is how people's mental capacities affect their learning and behaviour change, referring to the impact that a person's *biology* has on the learning process. He suggests that behaviour occurs as a result of both social factors (i.e. the impacts of the environment that facilitate learning), and personal factors resulting from biological events (i.e. a person's ability to perform particular tasks based on their mental capacities). In Bandura's later work (1986) he recognises this shift and advances 'social learning theory' to 'social cognitive theory'.

The core concepts which underpin social cognitive theory are:

Observational modelling (learning)

For individuals to learn an observed behaviour, they must have the cognitive abilities and physical skills in order to repeat that behaviour, and key factors such as 'attention, retention, and reproduction' affect an individual's ability to do that. From this perspective, biological features interact with observable environmental events.

Outcome expectations

For learning to be reinforced an individual's expected beliefs based on the positive or negative consequences of behaviour are a central motivating factor which impacts on behaviour change. Social expectations impact on *how* individuals conceptualise these and this influences a person's ability to decide whether or not to model particular behaviours. For example, if the consequences appear positive then behaviour is likely to be modelled. Therefore, these belief systems are fundamental for the modelling of behaviours to occur.

Perceived self-efficacy

This refers to the internal processes which individuals engage with when learning particular skills or behaviours. In order for someone to learn a particular behaviour or skill they must believe that they have the ability to *succeed* at a particular task. If an individual has developed high levels of self-belief they have a greater chance of developing effective strategies to facilitate learning, e.g. having belief in their parenting skills reinforces the ability to demonstrate parenting skills.

Goal setting

Individuals must have the ability to reflect on their own behaviours and set goals and challenges which are motivating factors. Goals represent the perceived outcomes of a particular behaviour, and individuals set learning goals to anticipate and develop strategies in order to achieve *desired* outcomes. Therefore, individuals can adjust their performances in order to achieve particular outcomes during the learning process, e.g. setting a goal to return to college.

Self-regulation

When behaviour is modelled during the learning process, humans have the ability to self-regulate their own behaviour in accordance with environmental factors. An individual can manage their own thoughts and behaviours in order to achieve a particular outcome, and can monitor their own progression when learning particular skills. This allows an individual the ability to develop particular skills based on the regulation of their own behaviours in order to facilitate the learning process. For example, regulating the self to fit within certain environments can be positive, as a person adapts to their environment, or negative where a person can mask their true self and manipulate others' perceptions.

As we can see, Bandura is no longer just referring to an environmental stimulus which produces a response, but he is commenting on how learning occurs due to an individual's own mental processes, i.e. cognition. In order for cognition to take place the individual must copy, reproduce and perfect a desired skill. Social cognitive theory defines the concept of cognition through a system of learning, and cognition takes place by an interaction between our physical selves and the social environment, which produces complex behaviours that construct our personalities, identities and notions of self. Bandura (1977, 1986) not only describes the input of information resulting in the output of behaviours – he also refers to how an individual's mental processes affect a person's ability to learn and reproduce behaviours and actions. It is important to note that, according to Bandura (1986), individuals can still *choose* not to reproduce an observed behaviour.

From computer science to cognitive theory

Similar to behaviourism, cognitive theory defines itself as a scientific discipline. Although cognitive theory develops out of behaviourism, it is also progressed by disciplines outside of psychology, specifically within the area of computer science. Although social cognitive theory enhances behaviourist research by making reference to mental processes in the form of cognition, it does not explain how learning/cognition takes place. The concept of how learning occurs through cognition was modelled on the breakthroughs in computer science that occurred in the 1950s (Miller, 1956). As computer science began to advance, psychologists examined these developments for inspiration, noting that computer systems reduce complex information into small units of data for storage and in order to perform complex tasks. Thus, computers store data as codes in order to represent complex information. For example, computers can solve complex mathematical problems, beat adults at chess, operate life-support systems, and run and maintain key operations at nuclear power-plants – all of this is possible because of a very simple model of coding. Hence, we can input information into a computer, the information is stored as code, and then those codes can be used to produce an output, i.e. complete a task that appears to be very complex (Miller, 1956).

Psychologists have used this method of information storage and retrieval to understand how neurological brain function works. Developments in cognitive theory advocate that the human brain operates in a similar way to artificial intelligence, i.e. taking complex information, breaking it down and storing it in codes. It then reproduces this coded information as an output which can often seem very complex (Miller, 1956). This develops the notion that knowledge is obtained by information being 'inputted' into the brain, i.e. via learning, these inputs are then processed and stored in the brain in the form of codes, i.e. through mental processes (cognition), and this is then reproduced in the form of complex outputs, i.e. behaviours. Cognitive theory suggests the mind should not be defined as an abstract concept (see Psychodynamics, Chapter 2) but as an information output of the brain. From this perspective, the brain is a complex biological computer where information is stored in multiple brain areas which interact through neurological pathways (electric pulses which transfer coded data). Therefore, cognitive theory views cognition as a system of decoding information in order to produce behavioural outputs, and these cognitive behavioural outputs result in the generation of our *consciousness*.

To understand how cognition works within the brain a motorway metaphor is often used. This defines cognition through the notion of a road map (see Figure 4.1).

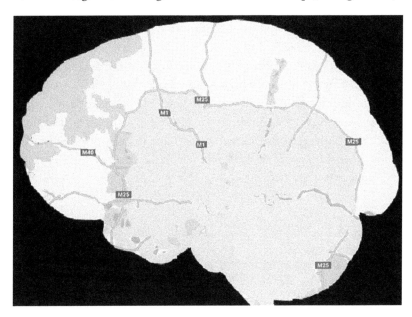

Figure 4.1

If we conceptualise the brain as a road map, then we are born with our motorways already in place. Our motorways are created by our genetics, which can affect how we learn or process information. At the point of birth, babies start learning new information which develops new cognitive pathways within the brain. The metaphor proposes that this cognitive development is represented by the A and B roads on the map (see Figure 4.2).

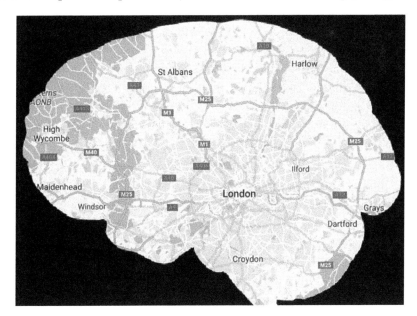

Figure 4.2

Although we are born with our motorways, through learning new information we develop a complex system of A and B roads that represent our neurological pathways established after birth. This suggests that behaviour is not only biologically determined (our motorways) but it is also affected just as much by our learnt environmental factors, which result in cognition (our A and B roads). From this perspective it is possible for cognition to compensate for any biological variations or 'weaknesses'; cognition can alter and sometimes override biological factors that individuals are born with. Therefore, cognition results in an individualised output which is referred to as the *mind*. This allows us to evolve language systems, develop complex relationships, create concepts such as culture, establish social networks and sustain societies. So cognitive psychology is the first school of thought that includes neurology within its explanation of human behaviour (Gross, 2015).

Activity 4.1

Using the concept of the road map, consider which aspects of your learning do you think were inherited (i.e. motorways) and which developed through your environment (i.e. A and B roads).

Stages of cognitive development

To understand how cognition takes place at different stages of an individual's life course, we must turn to the work of Jean Piaget. Piaget's research (1957, 1958) focuses on how cognition underpins childhood development. Piaget rejects the psychoanalytical approach of stages of sexual development and applies cognitive theory to comprehend childhood transitions. For Piaget, childhood development takes place in four observable stages of cognitive development ranging from birth to adulthood: the *sensory motor* stage, the *preoperational* stage, the *concrete operational* stage, and the *formal operational* stage. Although these stages are complex, a brief account of each follows, and they will also be covered in more detail in Chapter 6.

Sensory motor stage 0–2

The sensory motor stage is from birth to approximately two years old. Children develop their senses through touch and movement, and are only aware of the world around them based on information processed by their senses. Their senses are dominated by basic instincts, starting with the need for food, warmth and sleep, and progressing into skills such as basic speech and movement, in order for the child to interact with their environment. Children at this stage have not developed the complex learning skills which allow them to understand the concept of reality outside of their perception; reality only exists when the child observes it. For example, if a child views an object then it exists, but if the object is removed from view then the object disappears from the child's reality. At this stage cognition is learnt entirely from observation and touch.

The preoperational stage 2–7

The preoperational stage takes place approximately from two to seven years old. This is where basic language progresses into more complex forms of language. Although this is a period of significant development, children's problem-solving skills are still somewhat limited. In this stage children start processing more complex information from their environments. Thus, children recognise that objects exist even if they cannot observe them. During this period children learn basic problem-solving skills, such as how to open doors by turning handles. Role-play becomes a key facilitator of learning and cognition, as children start acting out what they observe around them or pretending to be fictional characters, e.g. acting out the roles of their parents or of a super-hero that they have observed on television. As a result of role-playing we see the emergence of other behaviours such as gender roles. During this stage children also start to develop cognition around peer interaction and basic social skills. As they learn from the environment around them the concept of stimulation within that environment becomes critical, i.e. the engagement and opportunities provided from the primary care givers.

Concrete operational stage 7–11

The concrete operational stage develops approximately between the ages of seven to eleven years. Children start developing more complex problem-solving skills. This is where children start developing more complex ideas, such as abstract thought and mathematical skills. They start understanding abstract concepts, such as how numbers can represent objects (i.e. statistics), and mathematics becomes very important as their problem-solving skills start to become advanced. Children progress to intermediate literacy skills and as their imagination develops they also start acquiring more artistic skills. With reference to cognitive development, art becomes a key skill which paves the way for further abstract thought.

Formal operational stage 11+

The formal operational stage is the final stage which takes place from the age of eleven years to adulthood. This is where children develop forms of advanced cognition and advanced social skills. Children start developing complex relationships outside the family, and they recognise the importance of these relationships. Children can comfortably engage in abstract thought and put themselves in other people's positions, which advances empathy and social conscience, acknowledging the rights and perspectives of people outside their community who they may never have met.

Similar to psychoanalysis, Piaget (1958) illustrates the importance of childhood development stages and their potential effect on adult behaviour. Unlike psychoanalysis, however, these stages are measurable and objective, and reveal how cognition takes place in a child's brain. Although Piaget suggests these key stages of development are universal in all cultures, he also acknowledges the important effect of the social environment on cognition; these stages can be affected by internal, social or cultural factors. From a social work perspective this means being aware of the influence of the environment a child is in and the opportunities for stimulation in order to develop their learning and cognitive development. Similar to psychoanalysis, individuals might not cognitively mature through all these stages, and this may impact on adult behaviour, but unlike psychoanalysis, behaviour problems can be accessed at any time, at a conscious level, which can result in further cognitive progress through learning, and result in behaviour change, i.e. being aware of lack of understanding and doing something about it. Piaget (1957, 1958) argues that cognition not only helps a child/adult develop new skills but also results in individuality, personality types, identity, gender formation and socio-cultural understandings of the external world.

Mental processes and schemas

From Piaget's (and Cook's, 1952) perspective, in order to understand how cognitive development occurs we must know how knowledge is decoded and stored within the brain. He develops the notion of a 'schema' to understand the decoding process – a cognitive framework which helps us organise, memorise and interpret complex information. For instance, in order to understand any form of information, e.g. 'a fish', we need to create a mental schema, i.e. a building block. The first stage is ACTION whereby we encounter a new object, i.e. the fish. If this is the first encounter then we do not already hold an existing schema so we need to ASSIMILATE the information. We need to remember the shape, size and colour of a fish; we need to have a concept of the environment where fish live, i.e. water; and we need to understand their basic behaviours. The brain stores these coded units of data to create a prototype of an object, i.e. ACCOMMODATION, so a new schema is created or an old one adapted. Thus, we learn multiple different concepts which we put together to form a single object to create a schema (i.e. our understanding of 'a fish'). A person might have only viewed a goldfish, but when presented with a blowfish, which is blue and a different shape, they can draw on their schema in order to recognise the object as a fish. As new information is encountered existing schemas are adapted and the process of ACTION-ASSIMILATION-ACCOMMODATION takes place in order to develop the building blocks of knowledge.

Example – social work learning

The way this book is constructed is based on this theoretical perspective of learning. It is anticipated that social work students may not have encountered social work theory before, so this book is written as an introduction. Concepts and principles are introduced and explained and then information is given for further knowledge development, e.g. more complex reading matter. The principle here is to build students' knowledge of theory – start at the first level and work up, i.e. building and developing new schemas of knowledge as students and then social work practitioners develop their experience.

Piaget (1952) suggests that children learn very basic schemas during the early stages of their lives, but as they absorb new information their schemas become more complex. Children will learn basic schemas which relate to objects, such as a chair, a table or indeed a fish, but as they learn *social* information their schemas become more complex. Older children will begin to learn schemas for gender roles, poverty, social class, criminality, ethnic groups, etc. It should be noted that these schemas are affected by the social and cultural environments in which they are learnt; learning takes place within a cultural environment, therefore cognition is significantly affected by environmental factors. For example, during role-play a child may recognise and copy the roles played out by their parents, and begin to distinguish the difference between gender roles within their family. The child may start identifying with a particular gender role, and they will learn everything they can about femininity or masculinity from their local environments. This will result in a learnt schema producing gendered behaviours which then influence the child's future interactions with others. This is beneficial for social work practice to help understand the potential repercussions, for example, of living in a home where there is domestic violence or substance abuse. Thus cognition is not a neutral process but is significantly affected by (and in turn significantly affects) environmental and cultural factors.

In cognitive theory, therefore, rather than describing a person's emotional journey which drives behaviour, the focus is on how information has been cognitively learnt during different stages of a person's life-course. Social work practitioners must attempt to comprehend how past experiences can affect a person's cognitive development and result in service users' behaviours and beliefs. Although cognitive psychology illustrates the importance of environmental factors as examples have shown, this approach also acknowledges how biological factors do influence the learning process – in cognitive theory we see an interaction between the biological self (nature) and the social environment (nurture), which constructs an individual's psychological profile. Therefore from a social work perspective this theoretical framework acknowledges that (a) service users have agency over their actions, i.e. control and (b) once they have access to new information/knowledge this could lead to behaviour change. So, a cognitive perspective suggests that people are able to adapt to their environments.

Case Study: Serious Case Review

When applying cognitive theory to the SCR concerning Child Z (2013) there are a number of risk factors that might affect MZ and FZ's cognitive development, impacting on their learnt parental skills. Cognitive psychology acknowledges how biological factors interact with a person's social environment and, as we can see in the case study, both FZ and MZ have been diagnosed with unspecified learning difficulties. Yet this diagnosis should not, on its own, be used to explain risk factors *per se*. Learning difficulties are experienced on a spectrum, and people with 'profound' forms of learning impairments have successfully raised children in a caring and nurturing environment. Cognitive theory does not advocate a deterministic approach when accounting for behaviour, i.e. that the presence of a learning difficulty automatically raises risks, as behavioural outputs which are influenced by cognitive development arise from the socio-cultural environment, i.e. nurture. So, by applying this perspective to the Serious Case Review, we can make an attempt to understand how the socio-cultural environment might affect the cognitive development for both FZ (father) and MZ (mother).

Both parents matured in deprived households where violence was commonplace, and so when MZ and FZ were constructing their schemas these could have been directly influenced by negative behaviours they observed. We can surmise that the schemas which relate to feminine and masculine roles may have been significantly affected by the violent interactions observed, which could lead to both MZ and FZ's schemas around motherhood and fatherhood incorporating aspects of violence and control. Further, as MZ and FZ grew up in an environment lacking stimulation we could consider the possibility that their cognitive maturity might have been affected by disrupted progress through Piaget's stages of cognitive development. From this perspective, the evidence of FZ's behaviour could indicate that he has not successfully learnt the role of responsible parent.

Activity 4.2

Consider what we mean by the idea of a responsible parent – how is this idea determined? Think of examples from your own childhood – how were you parented and what did you learn from those experiences?

Chapter Summary

As discussed, applying cognitive theory to social work practice does not explain behaviour exclusively due to biological factors. On the contrary, cognition takes place within a socio-cultural setting; hence learning is a form of socialisation which constructs all forms of behaviour and social interaction. Although behaviours are influenced by biological factors they are not determined by them, and people engage in destructive behaviours not because they are biologically programmed to do so but because of environmental factors that affect their cognition. Although basic schemas are constructed during childhood, humans learn new information throughout their life-course; thus, cognition does not stop after the fourth stage of development but continues until the end of a person's life. Schemas are learnt, but they can also be adapted and changed at any point in a person's life. Cognitive theory is also not a social deterministic approach, as service users have the cognitive ability to recognise their own behaviour and by doing so they can change it. The implications of this perspective for social work are significant, as cognitive theory presents practitioners with a somewhat optimistic view of behaviour and the possibility for change. This perspective asserts that behaviour is not pre-determined by the biological or the sociological, but it is fluid and constantly changing throughout people's lives.

Further Reading

Nicolson, P and Bayne, R (2014) *Psychology for Social Work Theory and Practice.* Basingstoke: Palgrave Macmillan.

Chapter 5

Humanistic psychology: A stairway to Athena

Stephen J Macdonald

Achieving a Social Work Degree

This chapter will help you meet the following capabilities, to the appropriate level, from the Professional Capabilities Framework:

PCF 1 Professionalism

- Describe the role of a social worker and the importance of personal and professional boundaries and behaviour, demonstrate ability to learn using a range of approaches;

PCF 2 Values and Ethics

- Understand the professional's ethical principles and their relevance to practice, and demonstrate awareness of own personal values and how these can impact on practice;

PCF 3 Diversity

- Recognise the importance of diversity in human identity and experience, and the application of anti-discriminatory and anti-oppressive principles in social work practice;

PCF 4 Rights, Justice and Economic Wellbeing

- Understand the principles of rights, justice and economic wellbeing, and their significance for social work practice;

PCF 5 Knowledge

- Demonstrate an initial understanding of the application of research, theory and knowledge from sociology, social policy, psychology, health and human growth and development to social work;

PCF 6 Critical Reflection and Analysis

- Understand the need to construct hypotheses in social work practice;

PCF 7 Intervention and Skills

- Demonstrate an awareness of a range of frameworks to assess and plan intervention and demonstrate initial awareness of risk and safeguarding;

PCF 8 Context and Organisations

- Demonstrate awareness of the impact of organisational context on social work practice.

Introduction

The chapter will examine humanistic psychology as a theoretical framework within social work practice. This perspective develops a holistic approach to conceptualise human behaviour and has had a substantial impact on social work theory and practice. Humanistic psychology can be described as a motivational theory, as it explores what inspires people to act and behave in particular ways. This perspective integrates subjective notions of identities, personalities and the notion of free will in conjunction with observable behaviours to understand human consciousness. The chapter will commence by examining the foundation of humanistic theory and how it progresses from two very different schools of thought from within psychodynamics and behaviourism. This will illustrate how humanistic psychology attempts to merge the concepts of universal behaviour, i.e. behaviourism, with that of the emotional development of the mind, i.e. psychodynamics, within a single theoretical framework. This chapter predominantly focuses on research by Carl Rogers and Abraham Maslow who are described as the founders of humanistic theory.

Carl Rogers and the emergence of humanistic psychology

In order to appreciate the history of humanistic theory there needs to be an acknowledgment of the work of Carl Rogers. Rogers (1951, 1959) originally trained as a psychoanalyst, which influenced key aspects of his research. Rogers (1951, 1959) believed the discipline of psychology had diverged into two very different ways of thinking about human behaviour, i.e. psychoanalytical and behavioural psychology.

Although these methods of psychology disregarded the other's interpretation of behaviour, Rogers endeavoured to merge both perspectives into a single holistic theoretical framework. He believed that it was possible to include both the subjective, i.e. the mind, and the objective, i.e. measurable behaviours, to develop a new form of psychology. Although Rogers attempted to draw together key aspects of psychodynamics and behaviourism he also rejected the core principles which underpinned both of these schools of thought. As discussed in previous chapters, psychodynamics explains behaviour as being determined by an individual's unconscious desires; whereas behaviourism considers that behaviours are formed by previous experiences of reinforcements. Rogers believed that both perspectives explained behaviour from a deterministic (i.e. entirely controlled) viewpoint, which he rejected.

What separates Rogers' (1951, 1959) humanistic approach from previous forms of psychodynamics is that he disregards the concept of the unconscious mind. For Rogers, individuals *can* understand their own behaviours and can understand *why* they act and interact in particular ways. From a humanistic approach people are conscious of their past, present and future desires. Rogers (1961) suggests there is no part of our mind that is inaccessible; therefore, to understand why people act in particular ways psychologists and social workers must ask individuals to rationalise their actions. From this perspective, humanistic psychologists can understand behaviour entirely through conscious processes from a person-centred approach. A fundamental principal of humanistic theory is that people's subjective experiences are interpreted at face value. Social workers do not and should not attempt to reinterpret service user stories. Practitioners need to attempt to understand these stories in partnership with individuals and these stories are viewed as an interpretation of the truth. Therefore, to truly comprehend human behaviour, we need to understand these behaviours from the perspective of the person who has experienced them.

Reflection Point

The question arises, however, whether we can ever completely understand the perspective of another person? What issues do you think could affect our understanding? (See also Chapter 10, Reflexivity.)

Although humanistic theory accepts that our past experiences influence our personalities and affect our decision-making abilities, it also suggests that individuals can reflect on these past experiences and understand how they affect their current behaviour; so it is then possible to make changes to their lifestyles. What makes Rogers' (1959, 1961) theory unique is that although emotional development *influences* human behaviour it does not *control* a person's actions. For Rogers (1959, 1961), behaviour is not determined and is fluid and constantly changing during an individual's life course. Similar to behaviourism, humanistic theory believes that human behaviours are not determined by genetic or biological factors. Although there is an acceptance of certain positive motivational factors, i.e. positive reinforcement, there is a rejection of any form of negative interventions which control behaviour. For humanistic psychologists, negative forms of control do not result in meaningful behaviour change and can cause harm to an individual (see some of the critiques of Behaviourist theory, Chapter 3). This can have a negative impact on the construction of an individual's personality and their constructed notion of 'self'.

Developing from the work of Rogers (1959, 1961), humanistic theory's fundamental belief is that humans have agency (power) over their own actions. Humans can perceive situations and make choices to act or interact in particular ways. Within humanistic theory there is an inclusion of the concept of 'self' within a social context. The 'self' is used to describe a person's inner personality, which influences their behaviours. For Rogers (1959), to analyse human behaviour we need to explore how people construct the concept of 'self'. Rogers advocated the significance of incorporating the concept of 'free-will' within an analysis of human behaviour. The concept of free will is central to how people behave both as a child and as an adult (in direct contrast to Behaviourism) (Rogers, 1959). What makes humans unique is the concept of free will, as individuals can understand their environments and make choices about how they act and behave in social situations. (See also Chapter 16, Radical Social Work for a critique of the concept of choice and free will in practice.) In Rogers' (1959, 1961) research, he indicates the importance of human 'agency' as individuals are in control of their own destinies. Interestingly, by including the concept of agency, what Rogers is highlighting is the importance of subjectivities. For Rogers (1959, 1961), in previous behaviourist research there is a rejection of human subjectivity, i.e. the mind, as this cannot be measured. For Rogers, it is human subjectivities that render us human. If we do not study the concept of individuality then we are overlooking the fundamental concept of what makes us human and separates us from other species of animals.

The hierarchy of needs and self-actualisation

Although Carl Rogers can be described as the founder of humanistic psychology, this school of thought has been significantly influenced by the work of Abraham Maslow. Both scholars illustrate the importance of understanding 'free will' and 'agency' in order to comprehend human behaviour. They also recognise how social environments affect a person's ability to have 'agency' over certain social situations. Within his work, Abraham Maslow (1943) illustrates the importance of developing a higher level of thinking, which he refers to as 'self-actualisation'. In order to understand what motivates our behaviour Maslow (1943) suggests we need to comprehend a hierarchy of needs which influence our social behaviours. A central feature to Maslow's hierarchy of needs is the concept of motivation. We are often not aware of the key motivating factors which underpin our behaviour; however, Maslow (1943) suggests that by becoming aware of these motivating factors this gives humans the ability to self-actualise. It should be noted that Maslow also recognises that the ability to fulfil these needs, and self-actualise, are significantly affected by a person's social environment.

For Maslow (1943), motivational factors are not linked to behavioural rewards or unconscious desires but relate to three domains. These three domains consist of our basic human needs, our psychological needs and our self-fulfilment needs. Maslow (1943) developed these three motivational factors into a five-stage model, which he names as the 'Hierarchy of Needs'. Maslow (1943) suggests that all humans have five stages of needs. These start in stage one with physiological needs and conclude in stage five with self-actualisation. Self-actualisation describes when someone reaches their full potential. Maslow's hierarchy of needs is usually represented as a triangle because the vast majority of individuals meet their basic needs but very few members of society progress on to self-actualisation (see Figure 5.1). In Maslow's (1943) model it should be noted that individuals must satisfy their basic needs in order to progress to a higher level of needs such as self-actualisation. Maslow's (1943) hierarchy of needs are as follows:

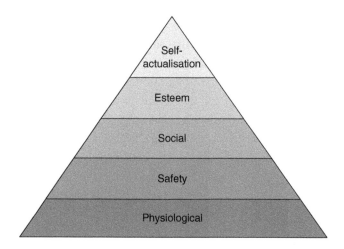

Figure 5.1   Maslow's hierarchy of needs

Basic needs

Stage one describes our physiological needs, which need to be met in order to keep a person alive. Therefore, this refers to access to food and water, sex, the ability to sleep and access to warmth. Maslow suggests that approximately 85 per cent of individuals manage to achieve their physiological needs in Western societies. Once a person has achieved the first stage of needs they can progress into the second stage. By not achieving the first stage of needs, i.e. not having access to food and water, this will dominate their motivations affecting a person's behaviour. This stage is particularly relevant to children who enter foster care – the first stage that needs to be met is their basic needs before higher level needs can be considered.

Stage two refers to people's need for safety and security. This makes reference to a person's ability to keep them and their family safe. Housing, the environment and living conditions become a significant motivational factor. Stability and law and order become vital to a person's wellbeing. Maslow suggests, in Western societies, about 75 per cent of individuals achieve the second stage of their needs. Therefore, a restriction in stage two of the hierarchy stops individuals progressing into the third stage.

Psychological needs

Stage three signifies the concept of love and belongingness. The idea and need for friendship becomes central to a person's psychological needs. A central motivating factor relates to people's abilities to cultivate romantic relationships and nurture friendships. Therefore, attachment with others becomes a central motivating force to grow relationships based on love and affection (see Chapter 6, Human Growth and Development). As humans are social animals, social interaction becomes a vital need. The importance of friendship, love, belonging, and sexual intimacy are essential to the well-being of an individual. For Maslow only 50 per cent of people in Western society achieve this level of needs.

Stage four relates to esteem. This stage refers to our self-confidence, self-respect and respect for others. Maslow illustrates there are two parts to this need. The first refers to our ability to succeed and master skills; directly referring to our level of confidence and competence. The second part refers to how this transpires into a person's reputation and social status. Fulfilling these esteem needs will build a person's self-confidence and self-worth and in turn this will motivate a person to have confidence in others. Having confidence in others allows individuals to develop respectful relationships which benefit themselves and people around them. However, low self-esteem and low confidence will restrict a person from achieving their full potential. Maslow suggests that only 40 per cent of people within Western societies achieve this stage. In Maslow's later version of his model, he adds cognitive needs, which relates to knowledge development, curiosity and exploration, as well as aesthetic needs, which result in an appreciation for beauty of humanity and nature.

Self-fulfilment needs

Stage five refers to Maslow's final stage in his model where a person reaches self-actualisation. Self-actualisation is the ultimate goal for people to progress to. If a person is successful in achieving the first four needs, there is the possibility to achieve self-actualisation. This describes the process of how an individual can reach their full potential. Individuals will have developed cognitively, creatively and spiritually and will have grown through their experiences and advanced their knowledge to a higher level. For Maslow approximately 10 per cent of the population achieve aspects of self-actualisation. In his later work he adds the concept of transcendent needs, which refers to individuals helping others to achieve self-actualisation. For Maslow (1970) only approximately two per cent of the population achieve this stage of the model. Central to self-actualisation is how individuals develop the need for creativity, problem-solving and the desire for knowledge, not for financial gain, but for the sake of knowledge. People who have reached this stage in Maslow's model reject social prejudices and are accepting in nature, have advanced levels of empathy and are driven by their social conscious rather than their own selfish needs. Therefore, self-actualisation refers to how individuals cultivate a social conscience and a global morality.

For Maslow (1943, 1970) and Rogers (1959, 1961) the aim of humanistic theory is to assist individuals to achieve self-actualisation. Maslow (1943, 1970) developed the model which emphasises how people are motivated to achieve a higher stage of consciousness. Both Maslow and Rogers however acknowledged how environmental factors directly impact on people's ability to progress to a higher stage. As suggested, according to Maslow (1943, 1970) only two per cent (i.e. transcendent needs) of individuals achieve self-actualisation, but this is not because they do not have the ability to achieve this level, but often it is due to restrictive social factors throughout a person's life. It must also be noted that these external factors can occur at any time in a person's life and the impact means that a previously met need now becomes unmet, e.g. losing a job or a home will lead a person to be motivated by basic needs again.

Multiple versions of self

Developing from a humanistic perspective, Carl Rogers (1951, 1959) established a new form of therapy – Person Centred Therapy. This form of therapy is client led, where service users are the experts concerning their own lives and the therapist's role is solely to facilitate change. Social work is often driven by a personal-centred approach, which is based on this form of therapy – it is used not just to facilitate change but also to understand the individual, i.e. the first stage of the assessment process. For Rogers (1951, 1959), Person Centred Therapy is a holistic approach with the concept of self-actualisation at its core. Rogers suggests that self-actualisation results in a fully functioning and healthy personality. Yet, problems can occur within an individual's life because there is a fragmentation to a person's concept of self. Roger (1951, 1959) suggests that the 'self' is divided into three separate parts: the 'perceived self', the 'actual self' and the 'ideal self'. If these three parts of our personality are very similar then this allows us to progress successfully through Maslow's hierarchy of needs towards self-actualisation; however, if these are dissimilar then this will disrupt our ability to progress. From a humanistic perspective, to comprehend why we behave in particular ways individuals must understand how their 'personalities' and versions of 'self' are formed.

The actual self

The actual self is how individuals construct and conceptualise their own personalities. For Rogers, the actual self is based in an individual's own inner-understanding of who they are that relates to their histories, beliefs, perceptions and aspirations – defined in humanistic psychology as a person's consciousness. Therefore, this approach implies that nothing in their consciousness is hidden from a person. Rogers observes that at points in a person's life other people can interpret a person's actual self differently within interactions. For example, a person who views themselves as helpful may be viewed by another as interfering. However, people have the ability to recognise this misinterpretation and potentially change their behaviours, circumstances, actions and interactions. The actual self is the portal of the person's personality, which the individual controls and can shape during their life course (Rogers, 1951, 1959).

Perceived self

The perceived self is how other people interpret a person's behaviours and define them as an individual. This is therefore an interpretation by others of an individual's own personality and identity. Individuals may not just have one perceived self as multiple people will interpret their personality in very different ways. For example, work colleagues might interpret a person's behaviour very differently from family members or friends. Rogers suggest that this is part of a person's personality which is not controlled by the person. Therefore, he emphasises that an individual cannot control their perceived self. It is a version of an individual's personality which is constructed by others who interact with that person within a social context (Rogers, 1951, 1959).

The ideal self

The ideal self is the model of how individuals would like their personalities to be perceived by others. This is how individuals would like themselves to be viewed in an ideal world. This could be influenced by peers, the media or socially constructed ideas. Individuals might construct the ideal self on how they perceive their perfect body image, their masculine/feminine qualities, or their intellectual abilities, etc. This is a version of themselves which they create and aspire towards. This ideal self is motivated by goals and aspirations, which are often linked to how a person constructs the notion of a 'perfect' being. Therefore, the ideal self refers to how people hope that others interpret their behaviours. From a humanistic perspective, this concept of the ideal self is constructed within a culturally specific environment, i.e. what may be ideal in one society may not be in another (Rogers, 1951, 1959).

Activity 5.1

1. What kind of person do you think you are? Try to be honest.
2. Ask the person sitting next to you what kind of person they think you are?
3. Does the other person's impression of you match with what you would like it to be?

Equilibrium of the self

A healthy and well-adjusted person's three versions of self should be very similar; the actual should be comparable to how others interpret a person's perceived self. If others view a person in similar ways to how the individual perceives themselves, then this might demonstrate a well-adjusted personality. Furthermore, if a person's ideal self is similar to the actual self then again this has a positive impact on their personality formation. This demonstrates that an individual has set realistic goals that are possible to live up to. So, if all versions of self are similar it makes it possible for an individual to successfully self-actualise.

However, problems occur if the three versions of self are very different – how an individual views their own identity might be very different to how others perceive their behaviours. Furthermore, if a person sets unrealistic goals to aspire to, and the version of their ideal self is dissimilar from their own actual self then this can create negative personality problems. In Rogers' (1951, 1961) Person Centred Therapy, he aspires to help people redefine these multiple versions of their personalities. He notes that people are only in control of their actual self and that realigning their actual self would assist people in becoming genuine, honest, caring and happy individuals. By doing so, people could choose to make positive changes within their lives which would eventually lead to self-actualisation. Rogers (1951, 1959, 1961) asserts that individuals can construct a genuine version of self and progress to a higher level of consciousness through self-actualisation.

Application to social work practice

The application of humanistic theory to social work practice gives a unique take on human behaviour as something which is inherently positive. Human behaviours result from key motivational factors which are affected by a person's basic needs. In order to understand why service users and carers act and interact in particular ways there needs to be an understanding of how social motivational factors affect their behaviours, i.e. in order to become an adjusted individual our basic needs need to be met. Once our basic needs are met we need to ensure that our psychological needs are embraced and so on. For a small proportion of society once our basic and psychological needs have been met this lays the foundation for self-actualisation. Within contemporary society, both Maslow and Rogers illustrate that only approximately 10 per cent of people within Western society progress to the stage of self-actualisation. From this perspective, it implies that the vast majority of service users and carers that social workers support will not have their basic or psychological needs met – as they are stuck with these needs. Because these needs are not being provided for, this results in many people displaying negative behaviours.

Case Study: Serious Case Review

By applying a humanistic theoretical approach to the SCR of Child Z (2013), this gives social workers a unique way of analysing the events described in this report. Central to humanistic theory is that individuals are inherently good and negative behaviours result from environmental and social factors. From this perspective the actions of MZ (mother) and FZ (father) result from their historical and contemporary social circumstances. As already illustrated both parents experienced abuse and neglect during their childhood. Therefore, their childhood was dominated by negative experiences. For both parents, issues of neglect might have restricted some of their basic human needs such as security, regular food, love, warmth and attachment. There is evidence in the SCR that both parents experienced behaviours that might have resulted in them not progressing through Maslow's hierarchy of needs.

Chapter Summary

Humanistic theory has developed a unique way of thinking about behaviour, emotional development and how our personalities are shaped within a social context and is particularly aligned to core social work values. The key concept that defines humanistic theory is the notion that individuals are experts in relation to their own behaviours. Professionals such as psychologists or social workers do not have the ability to analyse a person's behaviours and only have the skills to help the individual understand why they act in particular ways. Therefore, the social work practitioner becomes a facilitator rather than an analyst. This school of thought incorporates the importance of free will and choice. So, although people are not always fully aware of why they act in particular ways, practitioners can help service users comprehend their own behaviours. By doing this it can empower service users to make positive changes within their own lives. Therefore, a social worker is to facilitate positive behaviours in order for self-actualisation to take place.

Further Reading

Nicolson, P and Bayne, R (2014) *Psychology for Social Work Theory and Practice*. Basingstoke: Palgrave Macmillan.

Chapter 6

Human growth and development

Lesley Deacon

Achieving a Social Work Degree

This chapter will help you meet the following capabilities, to the appropriate level, from the Professional Capabilities Framework:

PCF 1 Professionalism

- Describe the role of a social worker and the importance of personal and professional boundaries and behaviour, demonstrate ability to learn using a range of approaches;

PCF 2 Values and Ethics

- Understand the professional's ethical principles and their relevance to practice, and demonstrate awareness of own personal values and how these can impact on practice;

PCF 3 Diversity

- Recognise the importance of diversity in human identity and experience, and the application of anti-discriminatory and anti-oppressive principles in social work practice;

PCF 4 Rights, Justice and Economic Wellbeing

- Understand the principles of rights, justice and economic wellbeing, and their significance for social work practice;

PCF 5 Knowledge

- Demonstrate an initial understanding of the application of research, theory and knowledge from sociology, social policy, psychology, health and human growth and development to social work;

PCF 6 Critical Reflection and Analysis

- Understand the need to construct hypotheses in social work practice;

PCF 7 Intervention and Skills

- Demonstrate an awareness of a range of frameworks to assess and plan intervention and demonstrate initial awareness of risk and safeguarding;

PCF 8 Context and Organisations

- Demonstrate awareness of the impact of organisational context on social work practice.

Introduction

At the point of qualification social work practitioners should be able to [d]emonstrate *and apply to practice a working knowledge of human growth and development throughout the life course* (BASW, PCF).[1] Knowledge of human development is therefore essential in social work practice in order to understand how human beings grow and develop throughout their life course. A psychological basis for this is also important in order to understand a person and how their personality develops. As stated by Nicolson and Bayne (2014), this is needed so that social work practitioners can try to understand service users and carers in order to engage more effectively, and so that they can understand and (to a certain extent) predict behaviour. However, it is also essential that the physical factors of growing and ageing are also understood, as well as the context in which the person is living, i.e. the social and environmental factors. Therefore it could be argued that a 'bio-psycho-social' approach is applied in social work practice.

An understanding of context issues and the course of development can be dependent on the specific theorist and their theoretical basis (Thompson, 2015), so in order to understand and apply a human growth and development (HGD) theoretical framework the main focus for this chapter will be on Erik Erikson. (Freud's psychosexual development and Piaget's cognitive development can be

---

[1] The term 'life course' will therefore be used throughout this chapter in line with the wording in the PCF, however it can also be referred to as lifespan.

seen in Chapters 2 and 4.) The reason for the use of Erikson is that his theoretical framework offers a crossover from psychological to sociological theories by setting out a psychosocial theory in which human beings develop through stages based on the physical development of age. Erikson's theoretical framework is particularly beneficial to social workers in practice as it offers a variety of perspectives on human behaviour and the influence of environmental factors and biology. It is evident from this position how the need for multiagency working in practice is demonstrated – the need to recognise the importance of the interpretation and focus of other professionals and for the social work practitioner to draw this together in a holistic view. (It is strongly recommended that Chapter 2 on psychodynamic theory is read first in order to understand Erikson's theoretical basis as a psychodynamic theorist – this helps in understanding the foundations of his theory.)

The life course

The concept of the life course, in its most basic sense, means the progression of human lives from beginning to end – from birth to death. It is cross-disciplinary with different understandings and interpretations from *biology, genetics, history, psychology, sociology, anthropology, philosophy, medicine and education*, for example (Crawford and Walker, 2010, p2). From a medical and physical perspective, for example, it can certainly also be seen that the life course begins before this, in the womb, and through genetic inheritance and the lifestyle choices of biological mothers. Considering this perspective, the NHS website indicates the dangers to unborn children of smoking during pregnancy: *babies of women who smoke are, on average, 200g (about 8oz) lighter than other babies, which can cause problems during and after labour, for example they are more likely to have a problem keeping warm and are more prone to infection* (NHS website). So it can be seen here how both medical and environmental aspects can impact on our life course.

The concept of *nature* refers to the genetic inheritance from parents and familial generations. Physical characteristics, e.g. hair colour, eye colour and height, are more easily accepted than, say, personality or behaviour (Beckett and Taylor, 2010). *Nurture*, however, refers to the way in which people are brought up, the environment they live in, cultural expectations, education and parenting, to name but a few (Beckett and Taylor, 2010).

Reflection Point

How much of your personality do you think is down to your genetic inheritance, how much is down to your social environment, and how much do you think is just individual?

Whatever our perspective is, there is no single, universal agreement as to how to explain the life course, its purpose or meaning, or how humans develop – just as there is no one grand social work theory that explains everything practitioners need to know or apply. One aspect that can be agreed upon, however, is change. No matter what happens, people and situations change and people act unexpectedly. Any event that takes place can affect one person one way and another person another without there seeming to be a reason for that. It is this, I would argue, that adds a significant layer of complexity to social work practice – and to understanding individual people. Erikson's theoretical frameworks for understanding HGD will now be considered, with the understanding that (as throughout this book) this is just one way of understanding and certainly not the only way.

Erik Erikson and psychosocial theory

Erik Erikson (1902–1994) was a German developmental psychologist who was initially a psychodynamic theorist interested in Freud's theory of psychosexual development. However, he developed his own perspective on human development, rejecting sexual development and instead specifically focusing on the role of the ego and the social environment. Erikson is the theorist associated with developing the concept of psychosocial theory (Newman and Newman, 2016). Psychosocial theory in essence refers to the interrelationship between one's psychology and the social environment. Erikson's first publication, *Childhood and Society* (1950), made these links between a psychodynamic approach and an anthropological one. Through this, cultural norms and values are transferred from caregiver to child through the way in which they care for the child (Newman and Newman, 2016). Erikson's theoretical framework, rather than being focused on sexual development as Freud's was, was more concerned with the development of skills and knowledge to help individuals navigate through social life, and how individuals feel integrated and valued in this (Newman and Newman, 2016). A further difference to Freud was that Erikson emphasised the importance of understanding change that takes place in middle and later adulthood and how this impacts on continuing personality development (Salkind, 2004). Freud argued that all developmental changes occur in childhood and their impact is continually felt in all adulthood. Erikson's theory, however, suggests that identity develops through stages or psychosocial 'crisis points' in our lives, which we move through biologically with increasing physical age. According to Erikson, *{t}he actual outcome for any individual would depend on how well the particular 'crisis', or challenge, of that stage had been successfully met* (Beckett and Taylor, 2010, p36), and it is the ego that manages, and attempts to resolve, these developmental crises (Newman and Newman, 2016). The psychosocial crisis refers to the conflict between a person's abilities at that stage of development and society's expectations. This manifests in an incessant requirement placed on individuals, usually for some sort of control at that stage (Newman and Newman, 2016).

In order for a crisis to be successfully navigated the person must reach a balance between the two 'polarities', which can be seen in Table 6.1. For example, the crisis of trust versus mistrust suggests two ends of a spectrum – to be able to trust, or to be distrustful (Newman and Newman, 2016, p233). If crises are successfully navigated then this can lead to the development of skills and knowledge that equips a person with what they need to transition through to the next stage. The stages take place in a biological and physical sequence, i.e. an individual moves through and onto each stage by the nature of growing and ageing. The actual development crises that take place are seen to have cultural influences, e.g. potty training being a significant development stage, and the age for this is particular to a Western cultural expectation. To achieve full ego integration all stages of the life course must be experienced. Therefore this is only experienced at the very final stage, of ego integrity versus despair – to become accepting of the self and of the life that has been led. While there are no opportunities to *turn back time* and return to an earlier stage of development in Erikson's theory, it is however possible to *review and reinterpret previous stages in the light of new insight and/or new experiences* (Newman and Newman, 2016, p230). The outcome of each stage and the resolution of the psychosocial crisis is rarely completely positive or completely negative, but does tend to be largely one way or the other.

Table 6.1 Stages of development

Age	Stage
0–1	Basic trust versus mistrust
2–3	Autonomy versus shame and doubt
4–5	Initiative versus guilt
6–11	Industry versus inferiority
Adolescence	Identity versus role confusion
Young adulthood	Intimacy versus isolation
Middle adulthood	Generativity versus stagnation
Older adulthood	Ego integrity versus despair

(Adapted from Erikson, E (1995 [1950]) *Childhood and Society*. London: Vintage Books)

Erikson's eight stages of man

Erikson identified eight stages of development through the life course. As with Freud, most of those stages take place in early childhood, but Erikson identified further stages that take place throughout adulthood – and each of these will be considered. However, it is not practical here to go into as much detail as needed to fully understand each of these stages, so this should be considered an introduction, with further reading being absolutely critical.

The first three stages of development are weighted heavily on the response of the primary caregiver/s to the child. If this response is positive and consistent then the child develops positively, if it is inconsistent or negative (or both) then the child can struggle to effectively resolve the developmental crisis. This focus is very important for social work practitioners (and any other practitioners) working within safeguarding children arenas. The influence and impact of the primary caregiver/s is essential in the child's development and is therefore an essential focus for social work. (See NHS *Birth to Five* website for specific examples of development milestones in the first five years of life.)

Trust versus mistrust

The first stage in Erikson's theoretical framework is referred to as Trust versus Mistrust. The concept of trust is an important aspect of life and is critical in humanity – the ability to trust others, to trust oneself, to trust in the world (Nicolson, 2014). The first time when a person engages with others is in their relationship with their primary caregiver(s)[2]. A baby is born completely dependent on this person in order to survive, i.e. for food, comfort and care. The development crisis at this stage is for the baby to trust the caregiver(s), and in order for that trust to develop the child needs to be responded to positively and for that response to be consistent. A lack of response to the child's needs or an infrequent response could hinder the child's development of trust both in the caregiver(s) and in the world around them. Remember, however, that at this stage this is *instinctual* as the child is unable to articulate their thoughts.

The similarity between this stage and Freud's first stage of psychosexual development (oral stage) is evident. The concept of attachment, i.e. the engagement in the relationship between the child and the primary caregiver, is also evident. This theory was developed by John Bowlby, where children have an attachment instinct and learn to develop love and trust with another human being, but if they are unable to develop this due to parental inconsistency or distance they can become *emotionally withdrawn and depressed* (Nicolson and Bayne, 2014, p49).

Further reading

In my experience as a practitioner and a lecturer I have witnessed a tendency for some social work students and practitioners to rely on Attachment Theory (and Systems Theory) to help explain situations they encounter. So, while the importance of these theories should be acknowledged, they are by no means the only ways to understand the vast complexity of human lives, behaviour, interactions and environments. Therefore, further reading is recommended here in order to better understand Attachment Theory, with this caveat in mind.

---

[2]While theories initially referred to one primary caregiver (usually the mother), the term caregiver(s) is used here to refer to whoever that person may be – be that the biological parent, grandparent, step-parent, guardian, for example.

The three seminal works of Bowlby are:

Bowlby, J (1969) *Attachment and Loss Volume 1: Attachment.* London: Hogarth Press.

Bowlby, J (1973) *Attachment and Loss Volume 2: Separation: Anger and Anxiety.* London: Hogarth Press.

Bowlby, J (1980). *Attachment and Loss Volume 3: Loss: Sadness and Depression.* London: Hogarth Press.

Mary Ainsworth developed Bowlby's initial theory further to consider the security of different types of attachment:

Ainsworth, M, Blehar, M, Waters, E and Wall, S (1978) *Patterns of Attachment.* Hillsdale, NJ: Erlbaum.

Remember also that Attachment Theory is relevant across the whole life course, including adulthood.

So, to successfully navigate this stage the child must develop trust in the primary caregiver(s). This does not mean that the child has experienced trust all of the time, but that on balance the weight is towards trust.

Autonomy versus shame and doubt

At this second stage of development, the crisis that needs to be overcome is the development of autonomy, or independence. This is the ability of the child to start to take some sort of control of themselves, and in Western society this is largely understood through the idea of potty training. That is, for the child to develop control over their ability to defecate (Freud's anal stage), i.e. to control their physical behaviour (Salkind, 2004). If a child is supported and encouraged in this way then they can develop a sense of control and autonomy. This involves the setting of clear and consistent boundaries by the caregiver(s); if however the caregiver(s) respond inconsistently, e.g. punishing the child for their behaviour based on their own mood rather than the actual behaviour, then the child can feel as though they are not right and therefore cannot be autonomous (Nicolson, 2014). Again, the importance of consistent and clear parenting is raised here, emphasising that the child is developing and that the caregiver(s) is key in managing that delicate process.

Initiative versus guilt

The key crisis in this stage is the idea of the child taking more control and developing ideas concerning what to do in their environment – exploring it and developing activities in it (Salkind, 2004). As the child enters school they begin to choose and develop friendships and seek praise regarding taking initiative (Nicolson, 2014). Again, the danger for the child comes in the form of the primary caregiver(s); their support and encouragement ensures the child develops confidence in themselves and their ability to make basic choices. A negative or inconsistent approach can lead the child to feel guilty about what they want to do not being right as well as a fear of being punished, of being *wrong*.

Industry versus inferiority

The first five years of life see a burst of development from birth and it is not until the age of five onwards that development slows. Gross and fine motor skills develop – expertise, sporting abilities and writing increases and according to Erikson, a period of 'industry' begins (Crawford and Walker, 2010). At this stage, children begin to describe themselves by social rather than physical characteristics, e.g. 'fun' rather than 'tall'. The child begins to see that they need to function in the world themselves – they need to be able to do this themselves as they spend more time apart from their primary caregiver(s) (Salkind, 2004). They begin to take pride in their accomplishments and so the issue of self-esteem becomes critical at this stage. The primary caregiver(s) therefore must provide for their child's physical needs, cognitive development and self-esteem, and nurture and encourage relationships with others, harmony and stability (Crawford and Walker, 2010, pp73–4). They must ensure that opportunities are given to the child in order for the child to develop the skills they need. The crisis is for the child to achieve a sense of ability, i.e. that they are able to apply themselves to something and have the skills necessary to do it. If, however, the reactions they encounter are negative or inconsistent then this can lead to feelings of incompetency (Beckett and Taylor, 2010).

Identity versus role confusion

If previous stages have been completed successfully then the child should enter this stage with at least some sense of security (Salkind, 2004). The onset of puberty is a significant period of physical change for children as they begin the physical transition into adulthood. There is a period of rapid change in which hormone levels rise, height increases, for females fat increases and for males muscles increase; for both, sexual organs change and develop. Erikson identified that physical changes in puberty lead to changes in choices, e.g. regarding sexuality (Crawford and Walker, 2010). As well as the physical changes from childhood, so also come social changes in which these children are expected to act with more responsibility (Salkind, 2004). Successfully developing the concept of the self at this stage is crucial, and if children are not supported and encouraged in this stage then this can led to doubt and confusion about who they are and their place in society. The role of the primary caregiver(s), however, diminishes at this point as the child steps further out into the world and the influence of peers, for example, increases.

Intimacy versus isolation

According to Erikson this is the stage of young adulthood (up to the age of 40). Only when we are secure in our identity (previous stage) can we take risks in social/ sexual intimacy. Empirical evidence to support Erikson's theory was later completed by researchers such as Kahn et al. (1985) who suggested that *new development tasks become progressively more difficult if other development tasks have not yet been completed* (cited in Beckett and Taylor, 2010, p117). It is at this first adulthood stage that the impact of previous crises being unsuccessfully negotiated begins to become more critical. This is the first period in which tasks relate to others and not just to the self, i.e. the forming of *relationships* (Salkind, 2004). The relationships do not necessarily mean sexual ones but ones that are based on friendship and understanding. If this crisis is not transitioned successfully then people will avoid intimacy and develop only superficial relationships with others, which will not be satisfying (Beckett and Taylor, 2010).

Generativity versus stagnation

This is the next stage of adulthood and generally covers the ages of 40 to 60. The idea of generativity refers to guiding the next generation. This does not necessarily apply to having children but may involve doing this in a different way, e.g. through a career. This is seen *as something associated with participating in society and working towards goals beyond one's own immediate needs, as well as just bringing up children* (Beckett and Taylor, 2010, p120). This stage involves a change in focus – becoming aware of one's own mortality and a growing concern with the wider community, not seen in previous stages. If this stage is not transitioned successfully the person can become stagnant and focused too heavily on personal needs (Salkind, 2004). The impact of being 'stuck' is that a person at this point can experience a physical impact in the form of mental health problems such as depression (Nicolson, 2014).

Reflection Point

Think about some of the transitions or changes in adulthood that could impact on a person at this stage.

Ego integrity versus despair

Factors that can impact on old age include class, gender, ethnicity, former occupation and particular cultural expectations of old age (Crawford and Walker, 2010). For Erikson this group concerns people aged over 60 (although this has been developed further due to advances in medicine and the rise in life expectancy). As opposed to earlier stages, there are no further opportunities after this one to make changes. Successful navigation of this stage involves reaching an acceptance of life for what it has been – 'ego integration'. A person who successfully transitions through this stage will be able to feel 'satisfied' with their life regardless of what happened (Salkind, 2004). Unsuccessful transitioning leads to dissatisfaction with life, despair, depression and hopelessness – this can appear as contempt for life, retreat, or becoming passive or isolated.

Case Study: Serious Case Review

To consider an application of Erikson's theoretical framework to the SCR of Child Z a significant amount of information is needed. First, a professional involved with the case would need to know the ages of all concerned in order to know what stage each person was at.

Individual	Age	(Erikson's) Stage
Child Z	9 months	Trust versus Mistrust
Sibling	20 months	Autonomy versus Shame and Doubt
MZ	20 years	Intimacy versus Isolation
FZ	23 years	Intimacy versus Isolation

History is significant in order to apply Erikson's theoretical framework. For FZ and MZ in particular, who were adults at the time, an understanding of their development throughout their own life course is essential in order to understand them at their present stage of development. However, the SCR (2013) states that there was an *absence of historical information [which] may have contributed to an apparent down playing of information about the parents' current circumstances and lifestyle* (p17).

Both MZ and FZ are at the young adulthood stage of Intimacy versus Isolation. However, were historical factors taken into account? MZ became a parent while in the previous stage of Identity versus Role Confusion – what impact might becoming a parent have had on her understanding of her *self*? There can be positive or negative outcomes to this, e.g. in becoming a mother she began to understand herself more and who she is, but if she had not transitioned successfully through previous stages she may be more confused about her identity. Regarding FZ, it is stated that in 1992 he was on the child protection register (as it was then known, i.e. a child protection plan) for physical abuse. His age at the time was approximately 12 years old so he would have been towards the end of Industry versus Inferiority stage or at the beginning of the Identity versus Role Confusion stage. The impact of physical abuse caused by his primary caregiver(s) could have had a negative impact on his ability to transition successfully through either of these stages. More information would therefore be needed to understand what happened and how he reacted to the situation.

Both MZ and FZ entered into parenthood relatively early, with the UK average being 28.3 years for a first child (ONS data). In their current stage of development MZ and FZ are concerned with the development of their relationships and their independence as adults. According to Erikson's theoretical framework, they are however not yet at the stage of Generativity, where they would be more concerned with the next generation. So what impact might this have? What this does is highlight the shortcomings of Erikson's theoretical framework, i.e. the fact that becoming a parent occurs at different ages (or not at all); so is the theoretical framework suggesting that, in terms of their development, they were not ready to become parents? This would be a dangerous perspective in social work, and a judgemental one, and it demonstrates how students and social work practitioners need to be careful when applying theories; they must remember the value-base of the profession and not apply theories from different disciplines without consideration of those values.

Finally, it is important to note that the issues raised in the application of Erikson's theoretical framework are just the tip of the iceberg. The main message indicated by the application of this framework is the importance of understanding the background of service users and carers in order to understand how they have and will transition through their life course.

Critique

There are constant debates as to whether or not Erikson and other theoretical frameworks on human growth and development can actually be referred to as a 'theory'. Many instead refer to them as a 'perspective', in particular because the social aspects of the frameworks are not developed, i.e. what events can cause specific consequences (Newman and Newman, 2016). Erikson suggests that responses to events can be individual, i.e. demonstrating agency on behalf of the person, but he does not give explanation or justification for these differences (Newman and Newman, 2016). The term 'theoretical framework' has been used throughout this chapter in order to address this critique, however, as already mentioned, this is not the only theoretical perspective that is relevant to students and social work practitioners, and therefore with knowledge of psychological and sociological theories, which can also be found in this book, readers should be able to engage in this debate between theories and form informed conclusions themselves.

Finally, Erikson's theory was developed by considering the life cycle of a man – a Western man to be precise. Therefore, his framework was both gendered and culturally specific. However, that does not mean this theoretical framework is obsolete, as it has since been adapted and developed to reflected cultural changes over the years.

Chapter Summary

This chapter has presented an understanding of human growth and development in social work by setting out the psychosocial theoretical framework of Erik Erikson, and demonstrating how it can begin to be applied to social work practice.

Further Reading

Erikson's is not the only theoretical perspective on HGD. It is recommended that students also read about and understand Freud's psychosexual development theories and Jean Piaget's cognitive development theories in the first instance before accessing further theories. These can be found in this book in Chapters 2 and 4.

Although reference is made to Attachment Theory in this chapter, further reading is needed in order to understand its nuances. As an introduction, the following book is recommended:

Howe, D (2011) *Attachment Across the Lifecourse: A Brief Introduction*. Basingstoke: Palgrave Macmillan.

Introduction to Part Two – Sociological Theories

Why are sociological theories beneficial?

It is essential for social work students to understand sociological theories in social work practice in order to look further than just at the service user and their individual pathology. As suggested in Chapter 1, the main theoretical basis for professional social work practice was psychological, but from the mid-twentieth century onwards that focus has shifted to include a more sociological basis. In essence, this meant a shift from the individual focus to a focus on the environment and the structures within that. Jane Tunmore's initial chapter on Social Constructionism sets this out clearly for students and practitioners to understand in terms of the key principles. Reference to classical sociological theories can be found in dispersed in various chapters in order to identify those particularly relevant to social work practice.

General Systems and Ecological Theories by Jane Tunmore, should be reasonably well known to anyone with experience in social work practice as it forms the basis of the assessment and intervention processes. However, while its practice model may be recognised there is often a lack of understanding of its fundamental theoretical basis; and in order to be effective in its application or indeed to challenge it, it must first be understood.

Catherine Donovan's chapter on Feminism and how its theoretical basis developed over time helps student social workers and practitioners to understand the wider basis of feminist thinking. This theory is as relevant today as it was at its inception, especially in the female-dominated social work workforce and the focus on mothers in safeguarding children, for example.

Finally, Mark Bradley is a current practising social worker in safeguarding children. His chapter on Reflexivity is aimed at taking students beyond reflection on action and into reflection in action – to consider the impact of action as it occurs in order to adapt practice in a fluid way. This is an extremely helpful theory for social work practice and understanding the impact of a practitioner's own actions and behaviour.

Chapter 7

Social constructionism and social work

Jane Tunmore

Achieving a Social Work Degree

This chapter will help you meet the following capabilities, to the appropriate level, from the Professional Capabilities Framework:

PCF 2 Values and Ethics

- Understand the professional's ethical principles and their relevance to practice, and demonstrate awareness of own personal values and how these can impact on practice;

PCF 4 Rights, Justice and Economic Wellbeing

- Understand the principles of rights, justice and economic wellbeing, and their significance for social work practice;

PCF 6 Critical Reflection and Analysis

- Understand the need to construct hypotheses in social work practice;

PCF 8 Context and Organisations

- Demonstrate awareness of the impact of organisational context on social work practice.

Introduction

The following social work frameworks and standards give very clear indications of a particular view of the role and nature of social work today. As well as the PCFs, an understanding of social constructionism will also support you to develop the critical and reflective stance advocated in the Knowledge and Skills Statements for Child and Family Social Work and Adult Social Work, and the capacity to critically examine the wider contexts for the situations social workers encounter. For example:

> *Explain and critically evaluate the role of social work as part of a system of welfare support to children and their families, including parents as vulnerable adults, and how this relates to the social contract between citizenship and the state and the role of family, kinship and community...*

> (Knowledge and Skills Statement for Child and Family Social Work, DE, 2014)

> *Supervision, Critical Reflection and Analysis*

> *They should apply imagination, creativity and curiosity to working in partnership with individuals and their carers.*

> (Knowledge and Skills Statement for Social Work with Adults, DH, 2015)

These statements could lead us to assume we know what social work is about, that these statements describe a shared common-sense view of social work. However, in this chapter we will be exploring a challenge to such assumptions. Social constructionism invites us to consider that everyday assumptions about the realities of our world are always being made and re-made in social interactions (Burr, 2015). So, in this example it would be argued that the notions of social work outlined in the PCF and KSS above are specific to a particular time and socio-political context and the shape and meanings we ascribe to social work are being made and re-made as it is practised. We can explore this further by examining definitions and expectations of social work over time. This reveals complexities and shifts in meanings and practices and prompts us to question the range of understandings available to practitioners in their everyday work within changing political and procedural contexts. Compare for example the classic definition of psychosocial casework by Florence Hollis in 1977:

> *It is... an attempt to mobilize the strengths of the personality and the resources of the environment at strategic points to improve the opportunities available to the individual and to develop more effective personal and interpersonal functioning*

> (Hollis, 1977, p1308 in Trevithick, 2012)

Trevithick goes on to argue *at the heart of casework – and a psychosocial approach – lies the relationship created between the service user and social worker* (Trevithick, 2012, p. 341).

Now consider the recent re-definition of social work by the International Federation of Social Workers:

> *Social work is a practice-based profession and an academic discipline that promotes social change and development, social cohesion, and the empowerment and liberation of people. Principles of social justice, human rights, collective responsibility and respect for diversities are central to social*

work. Underpinned by theories of social work, social sciences, humanities and indigenous knowledge, social work engages people and structures to address life challenges and enhance wellbeing.

(IFSW, 2014)

Both these definitions refer to individuals and their environment, both include the importance of relationships (though the IFSW definition uses a different language; 'engages') but it could be argued that focus and scope are very different. In the classic Hollis definition the focus is on improving an individual's capacity and functioning (albeit by some engagement with factors in the environment) whilst the IFSW definition, 37 years later, focuses much more strongly on rights and the need to engage in social change.

Activity 7.1

Have a look now at the PCF and KSS for child and family work - do the definitions above reflect what you read here about social work or can you see other key meanings?

Social work as a contested concept is, perhaps, not unexpected – social conditions/ the political context/notions of the role of the welfare state have shifted over time and whereas Hollis' description of social work reflected activities within Western industrialised democracies, the IFSW seeks to represent a wide range of global practices. We perhaps would not expect understandings and practices to be fixed and static in this instance. Social constructionism challenges us to take this acceptance of fluidity and change further.

Berger and Luckman (1966), in their seminal text *The Social Construction of Reality* propose more broadly that the reality of everyday life for everyone is socially constructed and that *the sociology of knowledge must seek to understand the processes by which this is done in such a way that a taken-for-granted 'reality' congeals for the man (sic) in the street* (Berger and Luckman, 1966, p15). This challenge of the *taken for granted* in social constructionism reflects the paradigmatic shift from modernism to postmodernism within social theory, which is outlined briefly below.

Rejection of positivism

In the natural sciences a positivist approach assumes that it is possible to identify objective facts or truths which are separate from individual interpretation. So, in the natural world there are seen to be sets of impersonal natural forces. The social sciences started from a position of trying to establish similar fixed, natural laws to determine human and societal behaviour. The challenge to this view is that human beings have 'agency', i.e. that individuals can make different decisions that may be constrained or shaped by societal forces, for example, but they can make choices to go with or against these. Each individual's interpretation of the situation is significant and the search for certainties from a positivist perspective is rejected as it does not reflect the process of human interaction (Thompson, 2010).

Rejection of inevitability of progress from increased scientific knowledge

Modernism assumes that the more we develop rational scientific understandings based on facts, rather than superstition and belief, the better society will progress. We can see these arguments, for example, being played out today in debates about the ethics of new advances in genome editing to remove the risk of hereditary diseases; a new advance in science but bringing with it debates about whether scientific advances inevitably mean progress and raising ethical debates about the impact on future generations and the possibility of 'designing' babies to have certain attributes (*Guardian,* Sept 2015). Postmodernism challenges the assumption of inevitable progress and points to the uncertainties in our capacity to predict consequences.

Rejection of grand narratives or meta-theories

Given these critiques of the positivist underpinnings of modernism, it follows that post-modernism is suspicious of grand narratives or meta-theories, i.e. that one theory or set of ideas can explain the whole of human development and behaviour (for example, behaviourism – see Chapter 3) or the way society functions (for example, Marxism – see Chapter 16). These particular explanations of the way the world works then offer specific ways of achieving change. For example, the central principle in Marxism is class relations so that social change could be achieved by changing these, e.g. by working-class revolution (Burr, 2015, p13). Furthermore, it is argued such meta-narratives inevitably exclude the possibility of other explanations and meanings, which might be developed within particular situations and at particular times.

Key concepts of social constructionism

Burr (2015) suggests that there is no single definition that would adequately encapsulate the range of ideas and activities being explored under the umbrella term of social constructionism but argues that there are key common features which she describes as *things you would absolutely have to believe in order to be a social constructionist* (Burr, 2003, p3).

From within a post-modernist paradigm then, social constructionists oppose positivism and *that what exists is what we perceive to exist* (Burr, 2003, p3). This means that the idea that there are realities that exist totally independently of our interpretation is rejected. Parton (2003, p8) goes on to argue that social constructionism insists we should *develop a critical stance towards our taken for granted ways of understanding the world, including ourselves*. So, for example, we should be 'ever-suspicious' of categorised aspects of the world into divisions which are sometimes exclusive of each other. Burr uses the example of gender and sex. She asks whether categories of 'man' and 'woman' do in fact simply reflect *naturally occurring distinct types of human being* with associated difference in behaviour and roles (Burr, 2003 and 2015). (See Chapter 9 for further discussion of social constructions of gender roles.)

Social constructionists would also question whether the notion of a 'child' is unambiguous over time and within different contexts, and that once different understandings of this term become possible then practices such as 'safeguarding children' also become open to examination. So, for example, in Victorian England, young children regularly worked long hours in industrial settings; their role being seen as a contributor to the family income. Today, the role of children of the same age is to learn through interaction in play and at school and expectations of the role of parents are very different. Underpinning this is a view that adults should protect children.

Activity 7.2

In relation to the SCR of Child Z, what do you think are the taken for granted assumptions about families where at least one of the parents has been referred to a substance misuse service?

Is there a taken for granted idea about how well parents who misuse substances can care for or protect their children? Provide a suitable home environment? Maintain a stable lifestyle? Are there different assumptions about the role of mothers and fathers?

Following on from taking a critical stance on taken for granted knowledge is the rejection of the idea of predetermined natural characteristics of the world or individuals. So, in psychology, social constructionists would reject the idea that people are born with individual sets of characteristics, traits or 'essences' which make them what they are. There is no 'pre-given' content like the forces of the id in Freudian terms (see Chapter 2), or particular personalities, e.g. depressive (Burr, 2003, p6). Social constructionism argues that not only do such inner essences not exist, but that the notion that people have such personality traits or inbuilt drives or traits can mean that people who are seen as having 'negative' traits may be pathologised or oppressed.

The central argument of social constructionism is that there is no *singular, objective reality that exists 'out there' in the world* (Hutchison and Charlesworth in Hutchison, 2003, p50). Instead, we create realities in our social practices and interactions. These shape our understanding of 'how to go on'. *Knowledge is therefore seen not as something that a person has or doesn't have but as something that people do together* (Burr, 2003, p9, author's emphasis). Gergen (1999) argues that social constructionism challenges the idea that language and our understandings of the way the world is are created within our own individual thought processes; instead our understanding of objects, of reality, emerge from within our everyday relationships and interactions. So, for example, social work students come to an undergraduate social work programme with an idea that they will attend lectures and seminars. From a social constructionist perspective there is no one 'thing' that is a lecture. Students come with meanings and understandings based on their interaction with current students, teachers at their school or college and media representations of what it is like to be a student. They come then with certain expectations of what is likely to take place and how they, their peers and the person known as the lecturer will behave. Lecturers come with their own experience of being a student, training and CPD about teaching practices, and the practices they have developed in being part of lectures and seminars. More broadly, *We are born into a world where the conceptual frameworks and categories used by the people in our culture already exist* (Burr, 2003, p7). Within the class group, including the lecturer, there may be very many different understandings of taking part in a lecture and seminar. As students and lecturers interact in the space known as a lecture they form new realities of doing lectures. Using this way of thinking it could be argued that students and lecturers in their everyday interactions could do lectures in any number of ways – by the lecturer standing up and talking and the students taking notes, or maybe by bringing in coffee and cakes and reading the papers together, maybe sharing crossword clues. The latter sounds very inviting and social constructionists would argue that this is a new and equally valid reality being formed within social interactions (and it could be the vehicle for some interesting explorations of the relationship between politics and social work of course!).

However, in most cases it is highly unlikely that these constructions of reality will develop outside a fairly limited range of ways of 'going on' in these situations, which have been developed over time and embedded in practices and ways of talking about objects. Even the example above is not very far from traditional lecturing activity. Berger and Luckman (1966, p72) used the term 'institutionalisation' to explain how certain practices become established and therefore *available to all members of the social group in question*. These practices establish 'this is how things are done' or understood and shape interactions and behaviour into particular directions rather than in a range of others that might be possible. Thus roles and role expectations are created and human conduct becomes controlled (p77). This is explored further when we look at language and discourse.

If then, *the relationships between man (sic), the producer and his social world… is, and remains a dialectical one* (Berger and Luckman, 1967, p78), it becomes clear that meanings and realities will change over time and in relation to different cultural contexts. Here we recognise the questions raised by the different definitions of social work at the beginning of this chapter. The way we define and categorise the world very much relates to the particular point in time in which understandings are being made and consolidated and the cultural context in which they are made. *Constructionists emphasize the existence of multiple social and cultural realities. Both persons and environments are dynamic processes, not static structures. The socio-political environment and history of any situation play an important role in understanding human behaviour* (Hutchinson and Charlesworth, 2003, p51).

There is an example of this in relation to child protection. Parton, in his review of changing conceptions of risk highlights the impact of historically specific factors such as the Baby P case and the reports and public outcry that followed this. As Parton notes *a number of influential commentators, including the House of Commons' Children, Schools and Families Parliamentary Committee (House of Commons, 2009), began to argue that the threshold for admitting children into state care was too high* (Parton, 2011, p886). Social workers began to change their practices even before new guidelines were released to reflect these influences; and there were nearly 50 per cent more care applications to courts in the second half of 2008–9 compared with the first half (CAFCASS, 2009, cited in Parton, 2011). Was this a real increase in levels of child abuse or a shift in the social construction of risk at this point influencing decisions (practices) about when and how action should be taken?

Social constructionism and language

If meanings and realities are constructed in everyday practices and interactions, then language is a central process. Social constructionism challenges the view that language merely represents or gives a picture of the world as it is known. Gergen (1999) uses Wittgenstein's idea of 'language games' to explore how the meaning of words cannot be understood until they take place within an exchange with its own socially constructed 'rules'. If we go back to our example of a lecture, the lecturer might begin the session by saying good morning – some students might choose to say good morning back, as this is part of the 'game' of greeting. However, if they responded by throwing things at the lecturer, this would be seen as totally outside the game. If in the middle of the lecture, the lecturer suddenly said good morning, this would be seen as meaningless. So the way we use language is shaped by the meanings and 'games' take place within interactions. So, as Burr (2003, p6) summarises, *when people talk to each other, the world gets constructed*. Language is not just a way of describing something that already exists; words do things as well as having meaning.

Social work training calls attention to the importance of thinking about the use of language in written and oral communication and the need to use clear and precise terms (Trevithick, 2012; Koprowska, 2014). Thus use of 'professional jargon' can exclude others (how many families in the community would have an understanding of assessment as it is understood by social workers?) and vague language like 'he has health issues' tell us very little (Dyke, 2016). This point is raised in the Serious Case Review where it is noted that on 10 December 2010 the TPM made a home visit and saw MZ and voiced her concerns about her *lack of engagement with antenatal care* (Para 175). Social constructionism argues that language actively constructs meanings and practices. If we look at the phrase 'lack of engagement with antenatal care' this needs to be understood within the specific historical and cultural context. This may include norms about the optimum age for pregnancy for example or expectations of the presence of professionals in the process of childbirth. Social constructionism makes no claims about which is right or wrong and has been criticised for a relativist position which might equally accept oppressive or discriminatory discourses but Teater (2014, p85) argues that *this does not mean that social workers should embrace attitudes and beliefs that are harmful to others.*

Tangled up in the examples above are issues of power – which stories get told and perpetuated, is there a space for challenge, to create different meanings? Burr draws upon Foucault's ideas of discourse and power to explore some of these questions in relation to social constructionism. Discourse is understood as *practices which form the objects of which they speak* (Foucault ,1972, p49 in Burr, 2003, p64). So particular uses of language, practices, actions and representations form particular versions of events, ideas about what is real or the truth about particular situations. As Berger and Luckmann (1966) said, this then shapes how we act, and controls behaviour. Keddell (2014, p71) used these ideas to examine the processes of risk assessment in child safeguarding. She argued that, *the discourses implicit in decision-making tools not only affect the ways client behaviour comes to be understood, but also have a direct impact on the relationship formed between social worker and client...*; and on the languages and practices used to describe and define service users and their families. She describes the key discourse is that risk is predictable (if only we use the right tools), and that therefore risk can be avoided or prevented – which sets up unrealistic and impossible expectations.

Foucault explored how and why different discourses became dominant, all-prevailing at particular points in time and he moved away from the notion of power as held by one group over another. He argued that a particular 'common sense' view of the world privileges acting in one way rather than another (so in the example above, avoiding risk rather than positive risk taking) and is maintained in practices which perpetuate particular discourse – and thus develop power inequalities as other discourses are excluded. This process is reinforced by drawing on wider discourses and ideas that characterise certain actions in a favourable light.

Case Study: Serious Case Review

An examination of the SCR for Child Z reveals how dominant discourses and the investment of those involved in perpetuating these can mean that alternative understandings are not heard. The family were being supported by the Family Nurse Partnership initiative and the report notes that *There is good research evidence that such strengths based support can work very well with many families living in similar circumstances to Child Z* (Para 81). However, it goes on to argue that the commitment to the FNP model and the possible need to evidence the benefits of a strengths-based model may have contributed to an over-optimistic assessment of the parenting capacity of MZ and FZ and the level of care being provided for the children. One discourse underpinning this is that of the need for evidence-based practice (EBP) in social work. Petersen and Olsson (2015) argue that the notion of EBP has become embedded in social work research, guidance and practices over recent years and has been seen as a way of reducing errors in analysis and decision-making.

Foucault also argued that where power relations are being enacted there will also be *contestation and resistance* (Burr, 2015, p80). Service users and carers may use a range of strategies to resist attempts to change or control their actions. It could be argued that MZ and FZ resisted professional intervention by subverting the use of assessment tools and missing many appointments in different settings.

Social constructionism in practice(s)

Parton (2003) argues that that social constructionism fits well with the *complex uncertainties of social work* rather than a 'technical-rational' approach which believes that there is a body of objective knowledge which can be rigorously applied and replicated in particular situations (p2). *Real world* problems, he argues are much more messy and indeterminate. This fits with the notion that social workers should always be aware of a possible range of hypotheses or understandings of a situation and that shifting circumstances are likely to undermine a particular fixed view.

PCF 6: Critical Reflection states that experienced social workers should *use critical thinking augmented by curiosity and creativity*. Teater (2014, p81) argues that it is only by coming from a position of curiosity that the social worker *can attempt to discover the reality of the client* – rather than making assumptions about this, or about what is best for the client (Parton and O'Byrne, 2000). This curiosity might also include questioning of a particular accepted view of the world or discourse, which is influencing the way professionals are reacting to information and events and making judgements and an interest in discovering other marginalised discourses. In the Serious Case Review it is noted that there was a tendency to be adult focused, to understand what was happening from assumptions about the parents, expectations of standards and lifestyles within a particular sub-culture; to the extent that the child's experiences (for example, the observation of the ambulance crew about the physical appearance of Z and lack of response to his distress) and 'voice' was not heard.

Parton goes on to argue that research with service users and carers emphasises the importance of the processes of talking and relationship building in order to arrive at mutual and co-produced understandings of what is happening and what is needed; to make sense of changes in people's lives. He relates this closely to the central principle of social constructionism that reality is constructed in social interactions and quotes research with experienced practitioners. Fook et al. (1996, 1997) and Fook (2000) articulated their understanding of the complexity of practice, the need to understand shifting contexts (and act within them) and the capacity to hold uncertainty as the processes of practice unfold. This reflects the notion of reflexivity in social work (see Chapter 10), working from a position of 'not knowing' and within a whole range of possibilities for understanding and responding, moving towards a 'mutual generation' of possible futures. So, a social constructionist approach it is argued, 'fits' with the realities of social work practice and encourages resistance to acceptance of taken for granted forms of understanding and 'stories' about families, certain groups of people and the ways people live their lives.

Social constructionist thinking can also be said to inform particular models of practice. Gergen (1999) points out that de Shazer and other supporters of solution-focused practice argue that persistent conversations which use problem-based language help to perpetuate a particular reality such as depression, whereas conversations about solutions are full of hope and promise, and support the person to create the possibility of a different reality. This can also challenge the power of dominant discourse, for example about the nature of depression and its impact, as embedded in mental health systems.

Parton and O'Byrne also look at the key process of assessment in social work, applying constructionist principles of questioning established discourses focusing on the individual rather than the individual in their context. Challenging taken for granted truths, and giving equal value to voices that are not traditionally heard and using collaborative conversations to create new realities, which include an analysis of risk but also look to develop safety for the child or vulnerable individual (s) now and in the future (Turnell and Edwards, 1997, in Parton, 2000).

Chapter Summary

This chapter has examined the key concepts informing social contructionist theory, which argues that realities are socially constructed within everyday interactions and that these realities are historically and culturally specific. This approach encourages social workers to question taken for granted knowledge and assumptions, and recognise the influence of dominant sets of ideas which shape the policies, procedures and structures of their practice. It highlights the key role of language in actively creating meanings and realities and therefore the crucial importance of conversations based on curiosity and collaboration.

Further Reading

To explore what 'constructive' social work might look like, see Chapters 7–9 in Parton, N. and O'Byrne, D. (2000) *Constructive Social Work Towards a New Practice*. Basingstoke: Palgrave Macmillan.

To explore Foucault's ideas about power further, especially disciplinary power, read Chapter 4 in Burr, V. (2015) *Social Constructionism*, 3rd Edition. East Sussex: Routledge.

Chapter 8

General systems and ecological theories

Jane Tunmore

Achieving a Social Work Degree

This chapter will help you meet the following capabilities, to the appropriate level, from the Professional Capabilities Framework:

PCF 2 Values and Ethics

- Understand the professional's ethical principles and their relevance to practice, and demonstrate awareness of own personal values and how these can impact on practice;

PCF 4 Rights, Justice and Economic Wellbeing

- Understand the principles of rights, justice and economic wellbeing, and their significance for social work practice;

PCF 6 Critical Reflection and Analysis

- Understand the need to construct hypotheses in social work practice;

PCF 8 Context and Organisations

- Demonstrate awareness of the impact of organisational context on social work practice.

Introduction

Social work has always had a focus on understanding the individual within their environment, and the impact of wider social factors on people's lives (Teater, 2014; Besthorn, 2013) and this focus is made explicit in current practice guidelines. For example, the 'assessment triangle' introduced in the *Framework for Assessment of Children in Need and their Families* (DH, 2000) and developed within *Working Together to Safeguard Children* guidance (HMG, 2015) is based on the principle that *an understanding of a child must be located within the context of the child's family (parents or caregivers and the wider family) and of the community and culture in which he or she is growing up* (p11). This is described as a child-centred ecological approach. Similarly, the new guidance for the implementation of the Care Act 2014 (DH, 2016) advises that *Local authorities must consider how the adult, their support network and the wider community can contribute towards meeting the outcomes the person wants to achieve* (s 6.10).

Both these statements give an indication that the context or environment can be explored at different levels, from immediate family to community, culture and wider society. The emphasis is very much on the importance of the *interaction* between the individual and these aspects of the environment. Already we can begin to see the emphasis on processes here – that problems, difficulties, crises are not isolated events, they occur within the ebb and flow of people's lives, and the networks of relationships around them. This chapter will explore two theories that focus on these processes. They are related but take a slightly different perspective on what is meant by context or environment. This difference impacts on both the way a situation might be understood, and ideas about where to intervene.

Systems theory

Systems theory sees the individual as existing in a web of relationships which they both influence and are influenced by, and any behaviour needs to be understood in the context of these relationships (Evans and Kearney, 1996, p14). It has been argued (e.g. Besthorn, 2013) that there were two important early influences on the development of systems theory. One was the functionalist approach of sociologist Talcott Parsons. He proposed that society is composed of social systems, which are *open systems, engaged in complicated processes of interchange with environing systems* (Parsons et al., 1961 in Calhoun et al., 2007, p421). Social systems are different from, say, a statistical group in society, e.g. the number of mothers over the age of 40 at any moment in time, because within them there is an interdependence of individuals/phenomena, which show a consistent pattern over time, e.g. the family. These structures might shift and re-shape according to differences in surrounding systems – e.g. changes in the structure of the family in relationship to changes in patterns of employment, gender roles, and innovations in birth control. One argument is that these systems interact, shift and change in order largely to maintain equilibrium (balance, stability) in society, to perpetuate established, overarching social structures and norms. However, because boundaries between systems are open, and there is interaction between them, significant changes in certain systems could cause 'disequilibrium' which challenge these established norms – for example, the challenge in this century to the conventional structure of the nuclear family. The interdependence of different parts of the system is crucial with a change in any one aspect of society impacting on the role and function of other parts, which is an important aspect of using systemic ideas to understand what has been happening in families for example, and their relationships with helping agencies. However, because these ideas are based on a functionalist view of society, there is an underlying emphasis on maintaining the status quo, and sustaining the individual in carrying out their roles (e.g. parent, breadwinner) within this – whereas social work values are more likely to emphasise empowerment and change.

The second theoretical perspective was the idea of Ludwig van Bertalanfy who was a theoretical biologist interested in the way organisms grow and develop. He developed a general systems theory, which rejected linear, cause and effect models, proposing instead that change results from interactions between the different parts of an organism and he sought to understand *how these different parts interact to purposely create a whole* (Teater, 2014, p17). Organisms were seen as systems which could be 'open' and influenced by external factors. Here is the key concept of the crucial importance of the context, or environment and the interactions between them. Change in one part of the system would result in changes throughout the system. He then took these ideas and sought to broaden them as a way of understanding the complexities of interaction within human systems. This meant he challenged behaviourist constructions of individual human beings responding to stimuli and conditioning (see Chapter 3), and the focus on the individual psyche of psychoanalytical approaches (see Chapter 2) and looked instead at the individual within their social and cultural environment and the interactions between the two. These ideas became more influential in social work in the 1970s when there were broader challenges to the profession's psychoanalytically underpinned focus on individuals and their immediate family (see Chapter 1), and a growing concern with the impact of structural factors within society such as class and inequality.

Activity 8.1

Think about the systems and sub-systems that connect and interact around you. For example, in the system that is your family, are their sub-systems, e.g. you and your brother or sister, your parents or parent and partner? Which wider systems are influential, e.g. university? Do you have a sub-set of peers within that? Try to think how these influence each other and overlap. What about if you encountered tensions in your relationships with your peers, how might that impact on other systems in which you participate? How might others within those systems react? Would this change your own views?

Evans and Kearney (1996, p28) argue that systemic thinking was also influenced by cybernetics – the science of machines and how they operate. They argue a key point from this way of thinking is the idea of self-regulation in response to feedback in human interactions. (See also, Teater, 2014, p23.)

Application to social work practice

These strands of thinking were developed by Pincus and Minahan (1973) and Goldstein (1973) into the unitary model for social work. This was an attempt to find an overarching theoretical approach to social work, which would incorporate the range of ideas that were informing practice. Pincus and Minahan operationalised these ideas into a model of four systems operating within a process of social work intervention:

> *Change agent system*: the system that is facilitating the change, for example the social worker, the agency, the legislation and policies that influence the resources and the work.

> *Client system*: the individual, family, community or other groups with whom the change agent system is working.

> *Target system*: the system identified as most appropriate to receive that intervention.

> (The Client system and the Target system may be the same)

> *Action system*: other systems that assist or work collaboratively with the change agent system to facilitate change.

> (Teater, 2014, p20)

Case Study: Serious Case Review

Using this model, in the case of Child Z (MSCB, 2015) it can be seen that the change agent system would be the Family Nurse and the Family Nurse Partnership programme, supported by the NHS Family Nurse Partnership Unit. The client system is the Child Z, his older sibling mother, MZ and father, FZ. The target system here is the same, although the primary target system appears to be the Child Z and MZ. The action system has variously included the FNP, mental health services, housing services, midwifery service, the probation service and Children's Services. Critics of this model (Evans and Kearney, 1996; Ross and Bilson, 1989) argue that it does not capture essential elements such as the interdependence of systems, and the influence of feedback in prompting change, so that it supports a description of a snapshot in time rather than an analysis of the processes which might lead to change.

Healey (2005) argues that although General Systems Theory and the unitary model were influential in the development of social work theory for practice they were not always well accepted by practitioners, partly because of the alienating nature of the language/key terms (see Teater, 2014, p29 for an overview). Healey (2005) argues that there was some resistance to the terminology used to explain some core concepts in systems theory such as homeostasis – the tendency for systems to seek to maintain equilibrium (balance/maintaining the status quo) – and the notion of disorder, when the system is disturbed (unstable/chaotic). In these terms the social work role was seen as identifying disorder and working with individuals and their social systems to achieve a steady balance again.

Using systems theory a social work assessment would want to identify the key systems and sub-systems in the situation presented to them, and identify the patterns of interaction between them and the impact of these on different parts of the system. The social worker would then be assessing where it would be best to intervene – a change in one part of the system will result in change to other parts (Teater, 2014). For example, where a child in a family is demonstrating distress, as a result of instability in the family, or earlier attachment difficulties (see Chapter 6, HGD), maybe in behaviour which is very challenging or worrying to others, systems theory would prompt the social worker to explore and consider the network of relationships between systems and sub-systems within the child's context and patterns over time. So, a chronology would not be just a list of events within the child's life, it would ask questions about what was happening around the child at this point. How did the systems around the child respond, what impact did this have on the child or family – did they begin to behave differently in response, were boundaries made more or less open as a result? What else is happening in other systems around the child – is the school system for example under stress and therefore less likely to be accepting or creative in its responses? In the interaction between the school system and the family system, what kind of feedback are parents picking up on – if it is negative, how does this impact? – do they become more defensive and are perceived as threatening, or do they close down and restrict the flow of information? What does this mean for the child? Is it more or less likely that the child's strengths will be reinforced to promote self-esteem and resilience? What is the influence of past interactions between social workers and the family or the school? What will be the impact on the family system, and then the child, of the social worker's position in relation to the school system? The overall context is key too – are we operating within a child safeguarding context? What impact does this system have on the range of sub-systems involved here? If it is possible to intervene, e.g. within the school system to build up resilience factors such as opportunities to succeed, or within the wider family to establish an alternative, consistent interested adult, a change in the child's behaviour as a result of these interventions will inevitably produce change in the family system as it seeks to accommodate the change and achieve equilibrium.

Activity 8.2

Think of an event in your own life, e.g. changing school or moving house. Think about the systems you needed to interact with in order to make progress. How did they interact with each other. Did you need to think about where to intervene to make progress?

Thus, systems theory recognises that *human systems develop patterns of relating over time* (Evans and Kearney, 1996, p15). There was also an argument that this approach had an overemphasis on maintaining the system – which might include a status quo, which may well sustain unacceptable inequalities such as patriarchy (Langan, 1985; Healy, 2005) (see Chapters 9, 15 and 16). However, the shift in focus from the individual to the individual in a complex network of interacting networks and systems has increasingly gained ground in social work theory and practice.

Key systemic concepts and application to SCR

Systems are made up of a number of sub-systems which interact together – the whole is greater than the sum of its parts. This may be the family and different sub-groups within it, such as children and parents for example, or an organisation or a range of agencies which make up safeguarding systems for children or adults. There may be a wider system of a worker and a family and different relationships or sub-systems within this – the worker and the child, the worker and the cared for person, the worker and the carer. In the SCR it is possible to see within the worker and family system, the sub-system of the worker and MZ. Most of the interaction took place between the FNP and MZ; and FZ was rarely present. Within the wider network of helping agencies there are was a sub-system of child-focused health services – the Family Nursing Partnership, midwifery services and the Vulnerable Baby Service for example.

Each system is embedded in a network of wider systems. So, children and parents in a family will operate within wider systems of extended family, schools, community groups, work-place environments, health systems, some of which will also overlap and interconnect. In a family where a parent has mental health problems, there will be interrelationships with GP services, wider mental health services and maybe housing or voluntary support services. This is very evident in the SCR where for example FZ was accessing mental health, addiction and probations services – systems which were also connected with each other and Children's Services.

A change in one part of the system or network of systems will create change in other parts of the system or network. The systems around the family in the SCR seemed to be in a state of flux at times, with uncertainties about processes for passing on concerns and sharing information. For example, the couple changed GP, which meant that some of the known history of the family was not shared, which could have an impact on the assessment of further indicators of concern.

> Some systems are more open than others – and therefore more open to change. Systems with more fixed boundaries will resist change. For example, in the SCR, the threshold criteria for the Vulnerable Baby Service were quite specific and resistant to efforts to involve them in supporting the family.

When these are applied to the context of social work, there are some important implications for practice. Systems thinking informs broad-based assessment practices which *identify the whole range of systems and networks* that interact around a person or family, including the worker, their agency and other agencies and focus attention on *patterns of behaviour* or happenings – moving away from seeing referrals or incidents as one-off events. This idea of patterns of interactions, the impact of changes in one part of a system on other parts, adds depth and complexity to social work analysis. Professor Eileen Munro in her influential review of child protection in England (Munro, 2011) uses systemic ideas to analyse existing issues and think about reform, and picks up this point, arguing that systemic thinking helps us to understand *long chains of causality, ripple effects*. It is important to understand these patterns over time and even generations within families (Burns and Dallos, 2014, p1). It also challenges practitioners to keep a focus on the *process* of what is going on, not just the content – including their own behaviour and their own impact on the range of systems involved.

> As a way of thinking and practising, a systemic view focuses on both the day to day interactions in families and their family traditions. Importantly it also focuses on the efforts professionals put into helping families and individuals to achieve change and how these in turn may become patterned, repetitive and even antipathetic to positive changes.
>
> (Burns and Dallos, 2014)

Systemic ideas then 'fit' very well with the process of hypothesising in social work – thinking about the range of possible explanations for problems people encounter, based on a wider view of the context, the network of systems involved and the ways in which these interact. They challenge practitioners to think carefully about the best way to intervene and to work reflexively as they receive feedback from their interventions into key systems and adjust accordingly.

Ecological systems theory/ecosystems perspectives

Healy (2005) describes general systems theory and unitary theory as the first wave of systems theory and the second as ecosystems theory or ecological theory. Besthorn (2013, in Gray and Webb, 2013) argues that this was a move to *clarify the abstractionism of general systems theory and its perceived lack of practical application*. These ideas were gaining ground within the fields of sociology and psychology and began to influence social work thinking too. Bronfenbrenner (1973), a developmental psychologist was particularly influential. His ecological systems theory proposed a model of the individual interacting within five nested and interdependent systems.

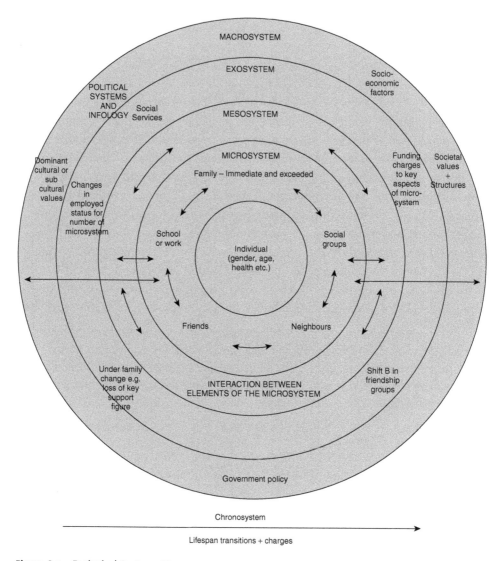

Figure 8.1 Ecological Systems Map

The Chronosystem reflects the transitions and shifts in a person's lifespan and how they affect the person's development over time – e.g. the well-researched impact of early attachment difficulties on relationships in later life.

(Adapted from Bronfenbrenner, 1979, pp8–9)

- The Microsystem is the individual's immediate environment, such as their family, classmates, work colleagues, neighbours.

- The Mesosystem is the interaction and relationships between these different elements of the microsystem. So, for example, if a child is witnessing domestic violence within the home, s/he may be less attentive, or demonstrate distressed behaviour at school, which may affect relationships with teachers and peers.

- The Exosystem refers to elements of the individual's context which indirectly affect them. So parents losing a job, a mother dealing with the loss of her own parent, the impact of a difficult Ofsted inspection at school, will affect elements of the child's microsystem and thus indirectly the child.

- The Macrosystem is the wider societal context which has an impact on the child's microsystem and determines the cultural and socio-economic context in which the child develops.

- The Chronosystem reflects the transitions and shifts in a person's lifespan and how they affect the person's development over time – e.g. the well-researched impact of early attachment difficulties on relationships in later life.

(Howe, 2011)

The ecological approach in social work maintains the focus on the person in context but in comparison with general systems theory focuses more directly on *how* the person interacts with their immediate environment. It draws from key concepts from ecology as applied to the natural world and the relationship we as humans have with life on our planet – and how sensitive ecological systems are to change. *Change one thing and you end up changing other things that are totally unexpected* (Howe, 2009, p109). Key proponents such as Germain (1979) took the view that human development and the physical and social environments of individuals and families needed to be assessed together to provide an holistic understanding of the situation and the possibilities for change.

Germain and Gitterman (1996) and Meyer (1993) led the way in developing ideas from ecology into practice models for social work, the most influential being Germain and Gitterman's *Life Model* (Healey, 2005). Gitterman and Heller (2011) emphasise the interdependence between people and their environment and the importance of understanding this relationship. As in systems theory generally, this leads the worker away from seeing one-off events, and a linear cause and effect model, to an exploration of the reciprocal exchanges between people and between people and their environment. This encourages social workers to shift from the idea of looking for *causes* of problems to be curious about *'What is going on?'* and *'How can the what be changed?'* rather than the *'who' should be changed'* (Gitterman and Germain, 2008, p54, in Gitterman and Heller, 2011, p205). This reflects the cyclical nature of ecological processes – the on-going exchanges between person and the environment and their responses to each other. Ecological theory emphasises the 'goodness-of-fit' between people and their environments.

> *...the 'fit' between a person and their environment is actually the fit between their need, goals and capacities to achieve them and the quality of their physical and social environments...*

(Wilkins and Boahen, 2013, p65)

This introduces the significance of the way people *perceive* the level of 'fit' between themselves (their physical, psychological, emotional strengths and resources) and their environmental resources (family, friends, support networks, physical environment, wider social environment). Gitterman and Germain (2008) explore the 'environment' in some depth. The physical environment is not only the natural environment but the built environment – made by humans, e.g. housing. The wider social environment includes *societal structures that shape the way in which the environment operates and orders itself, such as political legal and economic structures* (Teater, 2014, p25). Both influence, and are influenced by, cultural and social norms, e.g. about the nature of family life. So, for example, in a society where there has been a culture of the male breadwinner supporting the nuclear family (i.e. male parent, female parent and two children), housing provision is more likely to be based on individual units rather than communal living, and employment structures and patterns are likely to reflect inequalities between men and women.

It is suggested that when people face life stressors or challenges, the level of 'fit' will determine whether this becomes a problem. These stressors can include life transitions, e.g. an adolescent moving towards independence, the arrival of a new baby, or a difficult life event such as loss of a loved one, problematic relationships within families, communities or with agencies within the person's environment, as well as 'chronic environment stressors' such as poverty, social location, oppression (Healy, 2005; Teater, 2014). If people feel they have sufficient personal or environmental resources to meet the challenge, a positive 'fit', they will have the opportunity for growth and development as they move through it (Gitterman and Germain, 2008; Gitterman and Heller, 2011). Problems in living are conceived as *a result of stress associated with inadequate fit between people and their environments* (Besthorn, 2013, p76). Teater (2014) gives the example of a situation where an individual has to face a family member receiving a diagnosis of terminal cancer. As overwhelming and difficult as this may be, one person might have access to family support with the practicalities of managing hospital appointments, on-going emotional support and opportunities to maintain a social life; whereas another may already experience strained, non-supportive family relationships and has no access to wider community social and emotional support. It will be more difficult for the latter to develop a level of fit with their environment while trying to deal with this stressful life event.

Activity 8.3

Think again about the point of transition or significant life event in your own life. What were the factors in your environment (remember to think about the physical, emotional and social environment) that helped you to negotiate this? Were there any factors which made it more difficult? What did you learn from this experience?

Given this analysis, this approach steers the practitioner to develop a detailed understanding of the complexities of the interrelationship between the person and their environment. Gitterman and Germain's Life Model has four phases: preparatory, initial, ongoing and ending. The first two stress the importance of gathering information about the person and their environment as a preparation for entering their life. The second two focus on analysing the level of fit between the person and their environment, by looking with the individual at their personal biopsychosocial development (see Chapter 17), identifying previous coping strategies for example, or patterns of behaviour, and their current environment, identifying stressors and strengths, and possibilities for change. This way of developing an understanding the situation forms the basis for the development of mutually agreed goals, which are the basis for the ongoing phase of action and intervention to improve the 'level of fit' between the two by either, or both:

- helping the individual to develop better ways of adapting to the environment, e.g. by changing possibly unrealistic expectations, developing new skills, developing confidence, self-esteem and motivation;

- influencing significant aspects/people, e.g. family member, teacher, health professional, housing department within the environment to be more responsive or helpful to the person or to respond differently.

Case Study: Serious Case Review

Using these ideas to explore the situation outlined in the SCR we can see that although there had been involvement from various agencies at different points of time with the mother and father, and then the family unit, more intensive intervention was initiated at the point at which the family were experiencing a number of life stressors. Both were young parents and the birth of their first child had been followed very quickly by a second pregnancy – a significant 'life transition'. Their youth and a second pregnancy prompted the referral to the Family Nurse Partnership for support. The SCR also highlights wider 'chronic' stressors: the family lived in a deprived ward in Manchester and were living on benefits, with low expectations of achieving a more comfortable lifestyle. From the SCR evidence there also emerge factors of problematic relationships within the family (e.g. domestic violence) and within the local community. FZ had been involved in assaults and been the subject of assaults himself, as well being involved in other crimes such as theft.

In the *interface between the individual and the environment*, the SCR highlights the impact of difficult early life experiences: domestic violence; substance misuse and a degree of learning disability for both MZ's and FZ's *personal resources*. The family's immediate physical *environment* includes poor housing including longstanding difficulties in achieving repairs to the shower. The report does not specifically refer to support from extended family, and the immediate neighbourhood is a ward lacking in resources and with a high rates of unemployment and poverty.

The Family Nurse Partnership model declares that it takes a 'psycho-educational approach', with 'a focus on positive behaviour change' (FNP Unit http://fnp.nhs.uk/about-us). This suggests a focus on improving the individual's capacity to adapt to the environment in order to improve 'fit' and the report indicates an approach by the key worker which tried to focus on promoting confidence, enhancing skills in the care of young children. There is some challenge

(Continued)

(Continued)

from the SCR that this was at the expense of recognising the level of risk for Z. However, the FNP Unit also describes its model as being partly based on Bronfenbrenner's ecological model which means that attention should be paid to the person's environment. The SCR points out that the local community, though deprived, also provided some level of informal support, e.g. swapping baby equipment and there is evidence that support agencies around the family were trying to create some improvement to housing conditions.

From an ecological perspective, a worker would want to be working both at a personal level with MZ and FZ but very much considering the environment, and developing a detailed understanding of its strengths and limitations. This will guide the practitioner to identify ways to improve the environment. This could include securing greater co-ordination of effort among the wide range of helping agencies, e.g. interaction with the housing department to improve housing conditions. There appears to be evidence in the report of rather disconnected efforts being made to provide services and improve the family's environment, and to raise concerns about risk, but equally evidence of the parents not accessing resources which might alleviate the impact of life stressors, by missing appointments, dropping out of services. For workers from an ecological perspective this highlights the interrelationship between person and the environment and the importance of understanding what is happening, the pattern of events and responses from both the family and helping agencies over time.

Reflection Point

Having read this chapter consider some of the strengths and weaknesses of these approaches.

Chapter Summary

Systems and ecological theories identify the central importance of seeing the person in their context, and understanding that this is not a static picture. The individual is always interacting with wider systems/their environment. These interactions are reciprocal so that a change in one aspect will always produce a change somewhere else in the system. These approaches emphasise the importance of process, and of understandings patterns of interaction and behaviour over time. They draw the worker away from intervention focused primarily on work with the individual to a consideration of different strategies which seek to achieve change by intervening at different points in the systems/environment in which the individual is operating.

Further Reading

Healy (2005, pp 137–140) describes the phases of Germain and Gitterman's Life Model and applies this to a case study.

Chapter 9

Feminism and social work

Catherine Donovan

Achieving a Social Work Degree

This chapter will help you meet the following capabilities, to the appropriate level, from the Professional Capabilities Framework:

PCF 2 Values and Ethics

- Understand the professional's ethical principles and their relevance to practice, and demonstrate awareness of own personal values and how these can impact on practice;

PCF 4 Rights, Justice and Economic Wellbeing

- Understand the principles of rights, justice and economic wellbeing, and their significance for social work practice;

PCF 6 Critical Reflection and Analysis

- Understand the need to construct hypotheses in social work practice;

PCF 8 Context and Organisations

- Demonstrate awareness of the impact of organisational context on social work practice.

Introduction

Feminism and social work share many goals and core principles: social change and social justice, empowerment, activism, being non-judgemental and challenging oppression (Latting, 1995; Rose and Hanssen, 2010). In this chapter you will be introduced to the ways in which feminist theory can provide conceptual tools for making sense of human behaviour.

In truth it is better to talk about feminisms rather than feminism since there are many different feminist approaches to making sense of the world. There are commonalities across feminisms – for example, they place women or being female at the centre of their analysis and seek to understand women's (typically unequal) position in society. This also involves being interested in how power operates in society at micro (for example, between individual family members) and macro (between the state and its female and male citizens) levels. In theorising power, the concept of patriarchy is used which, put simply, is a label given to hierarchical social systems in which men are able to dominate positions of power and accumulate resources unequally compared to women and are able to exert power over women and other men. While Walby (1997) points to the changing nature of patriarchy and the position of women in society over time, she provides an analysis that focuses on six patriarchal systems that support a patriarchal society: the labour market; the gendered division of labour in the home/family; culture and its representation of women; violence against women; (hetero) sexuality; and the state. However, there are also differences between feminisms that are important and can reflect not only how human behaviour can be explained but also what agendas for change might follow on from that analysis.

(To illustrate application to social work practice, the SCR of Child Z will be referred to throughout this chapter.)

Four waves of feminism in social work

In their work, Phillips and Cree (2014) refer to four waves of feminism and their impacts on social work. The first wave, between the 1840s and 1920s, saw the emergence of liberal feminism, which, they argue, can be characterised as an approach based on the idea that women and men are equal but different. Many liberal feminists argued that the world of business or politics, for example, would benefit from the contribution of women's uniquely feminine characteristics on an equal playing field with men. Liberal feminism underpins the agenda promoting equal opportunities: demanding the state provide appropriate laws and policies to make society fairer so that women and men can compete equally. The Equal Pay Act (1970) is an early example of attempts to promote equal opportunities for women and men while more recently, in 2015, Shared Parental Leave was introduced to allow men to have the same involvement with their babies as women. Critiques of this approach point to the fact that what men have is predominantly used as the benchmark for equality rather than questioning the benchmarks in the first place (for example, should full-time employment be the goal we all should aspire to?). Others have pointed to the evidence that changing legal/societal structures do not seem to have the desired effect of improving attitudes/beliefs/prejudices about women. The focus on equal opportunities also assumes an individualist approach to human behaviour that can ignore other structural factors (such as age, social class, 'race' and ethnicity and so on) that shape and present barriers to choices.

In the second wave of feminism, between the 1960s and the 1980s (Phillips and Cree, 2014), liberal feminism was joined by Marxist or Socialist feminism and Radical feminism. Marxist feminism focuses on a dual systems approach to making sense of human behaviour: analysing the interacting impact of patriarchal and capitalist systems on social outcomes for women and men. In this approach the needs of capital (i.e. employers and/or shareholders) are understood to opportunistically draw on, reflect and reinforce patriarchal assumptions about gender roles, depending on local needs. Thus women are understood to be a surplus labour force who can be relied on in times of need by capitalist economies (for example, when men are away at war), or as a secondary labour force (with flexible hours and low, typically part-time wages, especially when they have dependent children) supplementing the wages of the primary breadwinners, the men. This can occur because women's primary roles are understood to be focused in the home, or primary sphere, being homemakers and mothers. Critiques of this approach point to the overemphasis on capitalism as a key source of inequality. These critiques, from Radical feminism, instead prioritise patriarchy as the dominant organising concept that provides an analysis of the ways in which women are systematically oppressed in all aspects of their lives and focuses on an analysis of their sex/body as the vehicle through which their oppression is maintained. Women's bodies and their sex is core to defining: their worth as (sexually and socially) attractive; their role as (primarily) mothers and carers of children and family; and their subordinate position in relation to men through domestic and sexual violence, sexual harassment, pornography and sex work/prostitution. Conversely, critiques of this approach point to the ways in which Radical feminism can (albeit inadvertently) construct women as passive victims of their fate, with little or no ability to act and have influence in their lives, i.e. to have limited or no agency, and no ability to resist their circumstances.

During the third wave of feminism, the 1980s to the 1990s (Phillips and Cree, 2014), these three feminisms were critiqued for too often foregrounding the situation and experiences of white, middle-class, heterosexual women who are able-bodied, as representative of all women. Black feminists, lesbian feminists, disabled feminists, international feminists, working-class feminists and others wrote and campaigned for theoretical approaches that were more inclusive of the different ways in which women (and men) were positioned in societies in unequal ways and the ways in which being Black, a woman and working class, for example, might result in very different experiences of society. Thus feminist analysis began to open up to and research the multiple identities that women might live and/or inhabit and to live up to its earliest core values to give voice to those who have historically been marginalised.

These critiques also illustrate another crucial piece of understanding about feminist social (and psychological) theory necessary to fully understand a feminist's approach and therefore to know how to apply that theory. This is about the root causes of human behaviour and whether sex, gender, or sexuality are understood in essentialist or social constructionist ways. Essentialist theories are characterised as reductive and present human behaviour as being either explained through biology (genetics, hormones, chemicals, being 'hard wired', and, most recently, neuroscience) or by assumption that there are universal ways of experiencing or living as a woman or a man and that, therefore writing about one group of women (or men) can be generalised to represent all women (or men). Essentialist differences are understood to be universal, across time, national, cultural and faith borders, and can be reduced to assumptions that all women (and all men) are the same. Gender differences are explained as the result of the different reproductive potentials women and men have which are assumed to lead to different interests in sex, family, parenting and the world of work. For example, women are assumed to have a maternal instinct that leads to them being nurturers and private sphere (the home) facing with an interest in, for example, peace or ecology while men are believed to be driven to have penetrative sex, to 'sow their seed' and establish a lineage but to otherwise be public sphere (the world of work, politics and war) facing.

Social constructionist approaches

Social constructionist approaches disagree fundamentally with essentialist approaches, arguing and evidencing that sex, gender and sexuality are products of society and the particular social forces (relating to the economy, politics, culture, ideologies, etc.) occurring in any historical moment (See Chapter 7.) Gender, sex and sexuality are understood to be separately constructed and historically, culturally and socially produced (Oakley, 1993), thus while women might share similar bodies and reproductive organs (their sex) there are many different ways to be feminine or to 'do' gender and there are many ways in which women might express or identify their sexuality which cannot necessarily be 'predicted' by their gender or their sex. Importantly, power is also theorised in ways that acknowledge the multiple ways that individuals and groups resist powerful ideas and structures in society. Foucault's ideas about power are also important for many social constructionists as he argued that in the modern state, power no longer belongs to a powerful group who exert it over subordinate groups but instead can be characterised in biopower and governmentality. In this approach, power is understood to circulate society through ideas, language and discourses that inevitably produce (differential) resistance, but also self-governance as dominant ideas become internalised and reproduced as situated or contingent 'truths'. We can see this illustrated in the SCR where MZ's resistance to being recognisably a victim works against her. MZ does not, apparently, behave like a 'victim' of domestic violence. She maintains a silence around this, retracts her only statement to the police, meets practitioners in venues that are not at home (managing what they see) and denies that she has experienced any domestic violence. If she had presented with more physical signs of violence or had continually rung the police, or had showed vulnerability and weakness in respect of FZ, might practitioners more quickly have picked up that she was, and responded to her as, a survivor of domestic violence?

Importantly, social constructionist approaches also critique theories of socialisation that argue gender is learnt or has developed by a certain age. Instead, social constructionist approaches, for example, in the work of Connell (2009) argue that gender is an on-going, negotiated set of behaviours, assumptions, beliefs, attitudes and expectations that are relational, i.e. that femininity and masculinity are constructed in relation to each other in everyday social situations. That gender is relational is a central aspect of understanding the dominant expectations that exist about masculinity and femininity (which includes the assumption that there is only one way of being either). Gender as relational has resulted in there being beliefs that what men are women cannot be and vice versa: women are victims, men cannot be victims. In the SCR we can see that MZ has difficulties getting the support she needs because she does not fit the picture of a victimised woman. Conversely, we might also ask why, apparently, little attention was paid, if any, to the fact that FZ had experienced abuse and childhood trauma as a result of living in a family where domestic violence occurred? If FZ was understood to have been victimised might he have been provided with more support for his own behaviour and wellbeing?

It has become increasingly understood that these gender binaries (male/female, strong/weak, aggressive/nurturing, perpetrator/victim) work to inhibit inclusive understandings about human behaviour. Binaries exist in many areas of social life but in relation to making sense of how women and men behave they can be both illuminating and restrictive. Theorists such as Connell (2009) and Rahman and Jackson (2010) have provided analyses of the ways in which being female or male have been constructed in opposition to each other: what is female cannot be male and vice versa. However, their analysis has also pointed to the ways in which these oppositions are ascribed unequal value insofar as what is associated with maleness (strength, leadership, rationality) is more highly valued that what has come to be associated with femaleness (vulnerability, weakness, being emotional, being supportive). While these binaries are useful theoretically to understand the social construction of gender in any particular social context, they are also restrictive in everyday situations for both women and men. For example, Connell (2009) argues that men are 'prepared' for violence insofar as they are expected and encouraged to focus on bodily strength, to be physically active and to be physical with others either in playful or aggressive ways. If boys fight parents might agree that this is wrong, but they might also believe that boys are doing what comes naturally. Conversely, girls are not prepared for violence: they are not encouraged to develop physical strength nor to engage much in physical activity, including games at school. They are expected to be uninterested in sport or other ways of being physical, certainly we do not expect them to get involved with aggressive behaviours. Such dominant gendered ideas and influences can make it difficult to respond appropriately when we have to make sense of situations of domestic violence, when men, for example, might give accounts of having been victimised by family members or when women do not live up to assumptions about being victims of violence.

Similar assumptions can be made about other aspects of family life such as parenting and this is illustrated in the SCR. It is clear that FZ's involvement with MZ's pregnancy or as a parent once the children were born was not a focus of either concern or work for practitioners. His absence when midwives, health visitors or social workers visited was not noted in the same way as the non-attendance of MZ at clinic appointments were. If practitioners had the same expectations of FZ as a parent as they had of MZ would this have made a difference to how they might have worked with him?

Reflection Point

Does 'parent' have the same resonance as 'mother' or 'father'? What are the gendered differences that get made invisible by referring to FZ and MZ as parents? When professionals say that they work with families is this true? What work did professionals do with FZ as a parent/father in this family? What expectations did they have of him as a father/partner?

Emergence of post-feminism

During Phillipson and Cree's (2014) third wave of feminism, from the 1990s to the 2000s, post-feminism emerged. In this approach, the very nature of the focus of inquiry is questioned: woman (or man) is understood as a socially constructed category that has no reality or truth except through and within its historical moment so what it is to be a woman is only ever as true as the immediate context within which woman is experienced and/or lived and is always contingent. Judith Butler (1990) introduced the idea that gender identities and sexuality are fluid and unfinished (akin to theorists like Connell's critique of socialisation theories) and can be understood as performance. In other words, Butler's, and others', work built on the idea, explained earlier, that sex, sexuality and gender can all be understood separately, to argue that they can each be deconstructed in order to resist heteronormativity. In other words, socially constructed norms of gender and sexuality can be disrupted and/or subverted in order to challenge norms of heterosexuality from which often come, norms of gender, sex and family. This approach also involves more of a focus on the individual to understand their own life and, according to Phillips and Cree, in feminism and social work, a focus on involving men in the development of strategies to challenge and support their role in families (see for example the work of Featherstone (e.g. 2009) on fatherhood).

Power is also understood to be 'slippery' rather than being 'owned' by particular social groups or individuals, for example, some feminist arguments would have had it that all men have power over all women. It is now understood that there are diversities among women and men and that in some contexts white women might have power over Black men. Drawing on Foucault's ideas about disciplinary power, power is conceptualised as being everywhere and relative since no identities or positions can actually exist. Feminists who draw on materialist and/or structuralist approaches to understanding the social world (they might be Marxist feminists or Radical feminists) have found post-feminist approaches deeply troubling because of the former's adherence to a feminist agenda that promotes social change. They argue that such an agenda becomes difficult to sustain through the classic feminist 'slogan' that 'the personal is the political' if personhood is understood as a fluid, temporary, position rather than as a member of a group with a shared set of experiences that can be reframed into political demands for social change.

Praxis (the co-existence of theory and practice as a goal and method for achieving social change) has always been central to feminisms and post-feminism appears to undo this. Social change has relied on there being identities (women) who share enough experiences of oppression and discrimination to warrant political action to agitate for change to improve the conditions of all women. Such oppression and discrimination can be measured, evidenced and 'felt' tangibly by those who are oppressed (low pay, the feminisation of poverty, homelessness, the results of violence and so on). Post-feminist claims that the identity 'woman' does not exist has also led to critiques of post-feminism as relativist, undermining the material inequalities between social groups (e.g. Jackson and Scott, 2010). There is some evidence of relativism in the SCR where it is clear that several of the professionals judged that the home environment in which FZ, MZ and their children lived was acceptable even though there were signs of chaos, dirt and unhygienic conditions and violence. Their assessment can be seen as relativist insofar as they are accepting standards of home life for MZ and FZ that they would not accept for themselves.

Such relativism can also be seen to be played out in some of the key professionals' assessment of the relationship between MZ and FZ. The SCR concludes that the signs of domestic violence and other violence were not recognised or taken seriously and nor was the *history of obsession/very controlling personalities often associated with low self-esteem; FZ's history and his childhood trauma of maternal death were all factors that were not looked at and the implications for his sense of identity and self-worth* (p58). We might ask why the fact that there were weapons displayed on the walls of the family home was not identified as a source of serious concern not just for MZ but also the children. The Serious Crime Act 2015 brought in the new crime of coercive control, in December 2015. This has been introduced to address domestic violence that is not necessarily physical in nature. Might knowledge about coercive control (which was introduced into the Home Office definition of domestic violence in 2013) have been helpful in making sense of either MZ's or FZ's behaviour?

Fourth wave of feminism

Phillips and Cree (2014) argue that the fourth wave of feminism began in 2008 and that we are still in that wave. Intersectionality which emerged as an academic concept in the 1990s, as both a theoretical approach to making sense of human behaviours and a methodology for collecting data about human behaviour, has increasingly been used in practice settings in the 2000s. Crenshaw (1989) was a pioneer of intersectionality in her work attempting to illuminate the ways in which African-American women experienced discrimination within the criminal justice system when they sought redress for domestic violence. Crenshaw's approach challenges us to understand that experiences cannot be described through an additive approach to identities, i.e. gender 'added' to 'race', because intersecting identities might *mutually and simultaneously* make up everyday experiences – your experience is *as* a woman who is Black. Experiences can also be the result of the *perceptions* of (and assumptions about) your identities by others (in this case professionals) within institutional systems as well as your own self-identified identities. Walby's (2007) approach to intersectionality focuses more on the institutional processes producing unequal outcomes than to the individual's location within those systems. This is illustrated in the SCR when FZ and MZ are assessed by professionals to have different standards of family life because of their gender and their social class, their learning disabilities and their family backgrounds. Because of this, professionals seemed not to be able to successfully identify coercive control or domestic violence, they had little or no expectations that FZ was or could be an involved father to his children and it was not noted that he did not bring his children to clinic appointments. They did not seem to act on their knowledge about his experiences as a child living in a home where domestic violence had occurred and assess him as having been victimised himself as a result. MZ is not identified as a potential victim of domestic violence yet is held responsible for being a responsible mother and it is noted when she fails in this by not attending appointments with her children. Thus the systems and professions of social work, health visiting, maternity nursing, probation and the police can be seen to fail this family because of the assumptions they made about their intersecting identities and their lack of knowledge about domestic violence and abuse.

Implications for social work

Within social work, there are attempts to maintain what is seen as the usefulness of post-feminism to promote understandings of a diversity of experience, de-centre the dominant group's experience, and provide ways of centring marginalised voices and experiences in intersectional ways. This is seen as essential not only to better understand the experiences of service users but also to honour their experiences and include them in the development of interventions, not only for their own, but more broadly for social, change (Morley and Macfarlane, 2012; Phillips and Cree, 2014).

The family has always been a site of analysis for feminism and is the site for assessment and intervention for social work. Families have been seen as both the cause of, and solution to, social problems. Taking a feminist approach to a family requires an understanding that the family can be a site of conflict, unequal power and abuse of power between women and men, between parents and children and between more and less able/resourced family members. For some families, for example Black families and lesbian-headed families, family can also be a haven in a racist or homophobic environment, a support for self-identity/self-esteem, important for a sense of solidarity and culture affirming. Being aware of how powerful ideas are about the nuclear family and its accompanying assumptions about (hetero)sexuality, gender roles and the division of labour in the home, including the gendered distribution of power is crucial in ensuring the service user and their (actual) family are centred in any assessment.

Gender binaries should also be kept mind when considering family life in order to challenge assumptions about motherhood and what mothers *should* do/be and the tendency to mother blaming, and beliefs about how sacrificial and unconditional a mother's love should be. Because of these beliefs female survivors of domestic violence are often treated harshly when they apparently do not protect their children from violent men/fathers (Hester, 2011), yet too often the violent men/fathers are invisible in professional contexts (Donovan and Griffiths, 2013).

Conclusion

Being able to understand the wider social context in which women and men live can illuminate the individual circumstances of any particular women: women, as single parents, as pensioners, as disabled people or parents of disabled child(ren), are among the poorest in society. At the same time, the underlying problem facing families where children are being assessed for child protection plans is overwhelmingly domestic violence (Department of Education, 2015). Feminism and social work share similar core values and principles as well as interests insofar as most social work practitioners and services users are women (Langam, 1992). Feminist research methodologies also parallel social work approaches to assessment: listening to and placing women at the centre of their own stories in order to understand their circumstances from their point of view. It is better to think about feminisms rather than feminism. Different approaches understand gender inequality differently and can have different agendas for change as a result.

A feminist approach can also enable a holistic understanding of the context in which the woman and her family live by being able to understand that there are links between gendered norms within the private and public spheres. Families are central to the work of social work and feminism and they are understood as both cause of and solution to social problems. Taking a professional approach that encourages recognition of diverse accounts of sex, gender and sexuality and that understands individual identities are intersecting can promote relationships of respect and trust even if these are also, necessarily, structurally unequal relationships.

Chapter Summary

This chapter provides a chronological account of several different strands of feminist thinking and how the underpinning ideas and values are understood to parallel those within social work. Using the SCR, the chapter provides illustrative examples of how feminist approaches can be used to critique the ways in which assumptions are made about gender and the division of labour in families and parenting. With its focus on domestic violence, the SCR also provides a way of applying a feminist analysis of structural and personal power both within intimate and family relationships and more broadly in society and in institutions of the state such as the police, social services and probation.

Further Reading

Domminelli, L (2002) *Feminist Social Work Theory and Practice*. Basingstoke: Palgrave Macmillan.

Featherstone, B (2001) Where to for feminist social work? *Critical Social Work*, 2001 (2): 1.

Home Office (2016) *Ending Violence Against Women and Girls Strategy 2016-2021*. London: Home Office.

Turner S and Maschi, T (2015) Feminist and empowerment theory and social work practice. *Journal of Social Work Practice: Psychotherapeutic Approaches in Health, Welfare and the Community*, 29 (2): 151–62.

Chapter 10

Reflexivity

Mark Bradley

Achieving a Social Work Degree

This chapter will help you meet the following capabilities, to the appropriate level, from the Professional Capabilities Framework:

PCF 1 Professionalism

- Describe the role of a social worker and the importance of personal and professional boundaries and behaviour, demonstrate ability to learn using a range of approaches;

PCF 2 Values and Ethics

- Understand the professional's ethical principles and their relevance to practice, and demonstrate awareness of own personal values and how these can impact on practice;

PCF 3 Diversity

- Recognise the importance of diversity in human identity and experience, and the application of anti-discriminatory and anti-oppressive principles in social work practice;

PCF 4 Rights, Justice and Economic Wellbeing

- Understand the principles of rights, justice and economic wellbeing, and their significance for social work practice;

PCF 5 Knowledge

- Demonstrate an initial understanding of the application of research, theory and knowledge from sociology, social policy, psychology, health and human growth and development to social work;

PCF 6 Critical Reflection and Analysis

- Understand the need to construct hypotheses in social work practice;

PCF 7 Intervention and Skills

- Demonstrate an awareness of a range of frameworks to assess and plan intervention and demonstrate initial awareness of risk and safeguarding;

PCF 8 Context and Organisations

- Demonstrate awareness of the impact of organisational context on social work practice.

Introduction

The notion of reflexivity has become progressively more important to social work education, theory and practice and therefore an understanding of reflexive practice is equally valuable to social work students and newly qualified practitioners alike (D'Cruz et al., 2007). In this chapter, the concept of reflection will be developed further theoretically towards the concept of reflexivity as a sociological theory. As well as being a methodological tool, reflexivity in its sociological form is useful for social workers as a means of *reflection in action*; this enables the practitioner to change their approach to any situation as it unfolds rather than *reflection on action,* which involves reflecting upon events after they have happened (Schön, 1983; Parton and O'Byrne, 2000; Fook, 2002). From this perspective, reflexivity can be considered to be the circular relationship between cause and effect with social work practitioners playing an influential role in any interaction between themselves and service users or carers (Knott and Scragg, 2013). This chapter will also apply reflexive thinking to an example of social work practice, to demonstrate how the ability to recognise the impact of one's words and actions, upon the responses of the service users and carers, encourages the consideration of one's own position and influence within any interaction.

Theory of reflexivity

The idea of something (or someone) being reflexive is not new to the English language with the first definition of the term, 'capable of turning, deflecting, or bending back', appearing in the *Oxford English Dictionary* in the sixteenth century. A meaning perhaps more relevant to modern social sciences, originates from the fields of philosophy and psychology: 'Of a mental action, process, etc.: turned or directed back upon the mind itself; involving intelligent self-awareness or self-examination' (Oxford University Press, 2016). The history of the term's use in relation to the social sciences (particularly sociology), however, is somewhat more complicated, as it has been used to describe numerous different theories by a number of different academics within the field.

The American philosopher, sociologist and psychologist, George Herbert Mead (1934), arguably provided the first comprehensive definition of reflexivity, which placed emphasis upon the social nature of humanity. Mead (1934) proposed that reflexivity was an essential condition within social interaction which not only enabled the development of our own self-awareness but, by *the turning back of the experience of the individual upon himself*, it was also possible for an individual to experience situations through the eyes of the other person (Mead, 1934, p134). This awareness, in theory, would enable an individual to reflexively modify or adapt their response to the given circumstances accordingly.

Alvin Gouldner (1970) suggested that by further understanding one's own place within society, it is possible to better understand others within their social worlds. To explain his view, Gouldner uses an analogy from fellow sociologist, Harold Garfinkel (1917–2011) in which he likens sociologists to goldfish swimming in a bowl, spending their time analysing other goldfish, without ever stopping to acknowledge that they too are sharing the same environment (water) with the fish they study. For Gouldner, reflexive sociology means getting into the habit of viewing one's own beliefs in the same way that we view the beliefs held by those we are observing.

Pierre Bourdieu's notion of reflexive sociology also refers to developing an appreciation of our own self and position within society in order to better understand the reality of others (Bourdieu and Wacquant, 1992). This concept is aligned with the work of Charles Wright Mills (1959) who wrote of the 'sociological imagination' and suggested that sociologists needed to involve themselves in the everyday experiences of their subjects and be willing to step into the other person's shoes, in order to understand why things happen the way they do. Reflexive sociology, therefore, requires us to be sceptical of our own views and judgements and to recognise that those we observe are doing exactly the same when observing us.

Reflexivity and social work

Within social work literature, reflexivity is also seen as a complex concept with a number of different interpretations and meanings, often used interchangeably with reflection (D'Cruz et al., 2007). However, reflexivity differs from reflectivity in that it provides immediate feedback and thereby affords the opportunity, if so desired, for the practitioner to modify or tailor their approach towards any given situation, according to the reaction received (Schön, 1983; Payne, 2002). In this way, the reflexive social worker is seen as both an *active thinker*, able to assess, react and intervene and as a *social actor*, aware of the significance of their role within the social work process, understanding of the impact of their participation upon their professional relationship with service users (Sheppard, 1998, p767).

In order to practise reflexively it is necessary to *bend one's thinking back on itself* and question the origin and rationale behind the knowledge, rather than simply accepting it (O'Sullivan, 2011, p10). The reflexive practitioner must therefore understand that, as well as being a provider of information and knowledge, they are also recipients of the same. As such they should appreciate that the knowledge which informs their practice originates from the dominant discourse to which they are exposed within their profession, together with their own social, professional and ethical conditioning. (See Chapter 15.) Practising reflexively therefore means being prepared to challenge 'professional norm circles' (those within an organisation who promote specific behaviour) and resisting the temptation of falling into non-reflexive or repetitive practice (Elder-Vass, 2012). Reflexive practice should also include the interrogation of previously accepted hypotheses or methods and it can therefore be argued that reflexivity or reflexive action may result from the analysis of, or reflecting upon, reflective practice (Ixer, 1999).

In the context of social work assessments, reflexivity is concerned with how we, as social workers, continue to question or critique our interpretations of risk and how the influence of our own professional identity impacts upon the conclusions that we make (Rojek et al., 1988). All people carry 'personal baggage' around with them and social workers are no exception; practitioners should therefore be encouraged to question their own values and assumptions and to assess the impact of these beliefs and their own professional practice on service users (Banks, 2006; Sheppard, 2006). Horwath (2007) goes as far as to suggest that practitioner reflexivity could be considered as a *missing domain* within the assessment process and refers to research conducted by McKeown (2000) who found that when it came to support for the family, the quality of the social worker's relationship with the family accounted for 30 per cent of the parental motivation to change (Morrison, 2010, p321). (See Chapter 14.) From this, it can be seen that a reflexive practitioner, aware of their own impact, will identify with the influence of their position and appreciate the significant positive effect that it will have upon the outcome of the assessment. Conversely, failing to take a reflexive approach to assessments may lead to inaccuracies and lost opportunities, which could have a negative impact upon their own practice and the lives of the people they support (O'Sullivan, 2011).

Implications for social work practice

It can be said that modern social work practice is *typically characterised by indeterminacy, uncertainty and non-linearity that demands attention to reflexivity* (Lam et al., 2007, p95). As a social worker currently practising in a busy team within a local authority, I can attest to the accuracy of this statement, the unpredictable nature of the situations confronted by practitioners and to the importance of practising reflexively. To illustrate this, I intend to refer to a series of interactions, within an example of my own practice. There is nothing remarkable about this scenario; on the contrary it is typical of any situation that any student or newly qualified social worker could encounter within their placement or early practice, and could realistically be replaced by numerous other examples to illustrate the value of reflexive practice. It is not, however, the purpose of this account to scrutinise practice or procedures, but rather to look beyond these frameworks to consider personal thoughts and experiences in an attempt to illustrate the value of applying a reflexive approach to practice. In order to guarantee confidentiality of all concerned and in keeping with the Health and Care Professions Council (HCPC) *Standards of Proficiency* (HCPC, 2012), the names of all persons, places and organisations have been changed or anonymised; the reflection however remains genuine, as does the practice scenario upon which it is based.

Case Study

Reflexivity in action

I was asked to make an unannounced visit to a family; the purpose of the visit being to observe the home conditions, to check that there was sufficient food in the house to sustain the family and also to ensure that there was no evidence of the parents using drugs in the presence of their children. I had attended the family home with a colleague earlier in the week to begin the assessment process, and at that time, it appeared that there was insufficient food in the house to sustain a family of six. Upon hearing this, the father of the children, Andrew, informed us that the contents of his kitchen cupboards were none of our business and left the house. As we left the home, the mother of the children, Beth, was informed that owing to the concerns raised by the police, there would need to be further visits undertaken and although there was no suggestion of drug use at that time, there were concerns regarding the lack of food. Beth confirmed that she and her partner had occasionally used cannabis and 'speed' (amphetamine sulphate), but never in the presence of the children and although Andrew did have previous convictions for assault, he would never dream of hurting her or the children. Beth also stated that she intended to go shopping to get some food that day and unfortunately, we had visited before she had the opportunity to get to the supermarket.

As I now drove towards the home address, I began to visualise different scenarios in my mind; imagining how I would be viewed by the family that I was about to visit and trying to envisage situations that I might encounter when I arrived at the house. Archer (2003) refers to this 'internal conversation' as the mental capacity to consider oneself in relation to one's social context (Burkitt, 2012, p462). I tried to imagine the effect that my attendance might have upon the family; how would I be viewed by these people whose lives I was going to descend upon without prior warning? How would I feel if I was being visited in the same way by Social Services? I wondered how they would respond to me as an unannounced and probably unwelcomed guest and also as an agent of the local authority.

Giddens (1991) suggests that reflexivity stems from the knowledge and understanding that a person has in relation to their position and role within society; this knowledge is used to

(Continued)

(Continued)

influence their 'social practices' (Burkitt, 2012, pp460–2). This theory is however challenged by Archer (2000, 2003) who accepts that reflexivity relies upon one's ability to consider their social position but insists that Giddens has overlooked the pre-existing capacities possessed by humans, which form the foundations of reflexive thought. According to Archer (2000), and drawing upon the developmental psychology of Piaget (1896–1980), a person's ability to think reflexively has much more primitive origins and develops in infancy as the child begins to explore and gain a greater understanding of itself and the surrounding world. (See Chapter 4.) This reflexive ability, which develops further as language is learned, *is prior to, and primitive to, our sociality* (Archer, 2000, p7).

Upon arriving at the address, I knocked on the door ensuring that my photographic identity card was clearly visible. As I waited for the door to be answered the 'internal conversation' continued... The door was answered by Beth, who was holding the youngest of her four children. Before I had chance to speak she said 'Oh it's you, what the hell do you want?' I explained to her the reason for my visit and, after a brief pause which was accompanied by an audible sigh, Beth invited me into her home. Once inside, I noticed another of her children sitting on the sofa in the front room watching television, however the volume of the television was at such a level that it would have proven very difficult to hold a conversation. I asked Beth if she 'wouldn't mind turning the television volume down so that we could talk' and, after a further pause, she agreed to my request.

Sheppard describes the reflexive practitioner as a 'social actor', a participant in a scenario in the *conduct of their practice... able to assess, respond and initiate action* (Sheppard, 1998, p767). In this instance, by asking Beth to grant me the seemingly small request of turning the television down, I was immediately assessing our relationship and concluding that by agreeing to do so, Beth had already gone some way towards accepting the authority that I represented. While this small concession on Beth's part may, on the surface, appear trivial or unimportant had she refused, I may have considered her refusal as an indication that perhaps she did not want to engage with me and modified my approach accordingly. Reflexivity involves considering one's response to an immediate context and then acting upon that decision, thereby making choices for further direction (D'Cruz et al., 2007, p.75). In this way it differs from 'reflective practice', which, according to Gibbs, is effectively *looking back on practice and practice incidents and adjusting future practice on the basis of these reflections* (Gibbs, 2009, p296).

Beth informed me that her partner, Andrew, would be back soon as he was dropping the other two children off at her mother's house which was a couple of streets away; however, as I began to discuss the purpose of my visit with Beth, her partner Andrew entered the house via the rear kitchen door. Andrew was stripped to the waist (a fact that I considered a little unusual as it was the middle of January and approximately 4 degrees Celsius outside) and upon seeing me appeared to become immediately agitated by my presence, demanding to know what I was doing in his home.

Based upon previous professional experience I was aware that some of the more noticeable signs of amphetamine use are increased body temperature, dilated pupils, 'jaw clamping' and a dry mouth; these physical signs can also be accompanied by increased feelings of restlessness and heightened aggression. In order to practise reflexively, a social worker must be able to react to each person's unique qualities and resist the temptation to stereotype or rely upon presuppositions; a failure to do so can lead to the practitioner making unsubstantiated assumptions, which can lead to missed opportunities to engage with families (Parton and O'Byrne, 2000; O'Sullivan, 2011).

Assessing Andrew's presentation, I had no reason to believe that he was under the influence of amphetamine or indeed any other illegal substance. I was, however, still aware of the police information with regards to the allegation of criminal damage and Beth's disclosure of Andrew's violent history. I therefore decided that before going any further, I needed to enquire into his lack of clothing as it may indeed have been associated with increased body temperature, one of the side-effects of amphetamine use. My request for an explanation was however, delivered in a subtle, non-antagonistic manner and in such a way that it reduced the possibility of receiving an aggressive response.

Sheppard (2006) comments that such an approach is important in reflexive practice as insensitive or aggressive questioning is likely to receive a hostile response and diminish the opportunity to gain the trust of the service user. By deciding to enquire further into the reasons behind Andrew's presentation, rather than simply continuing to explain the reason for my attendance, I was adapting my practice to the situation that had presented itself by mentally undertaking an immediate risk assessment.

Social workers can be asked to deal with particularly difficult situations when it comes to assessing risk, especially when there is a possibility of child abuse. Furthermore, the social worker may face criticism for taking action *or* for failing to act, when faced with the same set of circumstances (Carson and Bain, 2008). In such situations, while it remains important to maintain a non-judgemental attitude towards the service user, the social worker is inevitably influenced by their own life experience, values and social background (Biestek, 1961). Therefore, an ability to critically appraise oneself in action, together with the capacity to recognise that our beliefs and principles originate from our own life experiences, facilitates the development of self-reflexivity (Fook, 2002).

Andrew asked me to follow him out to the yard as he had something to show me. Again, by drawing upon my personal experience and by constantly monitoring his body language, I continually assessed the risk he posed to my safety. I was also mindful of a Health and Safety Executive (HSE) report that I had recently read that found workers in the social care sector had higher than average risk of being assaulted at work (HSE, 2014). As I made my way through the narrow kitchen, passing the knife block within which stood six presumably very sharp knives, the on-going mental risk assessment, the 'internal conversation' continued... Once out in the yard, Andrew pointed to a makeshift gym that he had assembled using a variety of ropes, pulleys and rusty weights. He explained that he had been 'working out' when Beth had asked him to take the children over to her mother's house for a couple of hours and, as she only lived a couple of streets away, he had rushed them round to see her without putting a top on. This interaction between Andre and I, which involved me showing my appreciation of his handiwork and him providing a perfectly feasible explanation for his state of undress, seemed to put him at ease and facilitated a conversation regarding the concerns that had been raised. By adopting this reflexive approach to practice, I was able to engage the family in the assessment process which subsequently identified a need for support.

The concept of 'relational reflexivity' occurs when self-reflexivity is shared with the service user and requires social work practitioners to appreciate that they are not independent of, nor separate to, any interaction by recognising that the language used is itself influenced by their own knowledge and experience (Parton and O'Byrne, 2000). Relational reflexivity can also enable the practitioner to remove barriers to engagement, challenge preconceived issues of power and gain a greater understanding of the issues that are of most importance to the client or service user (D'Cruz et al., 2007). In doing so, by giving the service user a 'voice' it may be possible to design and create a service that they want (Parton and O'Byrne, 2000, p76).

Chow et al. (2011, p142) describe reflexivity as a *slippery term* and there are also those who suggest that reflexivity and critical reflection are one and the same with the two terms being used as *interchangeable concepts* (Taylor and White, 2000; D'Cruz et al., 2007). In the social work context, however, reflexive practice centres upon one's ability to reflect in the 'here and now', to understand that every action or decision taken has a consequence and then to be able to adapt one's practice accordingly. The ability to *locate oneself in the situation and recognise how {one} influences and is influenced by the people and events being observed* is essential to practising reflexively (Fook, 2002, p.43). In this way, reflexive practice differs from reflective practice because the practitioner is not afforded the time to sit and contemplate or discuss the course of action to be taken. The ability to adapt one's practice 'in the moment' therefore becomes an essential part in the reflexive practitioner's skillset. In order to think and act reflexively in this way, while it is essential to have an understanding of the goals that you are aiming to achieve, it is equally important to understand your own strengths and weaknesses. As illustrated in the case study given, an appreciation of one's own professional and personal value base together with an awareness of the impact that this will have upon any subsequent actions or decision-making, is also central to practising reflexively. Involving the client, recognising their role in your practice and being prepared to challenge preconceived attitudes towards knowledge and power relations are therefore fundamental to becoming a skilled and reflexive practitioner.

Activity 10.1

Consider an interaction from your own practice – how might you have influenced the course of events by your own actions or behaviour?

Case Study: Serious Case Review

Reflexivity in action

Let us now examine how reflexive practice could be applied to an element of the SCR; this 'application' is not intended to be a critique or criticism of professional effectiveness but rather an opportunity to further demonstrate how reflexivity can influence practice. In the SCR (2013) it was reported that there had been four referrals to Children's Services within a twenty-month period, for incidents relating to domestic violence, neglect and physical injury to one of the children. Despite this, *both parents felt that professionals had readily accepted what they told them without sufficient challenge or skepticism* (p12). Parton and O'Byrne (2000) suggest that in statutory social work, there is a need for practitioners to challenge and to maintain an inquisitive stance; therefore, by applying a reflexive approach to interactions with the parents, the social worker would question whether the parents were presenting openly and honestly or simply providing answers to questions that were based upon their perception of them as an agent of authority. Questioning the impact of their own presence upon the actions of the family can therefore result in the number of *mistakes and lost opportunities* being reduced (O'Sullivan, 2011, p10). Additionally, the parents *acknowledged that they did not ask for help and support when they needed it for fear of what they perceived as potential consequences (potential removal of their children)* (p12). The reflexive practitioner will appreciate that their involvement in the lives of families is not a 'neutral event', but is rather determined by each other's 'personal biographies', which will influence the *power relationships that arise from the membership of differing social divisions* (Burke and Harrison, 2002, p232). By applying 'relational reflexivity' to practice, families become empowered, enabling them to have an input into any identified support or intervention; failure to take a 'reflexive approach to work' can lead to missed opportunities to make a positive impact on people's lives. According to Parton and Byrne (2000, p77), *[service] user uniqueness calls for a careful, thoughtful approach and reflexivity slows us down so that we can go faster.*

Chapter Summary

This chapter has discussed the concept of reflexive practice and its significance for social workers. Applying reflexivity to an example of social work practice, it has been shown to be an essential component of the social worker's 'toolkit' that should be practised at every given opportunity. By considering two of the comments made by the parents within the SCR, this chapter has provided suggestions how a reflexive approach could be applied to this situation.

Reflection Point

- Consider the impact of your presence, in a professional and personal capacity, upon the service user and reflect upon this in your assessment of the situation.
- Reflexive social workers are constantly questioning the basis for their own decision making process(es) and are prepared to adapt their practice accordingly.

(Continued)

(Continued)

I reflect + I change as I reflect = I am reflexive
(Parton and O'Byrne, 2000, p76)

Further Reading

D'Cruz, H, Gillingham, P and Melendez, S (2007) Reflexivity, its meanings and relevance for social work: A critical review of the literature. *British Journal of Social Work*, 37: 73–90.

This article examines the concept of reflexivity and its relevance for social work education, training, theory and practice. Through a critical review of social work literature, it also discusses how authors use the concepts of 'reflexivity' and '(critical) reflection' and 'reflectivity' interchangeably.

Introduction to Part Three – Ethics and Moral Philosophies

Treat service users and carers with respect.

(HCPC, 2016, p5)

This seemingly simple statement carries with it layers upon layers of complexity and raises so many critical questions. What does respect look like? How can respect be demonstrated if taking away someone's liberty, or taking their child into foster care, or removing services because of budget cuts, or declining services because of eligibility criteria? What does respect feel like to the service user or carer? What does it look like from the point of view of the practitioner? This first statement in the HCPC's Standards of Conduct, Performance and Ethics is a critical point for practitioners.

According to Banks (2012) professional ethics needs to consist of *meta*, *normative* and *descriptive* ethics. Meta means how we determine what is 'right'; normative means what is the morally right guiding principle to follow in a given situation; and descriptive means what moral opinions people, or in this case social workers, may have and how they act upon them. Professional ethics manifests itself in the following ways: *matters of right and wrong conduct, good or bad qualities of character and the professional responsibilities attached to relationships* (BASW, 2012). However, in practice it can be tempting for social workers to follow the final point in terms of professional responsibilities, without necessarily thinking through what this might mean in terms of the service user, or carer, or the wider implications. So, in order for practitioners to engage more critically with this, it is beneficial to initially remove reliance on legislation, policy and organisational guidelines.

A way to view ethical perspectives in practice, while considering the position of Banks (2012) and the HCPC (2016) as stated, is to strip away the concept of a service user or a carer and instead see the *person* and for the practitioner to also be a *person*. So, rather than considering specific statements of values and ethics in social work practice, this section will strip away the policy and guidance and instead take social workers back to the basics of human life and respect by considering moral philosophical positions in social work practice (Banks, 2012). For a philosophy degree students would question the mere existence of these philosophical positions, however, as has been the case in each chapter of this book, the existence of the theory itself will not be questioned, just its key principles and its application to practice. This will be achieved by looking at key philosophical positions: Deontology, Utilitarianism, Virtue Ethics, Ethics of Care and Radical Ethics.

Radical Ethics is less well considered in social work practice; however, it is the contention of this author, that it is imperative in social work practice today by combining political philosophy with the principles of Radical Social Work.

The main emphasis for all these chapters is not to answer questions but to raise them; and to raise them at a higher level away from everyday social work practice.

Chapter 11

Deontology

Lesley Deacon

Achieving a Social Work Degree

This chapter will help you meet the following capabilities, to the appropriate level, from the Professional Capabilities Framework:

PCF 1 Professionalism

- Describe the role of a social worker and the importance of personal and professional boundaries and behaviour, demonstrate ability to learn using a range of approaches;

PCF 2 Values and Ethics

- Understand the professional's ethical principles and their relevance to practice, and demonstrate awareness of own personal values and how these can impact on practice;

PCF 3 Diversity

- Recognise the importance of diversity in human identity and experience, and the application of anti-discriminatory and anti-oppressive principles in social work practice;

PCF 4 Rights, Justice and Economic Wellbeing

- Understand the principles of rights, justice and economic wellbeing, and their significance for social work practice;

PCF 6 Critical Reflection and Analysis

- Understand the need to construct hypotheses in social work practice;

PCF 7 Intervention and Skills

- Demonstrate an awareness of a range of frameworks to assess and plan intervention and demonstrate initial awareness of risk and safeguarding;

PCF 8 Context and Organisations

- Demonstrate awareness of the impact of organisational context on social work practice;

PCF 9 Professional Leadership

- Demonstrate awareness of the importance of professional leadership in social work.

Reflection Point

To start thinking in a morally philosophical mindset, consider the following question: when has it ever been morally right for a husband to physically hit his wife?

Points to consider:

- When this debate has been applied in teaching by the author, several students respond with reference to legislation – often, previous common law references to *moderate correction* (Myers, 2005). However, thinking philosophically needs to be more abstract – so reconsider the debate from this perspective: outside of law or policy, when has it ever been morally right for a husband to hit his wife?

Reflection:

- If known legislation is removed from the equation there is nothing to suggest that physical abuse from a husband towards his wife is acceptable. Perhaps there are social norms that have developed in certain environments but as a principle this is something that cannot be argued. Yet at certain points in time it is clear that law and policy in fact do not ensure people are treated with respect, care or consideration. This is something for the reader to consider throughout this and subsequent chapters as moral philosophy is considered.

Introduction

When working in social work practice it is important to remember there is more to a service user or carer than this role or position that has been allocated to them. What is meant by that is that it is important, in any kind of decision making, to recognise the person, the human being behind the role applied to them or the reason for the relationship. We must recognise that while a social worker may be fully aware of their professional role and their professional relationship with a service user or carer, the service user or carer may not see the relationship in that way. Social workers need to ensure when making decisions that they see the person, see the human being. In fact, allowing policy and legislation to hide their view of the person can lead to discriminatory practice. While policy and legislation may be based on sound principles, they *can and do conflict* (Beckett and Maynard, 2013, p9), so social work practitioners must act to ensure an organisation's decision does not take precedence over the rights of a person as a human being. Social work courses spend many years teaching students about values and ethics, yet moral philosophy allows students and practitioners to consider those important elements outside of policy, legislation and organisational guidance. As stated in the Introduction to Part Three, while there is a Code of Ethics in social work practice (HCPC, 2016), it is beneficial for social workers not to have to rely on specific reference to those codes but to have an intrinsic understanding of the value of human life, of the value of a human being, and of the value of the relationship between the social worker as a human being and the service user or carer as a human being. While it is also essential that social workers understand the limitations of their own role as a professional (Banks, 2012), what is even more necessary is to understand the person they are dealing with. The role that the person is allocated in the relationship with the social worker by its very nature means social workers will always have some power over them, but with that power, as we might think, comes great responsibility, and ethical thinking encourages students to recognise what that is by stripping away a mechanical reliance on law and policy so it becomes possible for social work students and social work practitioners to see the implications of their actions at a human level.

This will first be achieved by considering the moral philosophical position of Deontology.

Origins of Deontology

Deontology is a rule-based moral philosophy originally connected to the work of the Greek philosopher Plato, in relation to morals and reasoning (Beckett and Maynard, 2013). Plato was one of the first philosophers to be concerned with the concept of universal principles (Bensons, 1997). The concept of 'duty', from a Deontological perspective, is not based on the rules humans make for themselves through organisations (such as policy directives or codes of conduct), but in *certain unavoidable duties {human beings} have to one another* (Beckett and Maynard, 2013, p25). The German philosopher Immanuel Kant (1724–1804) developed Deontological thinking in his book *The Fundamental Principles of the Metaphysics of Morals* (1785). This was during the time of the Enlightenment, in which complete and unquestioning belief in God and the Church was being challenged by scientific development and the concept of 'reason'. The term Deontology developed from the Greek work *deon* meaning duty (Beckett and Maynard, 2013). According to Kant, the most important aspect of good in human life is that of *good will* (Kant, 1785, p81). It is not about the consequences of any action but about the intention of the action and the notion of *good will* itself.

We have then to develop the notion of a will which deserves to be highly esteemed for itself and is good without a will of anything further.

(Kant, 1785, pp3-4)

According to this philosophical position, the moral values that ensue are therefore *pure*; they are not tainted in any way by what people want but only by what is right (Akhtar, 2012). Respect is therefore a vital component of this philosophical position, tying in with the guidelines of the HCPC (2016). Deontology is underpinned by normative ethics, i.e. concerned with how people should act, how someone ought to act in a moral way (Beckett and Maynard, 2013).

Kant's concept of *Moral Absolutism* refers to the fact that decisions that are made are either right or wrong in their very act, regardless of the consequences. So it is the act itself that must be evaluated to ensure that in essence it is morally good and therefore the morally right thing to do (Bowles et al., 2006). The acts must be based on respect of the individuals involved in order for them to be morally right. Service users and carers must therefore be seen as rational beings, and therefore respected as such – so a social worker would show respect for these people because it is the right thing to do (Gray, 2010).

The 'categorical imperative', derived by Kant, is essential to the fundamental principles. He suggests:

Canst thou also will that thy maxim should be a universal law?

(Kant, 1785, p7)

So act as to treat humanity, whether in your own person or in that of any other, never soley as a means but also as an end.

(Kant, 1785, p16)

But what does this mean? Put simply, it means that we are all human, and so all humans should be worthy of fair treatment. Furthermore, each and every human's right to happiness is a worthwhile goal in itself, and should not be sacrificed in pursuit of any other goal. So, if we believe it is acceptable to treat one human in a certain way then we should be prepared for all humans to be treated in that same way. For example, if we think it is acceptable to lie to another person then we have to ask ourselves whether it would be acceptable for every person in the world to lie to every other person on the world, and if the answer is 'no' then it cannot be a universal transcending law and so we should not be prepared to treat *anybody* in this way, for *any* reason. Deontology, according to Dracopoulou (2015) is *'action deductionist*, i.e. the central aspect of the categorical imperative is to respect other people. This is the fundamental aspect, which must be acknowledged – not to use other people but to treat them with respect, which they automatically deserve. This is not a list of specific duties or guidelines but is a universal human law that can apply from any human being to another anywhere. Take the Children Act 1989 for example – at the time of writing, this is still the key piece of legislation that guides social work practitioners in safeguarding children in England and Wales. The statutes set down by this law could not be applied, say, in Namibia or South Korea for example as the legislation holds no status there. As Kant suggested, *{a} perfectly good will… could not be conceived as obliged therefore to act lawfully* (Kant, 1785, p16). So, in theory, the principle of Deontology *could*, as it is a universal basic duty of all human beings.

This chapter therefore focuses primarily on the key Deontological (also referred to as 'Kantian') principle of respect. This is the essential principle of the philosophy to follow, and the one which relates so well to social work practice. There are suggestions of other principles but these are ones that follow from respect. For example, is it showing respect if we lie? The reasoned answer to this would be no, therefore lying is wrong. When considering the concept of universal law as Kant suggests, could lying become a universal law? The reasoned answer again would be 'no', as if everyone lied then how would the truth ever be known?

Implications for social work practice

Applying a Deontological perspective to social work means that, regardless of their reason for having involvement from social work practitioners, all service users and carers must be treated with respect. While connecting to the HCPC (2016) Codes of Conduct, this can prove difficult in practice as social work practitioners are constantly challenged to put away their own personal values – yet they are also human beings, so social work practitioners should also be afforded respect themselves. What this might look like, in practice, is that social workers see the person in front of them – the person who may be in need; the person who may be angry or upset about the situation; the person who is not necessarily being honest; the person who may not want the social worker there. Yet that person needs to be seen first and foremost as the human being and be supported to be respected by those around them (i.e. advocacy). As Gray and Webb (2010, p10) state, *{a} moral stance which proposes that people ought to be allowed the freedom to choose is better than one which says that social workers have the right to manipulate and control* service users and carers.

An ethical dilemma occurs when there are *clear competing principles at stake* (McAuliffe, 2010, p48) for a social work practitioner (or any person) and there is not a clear course of action to take, or where values conflict in the decision-making process (Banks, 2012). Sometimes, social workers are placed in situations where they may feel they are being encouraged to tell lies or, at the very least, withhold the truth. This presents a dilemma for social workers from a Deontological perspective. Consider the following scenario.

Activity 11.1

Debate on the application of Deontology

A social worker is suspicious that a mother of four children on a child protection plan is allowing her former partner (not the children's father) to see the children, even though he is not allowed as part of the plan due to the risks he poses. The mother denies this but allows the social worker to talk to the oldest child alone at school the following day. When talking to the child (age 8) the social worker knows what information they want to find out – whether they have seen their mother's former partner recently. The social worker's knowledge of the child makes them believe that the child would not want to admit to this if he knew the consequences of admitting this, i.e. possibly being moved into emergency foster care. The ethical dilemma is: should the social worker be honest with the child about their intentions, risking the child then withholding information; or should the social worker withhold this information and talk to the child about other matters hoping that the child will, in the natural course of conversation, tell them about their mother's former partner?

From a Deontological perspective the key aspects to consider are thus:

- To withhold information from the child. Could this be seen as lying, therefore not treating the child with respect? Therefore not upholding a Deontological perspective?
- Or could this be considered differently? From a Deontological perspective is the child's mother not demonstrating respect to the child and therefore the social worker must act out of good will to redress this?
- Should the social worker not demonstrate respect for the child by explaining their concerns to the child and giving the child the opportunity to tell the truth?

Felix Biestek's Casework Principles, 1957

Felix Biestek was a Professor of Social Work in the USA who set seven key principles for social workers to follow which were based on Kantian Deontological principles of respect for people and that all people should be viewed as self-determining beings (Biestek, 1957 and Whiting, 2010).

1. Individualism

2. Purposeful expression of feelings

3. Controlled emotional involvement

4. Acceptance

5. Non-judgemental attitude

6. Rights to self-determination

7. Confidentiality

While these principles are underpinned by a Christian ethos (Whiting, 2010) and are almost 60 years old at the time of writing this chapter, it is possible to see how these can still be beneficial to social work practice today.

Individualism

Biestek (1957) emphasises that each person encountered in the course of social work practice must first and foremost be recognised as an individual and therefore as unique. So, while previous ways of working may have worked in context before, social workers should enter every new working relationship seeking to recognise the uniqueness of the individual, therefore understanding that they need to adapt the way they work to suit this particular service user or carer.

Purposeful expression of feelings

What Biestek (1957) was referring to here was that service users and carers must be allowed to express their feelings freely without condemnation. For example, if a parent becomes angry when accused of some form of abuse or neglect towards their child, they must be free to respond honestly, i.e. with anger, and should not be condemned for this, say for example being reported as a parent having problems with anger management.

Controlled emotional involvement

While not suggesting friendships should be made, Biestek (1957) did advocate that social workers need to be sensitive to the feelings of service users and to respond appropriately. So, going back to the previous example, an initial response to parental anger in such a stressful and difficult situation should first and foremost be understanding and recognition.

Acceptance

As well as recognising the uniqueness of individuals, Biestek (1957) identifies the importance of accepting the service users or carers for who they are rather than for the person the practitioner wants them to be. This means accepting both their strengths and weakness and respecting them for the person they are.

Non-judgemental attitude

When considering any issues of safeguarding in particular this is a key principle that Biestek (1957) advocates – not to ascribe either guilt or innocence to the service user or carer. In fact, the social worker should enter the situation in a completely open manner and not ascribe problems to the person themselves but to the behaviour or to the situation. So, for example, if there is evidence of abuse or neglect then the social worker should see this as the *behaviour* of a person and not an attribute of the person themselves.

Rights to self-determination

This emphasises the importance of allowing people to make their own choices about their lives. The very nature of the relationship between a social worker and a service user or carer can be seen as interfering as social workers are involved in the very essence of people's private lives – in their homes. However, it is important that the people they encounter are respected and given the freedom to choose. Biestek (1957) recognises the significance of the restrictions that law, policy and capacity place on this, although by respecting the person's rights first, a social worker can perhaps better explain when and why those freedoms may be curtailed. So part of the application of this principle is the importance of recognising a person's right to feel angry or upset about a situation and for the social worker to respect this.

Confidentiality

Respecting a person's right not to have information about them shared is imperative in demonstrating true respect for that person. This can become particularly problematic when dealing with matters of safeguarding where confidentiality can be overruled by law (Children Act 1989, Care Act 2014). However, the principle of confidentiality is still important, and therefore the decision not to maintain confidentiality is something that needs to be considered very carefully.

Case Study: Serious Case Review

In order to see how Deontology can be applied, the SCR concerning Child Z (2013) will be considered. It is reported that FZ (the father) used cannabis and had set up a cannabis farm in the family home. He reported to the Reviewing Committee that *he had not understood the seriousness of some of his lifestyle in terms of implications for a young child; this included his habitual use of cannabis that he had used since early adolescence* (p12).

First, the principle of respect is a fundamental principle that needs to be employed when working with this (or any) family. Regardless of the views of professionals on the actions or inactions of the parents, MZ and FZ, each of these people needs to be treated with respect. There is no doubt that this can be difficult for practitioners, especially when working in areas of child abuse, or in this case, a review of a child's death. It is understandable that practitioners could feel an emotional response to this situation. However, from a Kantian perspective they must still show respect towards MZ and FZ. This is especially important during the investigation processes. To demonstrate respect a person should not be judged as 'guilty' before any investigation has been completed; nor, however, should innocence be presumed. To treat MZ and FZ with respect would be to be honest with them about concerns and to try to work with them. When considering this perspective, it is not suggested that practitioners should 'collude' with parents, as this would not be demonstrating respect. To collude would mean to participate in lies and untruths so this would not be respectful.

Taking some specific details from the case, from a Deontological perspective the use of cannabis in itself would not necessarily be viewed as something to be concerned about (putting aside the legislative position in the first instance). When considering the concepts of respect and self-determination then FZ's lifestyle choices would need to be respected. He is a human being and from a universal perspective has the right to make choices for himself. Deontology would not look at the consequences of these choices *per se* so the implications of the cannabis use on others would not be a consideration. However, the act of doing something that was harmful would need to be considered. FZ himself has a universal duty to demonstrate respect for those around him, and in particular those he lives with – his partner and their children. Research suggests that *[p]arental substance misuse can have a detrimental impact upon child development placing children at an increased risk of developing a range of negative physical, emotional, behavioural, cognitive and social outcomes* (Woolfall and Summnal, 2010, p342). So whilst a Deontological perspective would not be concerned with consequences, it would be concerned with respect and could lead to the question of whether FZ was demonstrating respect towards his children. As Kant himself suggested, the having of a child *incurs an obligation towards the child and towards each other to maintain* the child (1800, p128). Their child belongs to them but is not their property and so the parents have an obligation to do the right thing for their child, i.e. that while a person has rights themselves they also have duties to others as those others have rights themselves (Kant, 1800, p65).

Chapter Summary

This chapter has set out the key principles of Deontology and demonstrated how these can be applied to help understand service users or carers in context by applying the principles to understanding aspects of a SCR. However, it has also recognised the importance of practitioners returning to law, policy and codes of conduct, as well as current research knowledge, in the implementation of this philosophical position in practice.

Reflection Point

- Remember that the focus of Deontology is that right and wrong come from the act itself regardless of the outcome.
- Duty from a deontological perspective does not refer to the duty of specific organisations or workers, but the duty of human beings to one another at a universal level.

Further Reading

The article recommended below demonstrates some of the difficulties in applying a Deontological approach in practice. Social workers identified the importance of personal autonomy (a key Deontological principle) but over-rode it in practice when considering risk. This is an important reflective point in social work practice – to consider how much personal autonomy is actually encouraged and prioritised.

Dunworth, M and Kirwin, P (2012) Do nurses and social workers have different values? An exploratory study of the care for older people. *Journal of Interprofessional Care*, 26: 226–31.

Chapter 12

Utilitarianism

Lesley Deacon

Achieving a Social Work Degree

This chapter will help you meet the following capabilities, to the appropriate level, from the Professional Capabilities Framework:

PCF 1 Professionalism

- Describe the role of a social worker and the importance of personal and professional boundaries and behaviour, demonstrate ability to learn using a range of approaches;

PCF 2 Values and Ethics

- Understand the professional's ethical principles and their relevance to practice, and demonstrate awareness of own personal values and how these can impact on practice;

PCF 3 Diversity

- Recognise the importance of diversity in human identity and experience, and the application of anti-discriminatory and anti-oppressive principles in social work practice;

PCF 4 Rights, Justice and Economic Wellbeing

- Understand the principles of rights, justice and economic wellbeing, and their significance for social work practice;

PCF 6 Critical Reflection and Analysis

- Understand the need to construct hypotheses in social work practice;

PCF 7 Intervention and Skills

- Demonstrate an awareness of a range of frameworks to assess and plan intervention and demonstrate initial awareness of risk and safeguarding;

PCF 8 Context and Organisations

- Demonstrate awareness of the impact of organisational context on social work practice;

PCF 9 Professional Leadership

- Demonstrate awareness of the importance of professional leadership in social work.

Reflection Point

To start thinking in a Utilitarian mindset, consider the following question: is it better to achieve the best outcome for the most number of people even if it means sacrificing the needs of the few?

Comment

It is important to think carefully about what it means to sacrifice the needs of the few. It is helpful for students and social work practitioners to put themselves in the position of the few – how would you feel to be the one whose needs were sacrificed to benefit others? How would you feel if it was your child/ren?

Introduction

Teleological ethics is a way of thinking that is concerned with an *end* or a *purpose*. So, rather than being concerned with an act in itself, this ethical perspective concerns itself with an overall goal, the outcome (Gray and Webb, 2010). Aristotle was a student of the Greek philosopher Plato and was concerned with philosophical positions that considered what was needed in order for human life to flourish. So, as opposed to the Deontological perspective, originating with Plato and then later with Immanuel Kant, Aristotle considered the importance of what was right in this world, rather than something that transcended human existence. Utilitarianism is a consequentialist theory based on a naturalist philosophy, the achievement of the best circumstances in order for humans to flourish; morality, and what is right and wrong, is concerned with achieving happiness for the beings in this world. The figures associated with the development of modern Utilitarianism are Jeremy Bentham and John Stuart Mill (Banks, 2012; Beckett and Maynard, 2013; Gray and Webb, 2010). According to Banks (2004) Utilitarianism is foundationalist as it seeks *to ground morality in one single principle* (p78), so making the concept straightforward in one sense and yet complicated to apply.

Jeremy Bentham

Jeremy Bentham was a British political philosopher (1748–1832) who was concerned with how laws should be derived in order to create an overall good. His view was based on a basic moral principle which underpins his devised philosophical position – the idea of utility and the greater happiness principle (Rosen, 1996). While this was not a new moral perspective he is considered to be the founder of what can be referred to as modern Utilitarianism (Rosen, 1996). His intention was to develop a *philosophical understanding of the law* in order that the law would be the representation of this moral principle (Rosen 1996, p xxxiii). The 'principle of utility' attempts to balance the positives and negatives associated with a particular action – this balance needs to maximise happiness and to minimise pain (Parrott, 2014). There is no difference in terms of one person's happiness over another; all are considered the same and the balance is one to one. So, from a Utilitarian perspective, if an action leads to pain for one person but happiness for two or more people then this would make the action morally right as there is more happiness than pain. Bentham identified what he called *two sovereign masters*, pleasure and pain (Bentham, 1988 [1789], p1). The intention of all life was to increase pleasure and minimise pain. However, to understand what is important to wider society, the individual's needs must be understood first. It is here where there could be a conflict between what an individual may want and what wider society may want (Baujard, 2010, p610). To address this, Bentham identified that outside intervention is needed if and when the needs of the individual and the needs of the collective collide (Baujard, 2010). The intervention of the law, for example, is imperative, in practice where social worker intervention may be necessary. (A caveat here, however, is that this is *Bentham's* interpretation and intention of the law.) In the introduction to this Part, readers were advised that they would need to see the human being; in doing so this means effectively putting the law to one side in order to refocus on the person rather than on their position under the law. What Bentham is suggesting is that the law is created and applied in order to apply the main moral philosophical principles in life, i.e. the law is the embodiment of moral philosophy from a Utilitarian perspective. Or at least that is what it *should* be, and it should be questioned if it does not embody this moral philosophy.

John Stuart Mill 1806–73

J.S. Mill was a classical economist (Rosen, 1996) who considered further Bentham's concept of utility (Kaminitz, 2014). This underpinning theoretical perspective led him to focus his concern on *the overall happiness of society*, and to do this he was concerned with the *development of their scientific ideas* (p234). As with a Deontological perspective, reason (and its application) is key to a Utilitarian perspective. Bentham focused on the principle of pleasure, but Mill identified happiness not just as pleasure but also as the absence of pain (Wright Mill, 1863). Also, he does not refer to just physical pleasure but emotional and intellectual pleasure. While the suggestion here is that this is natural to human beings, the focus is not just on the person's own happiness but on the greatest amount together, in society (Wright Mill, 1863).

Mill suggested that the morality of an action is evident in the action itself and in its consequences, but not in the motive for that action, or in the essence of the action. He suggests, for example, that in order to save life it would therefore be morally right to lie, cheat or steal if the consequence were to result in saving a life (Wright Mill, 1961). Lawrence Kohlberg was an American psychologist who researched the stages of development of moral reasoning. To complete this research, Kohlberg (1963) created a scenario, concerning a man called Heinz, for research participants to consider so that Kohlberg could understand the reasoning behind the decisions made. Briefly, Heinz's wife has cancer and a new drug could help her, but the pharmacist is charging more money for this drug and Heinz cannot afford it. The question is should Heinz steal the drug in order to potentially help save his wife's life? (Kohlberg, 1963) This is a useful scenario to consider from a Utilitarian perspective. But on the surface, applying the words of J.S. Mill as suggested above, the morally right thing for Heinz to do would be to steal the medicine. However, this does raise questions about how an act such as stealing could be viewed as morally right.

Rule Utilitarianism

The concept of Rule Utilitarianism developed out of objections to some of the problems with Utilitarianism (which then become referred to as Act Utilitarianism). Concerns were raised regarding Act Utilitarianism such as the notion that it leads to *counter-intuitive moral judgements* (Hill Jr, 2005, p161). For example, what evidence of consequences do people base their decisions on? Hill Jr (2005) suggests that too much emphasis on *wishful thinking* leads people to over-estimate anticipated outcomes of decisions. The acts from which these actions are based are therefore morally 'counter-intuitive' as they could involve lying, stealing, being hurtful to a person or persons, so long as the anticipated outcome is viewed as morally worthy of this sacrifice (as suggested in the previous section). Rule Utilitarianism recommends the concept of *ideal rules* (Hill Jr, 2005); to create rules of conduct which can be more easily applied in practice (Beckett and Maynard, 2013). So, from this perspective, a rule might be created that to lie would be the wrong thing to do, regardless of the immediate consequences. Referring back to the Heinz dilemma (Kohlberg, 1984), from a Rule Utilitarianism perspective the wider consequences of stealing could bring harm to more people than it would benefit. If it were possible to morally justify stealing then this could be applied in a scenario so that the overall consequence would be a world where anybody could steal should they see (or anticipate) an immediate benefit. For example, a couple stealing the next door neighbour's car because the neighbour is just one person and the couple are two so they would gain twice as much happiness as the single neighbour. It is easy to see how making such acts as stealing, lying or hurting morally justifiable could lead to the breakdown of society into one where individuals are just out for themselves.

Application of Utilitarianism

When applying Utilitarianism to social work scenarios, students and social work practitioners should first apply Act Utilitarianism and then apply Rule. So, any scenario should first be considered for the immediate benefits to the situation; then the wider consequences should be considered. That is, the consequences to the world if certain acts are then viewed as morally justified. Would the wider consequences be worse?

From Utilitarianism to Consequentialism

Students and social work practitioners may struggle to see how Act and Rule Utilitarianism can be easily applied in practice, so instead a more common term used is Consequentialism, which is the perspective they both ascribe to. While Act and Rule Utilitarianism are often now referred to as consequentialist, this actual term was first identified by the British philosopher G.E.M. Anscombe (1958), although this is not something she agreed with.

As suggested by Beckett and Maynard (2013, p27), one way to act morally is to consider *the consequences of actions*. As social work is an outcome-focused profession it would be impossible for social workers not to use and consider some element of Consequentialism, even if unconsciously. In effective decision making, consideration is always given to the intended consequences of certain actions. While this book is focused on consideration of understanding people, it must be noted that social work intervention is largely underpinned by a Consequentialist approach. Whether this is always from a moral philosophical basis however is questionable. Something for students and social work practitioners to consider is whether the actions and intended consequences do recognise the moral worth of the service user or carer, as a human being? And who are the considered consequences for – the service user, the social worker, the government or society as a whole?

Implications for social work practice

Let us refer back to the HCPC code, considered at the beginning of this Part of the book:

> Treat service users and carers with respect.

(HCPC, 2016, p5)

The concept of treating people with respect can become problematic when applying a Utilitarian approach. As has been seen in this chapter it is very possible, when applying Utilitarianism, to use a person as a means to an end. So, the needs of a service user or carer could in fact be sacrificed for the 'greater good'. This would seem to contradict the value of treating a person with respect. It could be argued that respect is shown in ensuring fair treatment for the larger number of people; however, referring back to the comments made at the start of this chapter, how would you feel if it was *you* whose needs were sacrificed? It is of great benefit for students and social work practitioners to put themselves or their family in the position of being the one who is treated as a means to an end. This is an excellent point for reflection – considering how you or your family members would feel.

Another useful code to consider from the HCPC where it is possible to see Utilitarianism in action is:

> You must take all reasonable steps to reduce the risk of harm to service users, carers and colleagues as far as possible.

(HCPC, 2016, p8)

What can be seen here are two key concepts: 'reduce the risk of harm' and 'as far as possible'. When considering the consequences of actions, 'as far as possible' gives us the caveat that it may not be completely possible to avoid risk of harm. So, from a Utilitarian perspective, it would not be expected that consequences were completely known or completely predictable, and there is room here for intended consequences not to be achieved. When considering reducing the risk of harm to service users, carers and colleagues, we can also see how decision making could over-rule the needs of the person concerned if its intended consequences were to reduce the risk of harm. Referring back to the scenario of talking to the child (see Activity 12.1, below), it is evident that not telling the child the intention of the conversation was aimed at reducing the risk of harm to this child and his siblings. So it could be seen that the practitioner in this scenario was applying a Utilitarian approach and following the Code of Ethics for practice. But again, a caveat here is to question whether or not this was really demonstrating respect?

Activity 12.1

Debate on the application of Act and Rule Utilitarianism

A social worker is suspicious that a mother of four children on a child protection plan is allowing her former partner (not the children's father) to see the children, even though he is not allowed as part of the plan due to the risks he poses. The mother denies this but allows the social worker to talk the oldest child alone at school the following day. When talking to the child (age 8) the social worker knows what information they want to find out – whether

(Continued)

(Continued)

they have seen their mother's former partner recently. The social worker's knowledge of the child makes them believe that the child would not want to admit to this if he knew the consequences of admitting this, i.e. possibly being moved into emergency foster care. The ethical dilemma is: should the social worker be honest with the child about their intentions risking the child then withholding information; or should the social worker withhold this information and talk to the child about other matters hoping that the child will, in the natural course of conversation, tell them about their mother's former partner?

From an Act and Rule Utilitarian perspective the key aspects to consider are thus:

- To withhold information from the child. This could be viewed as being for the greater good, i.e. safeguarding this child and his siblings. Therefore, the act of lying would not be morally wrong because the end would justify the means.
- Or could this be considered differently from a Rule Utilitarian perspective? What are the implications of creating a rule that it is acceptable to lie for the greater good? Would a society in which lying can be morally justifiable flourish?
- How are either of the Utilitarian perspectives demonstrating respect?

Case Study: Serious Case Review

Utilitarianism will now be applied to the same aspect of the case study from the SCR concerning Child Z (2013) to which we applied Deontology in the previous chapter. To reiterate, it is reported that FZ (the father) used cannabis and had set up a cannabis farm in the family home. He reported to the Reviewing Committee that *he had not understood the seriousness of some of his lifestyle in terms of implications for a young child; this included his habitual use of cannabis that he had used since early adolescence* (p12).

Any practitioner working with FZ and applying a Utilitarian perspective would need to consider what was in the interests of the greater good. Would it be better to have a world in which FZ was allowed to continue smoking cannabis and running a cannabis farm, or would outcomes be better if he were stopped? To do this, the consequences would need to be considered (Beckett and Maynard, 2013); of both his smoking cannabis and of the running of the cannabis farm. As Utilitarianism is a naturalist ethical philosophy, the concept of human flourishing needs to be prioritised (Gray and Webb, 2010). To do this, in a very practical sense for practitioners, is to consider research evidence about what is known about the consequences of certain behaviours.

Considering drug use in general, for example, research indicates that drug use has a negative impact on mental health (Lieb, 2015; Regier et al., 1990; Taylor et al., 2006). There are also links between drug use and problems in people's home lives which can lead to homelessness (Rosenthal and Keys, 2005). The *gateway hypothesis* suggests that cannabis is a gateway drug that leads users into further illicit drug use (Kandel et al., 2006). According to Secades-Villa et al. (2005) the probability of progression is 44.7 per cent, with the group most likely to progress being males aged 30–34, and there is a connection between the drug use and comorbid psychiatric disorders. According to the SCR report, FZ was aged 23 at the time of the incident, therefore does not fit with the risk age, however he did experience comorbid disorders: *FZ's mental health and self-harm issues, previous hospitalisation for depression and self-harm in 2009, current offence of possession of bladed article which involved FZ stabbing himself* (Child Z, 2013, p32).

It can therefore be seen clearly from this research knowledge that taking an Act Utilitarian principled position would suggest that anyone using drugs does not achieve the greater good – either for themselves or for those close to them. Therefore, the needs of that individual could be sacrificed for the greater happiness of more. FZ's cannabis use and the running of the cannabis farm should therefore be stopped, even if he does not agree. However, while there are clear implications here, this also raises another question: could some of these negatives not be balanced against FZ's decision to choose to do something that makes him happy so long as it does not impact on others? When considering the act itself, is the use of cannabis morally wrong? Looking at the consequences again from the research evidence given above, it could be argued that based on the probability argument (Secades-Villa et al., 2005), it is more likely that FZ will *not* use cannabis as a gateway drug to more illicit substances, as more than 50 per cent of people do not. So, if this is the case, where in the consequences can it be argued that the act taken by FZ is morally wrong? It is here that some of the evidence referenced in the previous chapter on Deontology needs to be re-considered. Research by Woolfall and Summnal (2010) found that *[p]arental substance misuse can have a detrimental impact upon child development placing children at an increased risk of developing a range of negative physical, emotional, behavioural, cognitive and social outcomes* (p342). So, here it can be seen that there are potential negative consequences to FZ's children – so using the principle of utility it can be seen that the balance is tipped towards causing pain, and therefore the act is morally wrong because of these consequences.

What should be evident from this reasoning is the complexity of applying Utilitarianism to social work practice dilemmas. It is certainly possible that two people applying the same moral philosophical perspective could come out with different decisions. And it is likely that there is research evidence that contradicts that used in this scenario. So, how can social work practitioners be confident of the making the right moral decision from this perspective?

When applying the Rule Utilitarian approach to a dilemma, the further implications of parental substance use and wider consequences need to be considered. If, as Woolfall and Summnal (2010) suggest, there are far-reaching negative consequences for children of parents who substance misuse, then a 'rule of conduct' should be applied (Beckett and Maynard, 2010). So, a rule of conduct could be that parental substance use from a Utilitarian perspective is morally wrong due to the potential negative impact on children. However, a note of caution needs to be given here – this does not mean that social workers should make moral *judgements* about parents and their choices concerning substance use. It is imperative that whatever philosophical approach is taken, social workers must still act out of respect, due to the professions value base. Would taking the view that a parent is morally wrong do that?

Research Summary

When reading about moral philosophy and considering its application to social work practice, it is important for students to understand the original key texts. As different authors write about these perspectives over time, opinions and interpretations can change and be reflective of the time in which they were written. Therefore, as students and social work practitioners develop their academic and practice knowledge they should become more confident in accessing original texts. From this they can then begin to consider their own interpretations. This is particularly important when applying moral philosophy in practice. The act of application is particular to the scenario being considered and the social work practitioner's understanding and interpretation of that scenario. Using a Utilitarian perspective can be beneficial as it encourages practitioners to use research evidence in order to evidence the potential consequences. However, with all application of theoretical perspectives in social work practice, practitioners need to be mindful that research evidence is not necessarily 100 per cent accurate and therefore all individual circumstances need to be considered and evaluated.

Chapter Summary

In this chapter the moral philosophical positions of Act and Rule Utilitarianism have been considered in order to provide students and social workers with an understanding of the consideration of best outcomes in social work practice.

Reflection Point

- From a Utilitarianism perspective it is not the act itself which is good, but the consequences of it, and that it brings out more pleasure than pain.
- Act Utilitarianism considers an individual act.
- Rule Utilitarianism considers the application of rules that bring about the most pleasure over pain, e.g. not lying.

Further Reading

Two journal articles are specifically recommended for further reading:

Robson, D (2014) Moral regret in mental health social work. *Ethics and Social Welfare*, 8(1): 86–92.

This journal article is an example of the application of Utilitarianism in social work practice.

Hill Jr, T E (2005) Assessing moral rules: Utilitarian and Kantian perspectives. *Philosophical Issues*, 15: 158–78.

This article presents a good debate between Act and Rule Utilitarianism.

Chapter 13

Virtue Ethics

Lesley Deacon

Achieving a Social Work Degree

This chapter will help you meet the following capabilities, to the appropriate level, from the Professional Capabilities Framework:

PCF 1 Professionalism

- Describe the role of a social worker and the importance of personal and professional boundaries and behaviour, demonstrate ability to learn using a range of approaches;

PCF 2 Values and Ethics

- Understand the professional's ethical principles and their relevance to practice, and demonstrate awareness of own personal values and how these can impact on practice;

PCF 3 Diversity

- Recognise the importance of diversity in human identity and experience, and the application of anti-discriminatory and anti-oppressive principles in social work practice;

PCF 4 Rights, Justice and Economic Wellbeing

- Understand the principles of rights, justice and economic wellbeing, and their significance for social work practice;

PCF 6 Critical Reflection and Analysis

- Understand the need to construct hypotheses in social work practice;

PCF 7 Intervention and Skills

- Demonstrate an awareness of a range of frameworks to assess and plan intervention and demonstrate initial awareness of risk and safeguarding;

PCF 8 Context and Organisations

- Demonstrate awareness of the impact of organisational context on social work practice;

PCF 9 Professional Leadership

- Demonstrate awareness of the importance of professional leadership in social work.

Reflection Point

Consider the following issue – can a person do the right thing without actually being a good person?

Some of the issues to consider here are the intentions of the person; they could very well do something that appears to be good either because of the action itself (Deontological), or the consequences of the action (Utilitarianism) – but what of the person? Can the act be good if in fact the intentions of the persons are not?

Introduction

Virtue Ethics was originally referred to as Eudaimonism and was associated with the Greek philosopher, Aristotle (Beckett and Maynard, 2013). Eudaimonism refers to the idea of human flourishing and Aristotle's focus was on the idea that the collective good life for all was more important than the individual (Webb, 2010). The good of the collective state should ultimately be in line with the good of the individual and the equilibrium needs to be met through the character of the individual.

This philosophical concept re-emerged in the late twentieth century as a reaction to the principle- and rule-based philosophical ethics such as Deontology, Act and Rule Utilitarianism (Webb, 2010). The significant issue with taking a reasoned and principled approach to ethical decision making was that this does not require the person acting to actually be a moral person – only that their *acts* were moral. These principles ignored the *important features of the moral life and moral judgements, including character, motives and emotions* of the person and the significance of the relationships between people (Banks, 2012, p69). This is especially true because of these ethical perspectives being based on *reason*, i.e. the intellectual virtues suggested by Aristotle (Webb, 2010). Virtue Ethics shares a similarity to Act and Rule Utilitarianism as it is a naturalist philosophy, i.e. what is needed in order to ensure human flourishing

(Beckett and Maynard, 2013). However, it is also based in social constructionism (see Chapter 7) as Virtue Ethics requires knowledge of what characteristics are appropriate and needed *in the current time period* in order for humans to flourish. Therefore, this philosophical perspective is not transcending (like Deontology) but exists very much in this world, today.

When considering the level of reasoning that is required in order to ensure ethical decision making is made, it can be argued that principle-based concepts are far too abstract to be inherently useful in everyday life. Such principle-based concepts require each situation to be analysed to a micro-level in order to ensure either the act or the outcome are ethical (Statman, 1997). A different approach to ethical thinking suggests that *a good act is one that ensues from the good intentions of the actor* (Gray and Webb, 2010, p13). So, what this means is that a person who is inherently a good person would act in a way that was good, and that goodness would be focused on human flourishing. The focus here shifts to the person and their traits and characteristics. Therefore, complex situations would not have to be reasoned with or analysed to such an extent – a good person would act in a good way automatically, it would be natural.

Virtues

When thinking about how people in society describe other people, it is often through the use of character traits – for example, kind, considerate, horrible, selfish, etc. Virtues are in fact *fixed character states* (Gray and Webb, 2010, p13) that develop from habits of behaviour and the development of knowledge and experience. Originating in the work of Aristotle, as previously suggested, Virtue Ethics was the consideration of the relationship between the *individual character, morality and public life* (Webb, 2010, pp109–10). The focus on the individual character and the way in which it negotiates with morality and public life is significant. For a naturalist philosophy the focus needs to be on human flourishing and therefore this relationship is significant. The main concern for the individual is outside of themselves and what they need, and instead is concerned with what the wider society needs.

Prior to Aristotle, Socrates suggested that virtue was not something that could be taught as such, but *is something possessed to one degree or another by everyone* (Bensons, 1997, p327). According to Aristotle, there are two particular types of virtue: intellectual virtues, which consist of wisdom, prudence and understanding; and moral virtues, which consist of liberality and temperance (Webb, 2010). Moral virtues are acquired out of habit, such as temperance, but intellectual virtues, such as wisdom, are developed from experience, education and the acquiring and development of knowledge. Reason is the primary intellectual virtue which is natural to use when making decisions regarding how to ensure human life flourishes. According to Aristotle, people should live moral lives rather than just follow rules, as could be done when applying Deontology or Utilitarian moral philosophies. To actually live a moral life would suggest the habit-forming of particular traits, which would then become natural to the person. Virtue Ethics can be referred to as the fusion of the head and the heart (Banks, 2012; Oko, 2011; Beckett and Maynard, 2013; Gray and Webb, 2010), i.e. that logically human beings will flourish if collective ideals are sought, and that goodness would also focus on this outcome. The difficulty, however, is that the list of what could be viewed as *good virtues* could in fact be substantial (Clifford, 2014).

Because of this, the concept of the *golden mean* is significant in Virtue Ethics, as this is where balance can be found in terms of good character, i.e. a happy medium. For example, it could be argued that a balanced position would be courage – the extremes of this position would be either recklessness, on one side, or cowardice, on the other. So, from a Virtue Ethics perspective, it would be argued that courage is balanced between those two positions and so would suggest itself to be a virtuous character trait. This can be seen in the idea of having the courage to act in a situation to do the right thing – for example, having what could be a difficult conversation with someone but managing it carefully. A social work practice example might be the need to have a conversation with a family about considering temporary foster care for their children. This could be a very difficult conversation and would need to be managed very carefully. The reckless path would suggest brutal honesty, saying it like it is – for example, just stating the fact that the family either agrees to the foster care or an emergency or interim care order will be sought (Children Act 1989). The cowardly path would be to avoid the situation or to get someone else to do it, or to drop hints – for example, suggesting that this is not the decision of the social worker but someone else's; or that it is out of their hands and not something they have instigated. A virtuous person would act out of kindness and consideration and would have the courage to speak up when needed; to address the situation with the family, explaining the concerns and benefits, and being honest but not brutally so.

Activity 13.1

Can you think of other examples of virtuous character traits and what their extreme versions might be?

Implications for social work practice

The concern of Virtue Ethics with the welfare of people beyond the individual is significant when considering its application to social work practice. According to the IFSW and IASSW (2014):

> *Social work is a practice-based profession and an academic discipline that promotes social change and development, social cohesion, and the empowerment and liberation of people.*

Nowhere in this statement does it suggest anything about personal gain, instead it suggests something about the characteristics needed to be a successful social work practitioner – someone concerned with the welfare and wellbeing of others. According to a recently qualified social worker, to *know that you helped another person in some small (or sometimes big) way is one of the greatest rewards you can get* (Lovell, 2015). The focus of being a good (i.e. virtuous) social work practitioner is on the good that is achieved for others rather than for the self. This comes not from the action or the consequences but from the intention, even though the positive consequences are part of the intention of a good practitioner.

It can, however, be difficult to specifically connect Virtue Ethics to the HCPC Code of Ethics. According to Pullen-Sansfacon (2010), Virtue Ethics has not been considered in social work ethics as much as Deontological or Utilitarian perspectives. However, it is increasing in popularity, and Banks and Gallagher (2009) for example specifically refer to how professional wisdom can be developed in social work practice. They refer to the following characteristics of a good social worker: professional wisdom; courage; respectfulness; care; trustworthiness; justice; and professional integrity. So, when taking this perspective, it is in fact *more* evident to see the connection with the HCPC codes, such as to challenge discrimination; to keep within your scope of practice; to be honest and trustworthy (HCPC, 2016).

Activity 13.2

Debate on the application of virtue ethics

So, referring back to the concept of the *golden mean* (i.e. a happy medium), consider this in relation to following issue:

A social worker is suspicious that a parent of four children on a child protection plan is allowing their former partner to see the children, even though he is not allowed to as part of the plan due to the risks he poses. The mother denies that the man is having contact with the children, but allows the social worker to talk to the children alone at school the following day. When talking to the oldest child (age 8) the social worker knows what information they want to find out – whether they have seen their mother's partner recently. The social worker's knowledge of the child makes them believe that the child would not want to admit to this if he knew the consequences of admitting it, i.e. possible foster care. The ethical dilemma is: should the social worker be honest with the child about their intentions, risking the child then withholding information; or should the social worker withhold this information and chat to the child about other matters, hoping that the child will, in the natural course of the conversation, tell them about their mother's partner?

(Continued)

(Continued)

In order to apply a Virtue Ethics perspective the key aspects to consider are thus:

- What would a good social worker do? Would a good social worker lie or withhold information?
- Would a good social worker address the issue with the child directly and be honest and respectful?
- What virtues and characteristics can you see in the possible actions of the social worker in this scenario?

A significant problem with Virtue Ethics, and especially with its application to social work practice, is how particular virtues are identified and defined (Pullen-Sansfacon, 2010; Clifford, 2014). As previously suggested, there is a relationship between the individual, morality and the state (Webb 2010), and that virtues have been suggested and connected to the HCPC codes, such as to challenge discrimination. Yet how can a social work practitioner act virtuously and respect this status if it is in fact the actions of the state that can appear to have been discriminatory; for example, in cutting funding to essential services that leave vulnerable people without support? If a social worker removes services from a service user based on this, can that in any way be acting virtuously? According to Virtue Ethics the role of the social work practitioner is then to challenge that, but how? How can a social work practitioner challenge the state in a virtuous manner? Would it be virtuous for practitioners to take strike action, for example, against these cuts? This would certainly be courageous, but could it also be argued that this may be reckless? Are there implications to the collective over the individual if strike action is taken? Let us consider the Junior Doctors' strikes in 2016 as an example; on the one hand they are challenging the government (i.e. the state), suggesting that the new contracts being enforced on them will put patients at risk; on the other hand the strike action itself means that medical care was withdrawn from some, so potentially putting them at risk. Can this therefore be argued to be virtuous? As with all moral philosophical positions (as you will see from reading this part of the book), there are no easy answers... In fact, the consideration and application of most moral philosophical positions tend to raise more questions than answers.

Donaldson and Mayer (2014) suggest, however, that a core virtuous principle for social work should be *justice*, which they view as both a personal and a social virtue. *It is personal in that it requires a disposition to the good; it is social in that it is manifest in one's interactions with self and others, and in how one pursues the arrangements of social institutions and communities* (Donaldson and Mayer, 2014, p208). Because of the differences in concepts of what virtues are relevant to social work, there can be difficulties in the application of Virtue Ethics to practice. For example, at what point does a social work practitioner become a 'good' social work practitioner? If experience is needed in terms of knowledge development (Webb, 2010) then at what point does the social work practitioner have enough to be considered virtuous, and what do they do in the meantime while they are gaining this experience? The answer can still be found in further consideration of the application of Virtue Ethics, in that, as a virtuous person, they would naturally recognise the limitations of their knowledge and would act accordingly because of their character (Banks, 2012). The principle of good character traits is significant when considering what makes a good social work practitioner; a social work practitioner who is inherently good and who knows their limits.

Case Study: Serious Case Review

Virtue Ethics will now be applied to the same aspect of the case study from the SCR concerning Child Z (2013) as the previous chapters on moral philosophy. It is reported that FZ (the father) used cannabis and had set up a cannabis farm in the family home. He reported to the Reviewing Committee that *he had not understood the seriousness of some of his lifestyle in terms of implications for a young child; this included his habitual use of cannabis that he had used since early adolescence* (p12).

A virtuous social worker would *simply* act (although of course simply does not really do justice to the complexity that lies beneath this), and in doing so would be doing the right thing. But how can it therefore be known what this is? Might a virtuous social worker carefully challenge FZ about whether his statement about not understanding the *seriousness of some of his lifestyle* was really true? Is this really an honest response on the part of FZ or possibly a defensive one? This can be considered by applying the concept of *golden mean*; for example, again considering the virtue of courage. Certainly a virtuous person would challenge something if they were concerned that it appeared not to be true and would do this carefully and respectfully with FZ. Perhaps FZ could be asked questions about what he saw in terms of good outcomes from his behaviour towards his children in order to establish his knowledge? His understanding of the impact of cannabis use could be discussed with him. This example would follow the concepts suggested by Banks and Gallagher (2009) of professional wisdom, courage, respectfulness, care, trustworthiness, justice and professional integrity. So it is important to remember that, from a virtuous perspective, it is not the act or the outcome that is right or wrong, but what the person does based on their virtuous characteristics (Banks, 2012; Beckett and Maynard, 2013; Gray and Webb, 2010; Oko, 2011; Webb, 2010).

What is also significant in considering the application of Virtue Ethics to this example is that a virtuous person would need to be able to recognise the limitations of their own knowledge and skills (Webb, 2010). The SCR indicates that a cannabis farm was found in the house but that the nurse working with the family had not identified any signs of substance use while working with the family and was not aware of the cannabis production in the house. According to Galvani et al. (2013), *evidence shows that practitioners across the spectrum of social work and social care practice are working regularly, if not daily, with people using substances* (p889). However, in terms of training and knowledge, few social work practitioners in their research felt prepared or equipped to address these issues (ibid., p901). Bearing this in

(Continued)

(Continued)

mind, a social work practitioner (or nurse) who was working with FZ may not themselves have the knowledge to understand how to identify signs of substance use or the potential implications of substance use on FZ or his family. If this were the case, then a virtuous social worker (demonstrating their professional wisdom) would have to recognise this and take action in order to obtain appropriate knowledge. According to the HCPC (2016), in section 9 *Be Honest and Trustworthy*, social work practitioners must *be honest about [their] experience, qualifications and skills* (p9). It can be argued that this relates directly to a virtuous characteristic of a social work practitioner – to be able to recognise when they do not have the knowledge necessary to act and, as suggested by Whiting (2010), to demonstrate *humility*.

The very existence and nature of a SCR suggests virtuous characteristics of those in the profession having the courage to admit when something has gone wrong, when an event has happened that was neither expected nor anticipated. While a Utilitarian perspective would attempt to anticipate the consequences, it is not possible to see the future, only to make educated and informed judgements – but these are still fallible. Therefore, Virtue Ethics recognises that a person of virtuous character would always do the right thing, but this does not mean that the outcome would always be right, and so the virtuous person would recognise this and acknowledge their limitations and mistakes.

Research Summary

When reading about a moral philosophy and considering its application to social work practice, it is important for students to understand the original key texts. As different authors write about these perspectives over time, opinions and interpretations can change and be reflective of the time in which they are written. Therefore, as students and social workers develop their academic and practice knowledge they should become more confident in accessing original texts. From this they can then begin to consider their own interpretations. Students especially should not be afraid of disagreeing with key texts or work from any authors – there are always different ways to interpret information, the only key requirement is that the alternative argument is validated and backed up with evidence as well.

Chapter Summary

In this chapter the moral philosophical position of Virtue Ethics has been considered in order to provide students and social workers with an understanding of the consideration of what makes a *good* social work practitioner and how consideration needs to be given to the character and intention of the practitioner themselves.

Further Reading

A journal article and a book chapter are specifically recommended for further reading.

Pullen-Sansfacon, A (2010) Virtue ethics for social work: A new pedagogy for practical reasoning. *Social Work Education,* 29(4): 402–15.

Webb, S (2010) 'Virtue Ethics' in M. Gray and S.A. Webb (eds) *Ethics and Value Perspectives in Social Work.* Basingstoke: Palgrave Macmillan.

In considering different types of virtues, the following journal article is recommended.

Clifford, D (2014) Limitations of virtue ethics in the social professions. *Ethics and Social Welfare,* 8(1): 2–19.

Chapter 14

Ethics of care

Lesley Deacon

Achieving a Social Work Degree

This chapter will help you meet the following capabilities, to the appropriate level, from the Professional Capabilities Framework:

PCF 1 Professionalism

- Describe the role of a social worker and the importance of personal and professional boundaries and behaviour, demonstrate ability to learn using a range of approaches;

PCF 2 Values and Ethics

- Understand the professional's ethical principles and their relevance to practice, and demonstrate awareness of own personal values and how these can impact on practice;

PCF 3 Diversity

- Recognise the importance of diversity in human identity and experience, and the application of anti-discriminatory and anti-oppressive principles in social work practice;

PCF 4 Rights, Justice and Economic Wellbeing

- Understand the principles of rights, justice and economic wellbeing, and their significance for social work practice;

PCF 6 Critical Reflection and Analysis

- Understand the need to construct hypotheses in social work practice;

- Demonstrate an awareness of a range of frameworks to assess and plan intervention and demonstrate initial awareness of risk and safeguarding;

- Demonstrate awareness of the impact of organisational context on social work practice;

- Demonstrate awareness of the importance of professional leadership in social work.

Introduction

Ethics of Care is a moral philosophical position that developed in the 1980s. However, its basis can be seen in relationship-based ethics that already existed although were not *officially* recognised before this time. In a social work context it can be seen in the relationship-focused practice of the likes of Elizabeth Fry (1780–1845) and Octavia Hill (1838–1912) (Howe, 2009). It can be argued that Ethics of Care is in essence a critique of the Deontological and Utilitarianist positions, which can be, together, referred to as Ethics of Justice. In her seminal work *In a Different Voice*, Carol Gilligan (1982) observed **two distinct voices** in speaking about morality in the interviews she conducted with female college students: concerning *identity* and *moral development*. She was clear that the difference was in the 'theme', in the way of thinking; and it was through empirical evidence, she argued, that this was then associated primarily with the thinking of women. *The moral imperative that emerges repeatedly in interviews with women is the injunction to care, a responsibility to discern and alleviate the 'real and recognisable' trouble of this earth* (Gilligan, 1982, p100). Gilligan's interviews with women identified concern for others and about not hurting or doing harm to others. This is the basic principle of Ethics of Care (also referred to as a Feminist Ethic). To understand the distinct difference, it is important to first look at the concepts of earlier ethical thinking.

Ethics of Justice

To understand how morality is developed it must be understood in the context of how identity is developed. Gilligan refers to developmental psychologists as falling into the trap of *observational bias* in the development of their theories as they observed the *male life as the norm*, Freud being a significant example (Gilligan, 1993, p6). (See Chapter 9 for context.) Lawrence Kohlberg (1927–87) was an American developmental psychologist whose work was concerned with understanding moral development within identity. His findings suggested cohesion between moral reasoning and concepts of justice and fairness. It was these which Kohlberg identified as the highest states of moral development (Kohlberg, 1981). Yet, according to Gilligan, relationships and concepts of dependency, it could be argued, are experienced differently by men and women. Gilligan therefore identified a significant difference between the way men and women made moral decisions, and she referred to the work of Kohlberg and others as identifying male thinking as an 'Ethics of Justice'. The ethical principles that have been presented concerning Deontology and Utilitarianism (Act and Rule) can be identified together as Ethics of Justice. This is because they are concerned with the fair distribution of goods and services, etc. These moral principles are both universal and absolute, and the application of these is completed from an abstract position; too much emphasis is placed on the *rational and impartial nature of ethical decision-making* (Banks, 2012, p69). Kohlberg's research made the suggestion that women remain in an *inferior* stage of moral development (Kohlberg, 1981). In her research, however, Gilligan found that women reasoned *differently* to men, but that this difference must not therefore be observed as inferior, as suggested by the 'observational bias' towards a male perspective (Gilligan, 1993).

Ethics of Care

Gilligan referred to a moral ideal as one that was focused on attention and on response, not on remaining principled or abstract (Gilligan, 1982). These principled and abstract responses in fact ignore some significant and important aspects such as *the character, motives and emotions of the moral agent* (Banks, 2012, p69). To understand female moral reasoning, Gilligan emphasised the importance of responsibility in morality, i.e. responsibility and obligation to others. She found in her research that women's understanding of morality very much focused on the concept of not causing harm or hurting another, and that in some way morality is able to be used to resolve conflicts in a way that does not harm others; *{t}he moral person is the one who helps others* (Gilligan, 1982, p66). At first glance a reader may see similarities between this and the concept of Virtue Ethics (see Chapter 13), and certainly concepts of a good character do refer to this. There are indeed some similarities between Ethics of Care and Virtue Ethics, particularly regarding the importance of character, human qualities and motives of the person. However, the significant difference is in the focus on the relationship between the carer and cared-for, recognising the dependency and vulnerabilities in this relationship (Banks, 2012; Beckett and Maynard, 2013).

Virtue Ethics focuses on the character traits of the individual in terms of their contribution to the collective happiness, but the focus of Ethics of Care is very specifically about not causing harm, rather than about virtuous characteristics *per se*. So, while 'care' may be considered a virtue, from an Ethics of Care perspective, it is seen instead as an attribute (Banks, 2012). The virtue of 'care' could be displayed without there being a real connection, i.e. relationship between the carer and the cared-for. What is essential in Ethics of Care is that the individual must accept *responsibility* for the decisions that they make, and that those decisions are intended not to cause harm. Along with accepting responsibility comes the recognition of the importance of relationships and, in particular, relationships with others. According to Gilligan, for women, their identity is tied up with the context of relationships and with *responsibility and care* (1982, p160). This different way of thinking about morality shifts the focus from more abstract universal principles to the everyday concept of care and concern for others, avoiding harm, and recognising the importance of the relationships between people; so Ethics of Care becomes a *social* activity (Banks, 2012).

Gilligan (1982) argued, therefore, that ethical and moral issues were (and are) emotional issues and so emotion should not be separated from them. Being concerned for the welfare of others or for the discrimination they may face is an imperative human need and human concern. Therefore, this should be embraced and not removed from ethical decision making. Rather than being about rules, she views moral decision making as being about the quality of caring for another (Beckett and Maynard, 2013). Also, rather than human beings being independent and autonomous, they are in fact dependent upon each other – dependent upon each other for care.

Rather than being set out from a universal, abstract and principled perspective, Ethics of Care is therefore relational and context specific. Care and relationships are dependent on the individual situation in which a moral decision is needed. It could be argued that this perspective fits better with a social work perspective as it requires understanding of individual situations in order for morally right decisions to be made. However, that is not to say that Deontological, Utilitarian or indeed Virtue Ethics perspectives are not applicable. To some extent, Ethics of Care may appear to be easier to apply, but the danger with this is in understanding the key principles of care and of relationships rather than just a process. A social worker could perceive themselves as applying this moral philosophy without actually doing so; this is where the concepts of care and concern need to be distinct from the concepts of care and control.

Care and concern versus care and control

When considering social work practice, the concept of care and concern is pivotal. As Thompson (2015) suggests, social work is often referred to as a *caring* profession; however, he raises the issue that the work of social work practice is also about a form of *social control* (p3). The reason for this is that social work practice is not just about an individual but about the wider community, and sometimes these priorities come into conflict. It must also be recognised that the actions of social work practitioners will either *support and reinforce the status quo*, or they will *challenge it*, but they can never be neutral (Horner, 2013, p25). Therefore, what must be recognised in any social work practice is the existence of control. Along with the role and duties of the social work practitioner comes the power to make decisions about other people's lives. So, while the principles of the profession may well originate with care and concern, there is no doubt that when implemented it can manifest as care and *control*. (See Chapter 16

Radical Social Work to understand some of the conflicting values in this.) If control elements take over then this can enforce oppression onto individuals – something that Ethics of Care does not ally itself with (Thompson, 2015). So, how is care achieved from this perspective while recognising elements of social control but without that control becoming oppressive? And how can it be applied to avoid reliance on abstract principles, as in Deontological and Utilitarian perspectives?

Activity 14.1

Consider the difference between the two extracts below:

An unaccompanied minor has just arrived at the local authority and needs an assessment and temporary accommodation.

Asha is a twelve-year-old girl who is waiting in the reception area. She is frightened and is alone. Her parents have died and she needs your help. She needs a place to stay and she needs to feel safe.

The first of these statements may be factually correct, but avoids an emotional response or connection to the situation or to person. The second (however minimally) begins to recognise the person – Asha, the girl who is alone and without support, the girl who needs help. In applying Ethics of Care as a philosophical perspective the humanity of Asha must be seen, along with recognition of the relationship she is seeking to help her feel safe, and recognition of the responsibility of social work practitioners to provide that. That is not to suggest that any social work practitioner involved should become a surrogate parent to Asha, but to ensure that they *care* for her and have *concern* for her wellbeing.

Case Study

Personal reflection

I want to reflect on an interaction I had with a service user who contributes to the social work course that I teach on - to protect his anonymity, I will call him David. We were discussing the concept of Ethics of Care and the difficulties social work practitioners may have because the nature of their relationship with the service user is a professional one, i.e. they met the service user because the service user needed a service from them. However, the service user's perspective may be different. This reminded me of practice situations I had encountered, for example, receiving Christmas cards from service users, or being invited to important events such as weddings or Christenings. My professional role as a social work practitioner prevented me from accepting these. Yet in my discussion with David it became clear that his view was different. To him his social worker was a very important person in his life – a significant person – and not someone he considered just as a professional; someone just doing their job. Instead he had considered his social worker as a friend, yet he was a friend who always declined his invitations to go for a drink at the local pub. This realisation for David was significant - a realisation that his perception of the relationship was different to the social worker's. This was disappointing for him.

Activity 14.2

There will undoubtedly have been times when social work students and social work practitioners have encountered similar situations in practice such as gifts, invitations or Facebook friend requests. Rather than consider the professional obligation to decline, consider for a moment the reason for the service user's actions - consider how they perceive the relationship.

It is important when applying Ethics of Care to reflect and empathise with the service user or carer and the way in which they view the relationship with the practitioner. Social work practitioners can be involved in a person's day-to-day life and their support and presence can become important. Before this relationship is dismissed because there are professional boundaries, it is important for it to be *recognised*.

Tronto's political theory of care

Following Gilligan, Joan Tronto (1993) developed what she referred to as a *political theory of care*. It was her perspective that care alone was not sufficient and that justice and shared power were also important. She suggested that the concept of care is a basic aspect of human nature – we both depend on others and care for them. While the concept of care itself was culturally specific, the basic concept was in *taking the other's needs as the starting point of what must be done*, i.e. putting the other person first (Featherstone, 2010, p76). According to Tronto (1993) there are in fact four phases of care:

1. Caring about – to recognise the need others have for care.

2. Taking care of – to actually accept the responsibility of care for another.

3. Care giving – to give care to another.

4. Care receiving – to receive care from another.

Connected to these four phases, Tronto (1993, and cited in Banks, 2012) argued that there are four ethical elements of care:

1. Attentiveness – it is essential that needs are actively sought, that attention is paid to where care may be needed.

2. Responsibility – the acceptance of the responsibility to care for others should become natural to each individual and not based on rules, regulations or principles.

3. Competence – it is imperative that the care giver is competent to give the specific care needed by the cared-for, i.e. has the necessary skills and knowledge.

4. Responsiveness – the individual in receipt of this care needs to be able to understand the care given and the care giver needs to be alert to any issues of abuse or concern in the way an individual responds and in terms of their vulnerability.

Tronto was explicit in this not being about women's morality but about an Ethics of Care, which is made up of the values that traditionally are associated with women, such as love, care, nurture, concern and peace. It was not enough just to have concern for others – it was necessary to accept the responsibility of being responsive to it and taking action (Featherstone, 2010). To operate within an Ethics of Care, all aspects set out by Tronto would need to be applied, and in that application it should not be sentimentalised or romanticised (Featherstone, 2010).

Ethics of care in social work practice

The underlying concept of Ethics of Care and its focus on care, concern and relationships can be identified in the following HCPC codes:

> *1.5 You must not discriminate against service users, carers or colleagues by allowing your personal views to affect your professional relationships or the care, treatment or other services that you provide*
>
> *10.1 You must keep full, clear, and accurate records for everyone you care for, treat, or provide other services to*

(HCPC, 2016, p12)

In the codes there are 47 references to care/carer, indicating the nature of the relationships involved – being a carer or caring, and being cared for. The concepts of care are entrenched in the HCPC codes and are therefore a requirement of the social work profession. As suggested by Featherstone (2010), a difference between those who apply to study the social sciences and those who apply to study social work is that social scientists tend to be focused on *what makes people 'tick' and understand{ing} society* whereas social workers are concerned with engaging with others (p83). So, by the very nature of the person applying for social work they are immediately engaged with an Ethic of Care.

Returning to the origins of theory in social work, it can be seen through the work of the likes of Elizabeth Fry and Octavia Hill that it could be argued the importance of care and of relationships has always been a fundamental and significant aspect of the morality of social work practice. The difficulty in applying Ethics of Care to social work settings, however, comes from the restrictions placed on the 'relationships' by codes of conduct (HCPC,

2016) – something which would not have been a concern for Fry or Hill. The meeting point, interaction and involvement between a social worker and a service user and/or carer is defined by *professionalism*. The relationship is therefore different to one that may be formed between, for example, family, friends or neighbours (Beckett and Maynard, 2013). It could be argued that this changes the nature of the relationship from informal to formal. However, it can also be argued that nothing has changed; that in order for a social worker to apply Ethics of Care in practice they must recognise themselves as a human being and the service user or carer as a human being. As suggested by Beckett and Maynard (2013), Ethics of Care alludes to human qualities; this moral philosophical position was not in itself applied to social work practice but to human beings' relationships and responsibilities to each other. Therefore, it is from this perspective that it should be considered and applied. The caveat for any and all of the theories presented in this book is that there is no one-size-fits-all approach, and so social workers in practice would and should consider different perspectives on the same situation before making a decision.

Critical evaluation

It can be argued that in identifying a difference in moral reasoning between men and women that Gilligan is, in essence, reinforcing gender stereotypes both for and against both genders, i.e. women as caring and men seeking justice. While Ethics of Care is sometimes referred to as Feminist Ethics or a Feminist Ethic of Care, it is *both dangerous and misleading to attribute* this Ethics of Care to just women (Banks, 2012, p78). It is essential when considering and applying Ethics of Care that is not associated as being gender-specific but *gender-neutral*. In fact, Gilligan (1993) herself argued that there is no hierarchy between Ethics of Justice and Ethics of Care, they both should be considered equally. The concept of care therefore should not be considered as a feminist oppression but as important for all human beings (Featherstone, 2010).

It can also be seen, from Gilligan's original philosophical perspective and the ethical principles set out by Tronto, that the ideas of control and protection are not included. So, while this theory emphasises the applicability of care, and this is indeed a significant part of social work practice, referring back to Thompson (2015), we must ask how the social control element can be recognised and addressed by this philosophical perspective? There is a suggestion in Tronto's work that the act of caring would become natural if barriers to the morality of care were removed (Featherstone, 2010); so in effect there would be no need for control. It is suggested by Featherstone (2010), however, that most critiques of Tronto's work focus on the lack of a clear psychological analysis of the self and motivations towards care. So, the justification is not evident that removing barriers would lead towards a disposition to care.

Activity 14.3

Application to practice

Consider the following dilemma, which was experienced by a social work student in a practice situation in 2015:

> Sarah is a 73-year-old female with dementia who lives in a residential care home. However, every day she asks to go home and requests that the staff call her a taxi. When staff members have tried to explain to Sarah that she now lives in the care home, she would become aggressive and punch and kick out at staff. She would then refuse to go into the dining hall for meals as she believed her taxi would be coming. Staff members found that if they told Sarah her taxi would be coming after lunch, she would remain calm and go to eat; this led to other residents of the care home doing the same.

Now apply the principles of the Ethics of Care to this scenario; consider the importance of care and concern as opposed to care and control.

Case Study: Serious Case Review

In applying Gilligan's perspective of the Ethics of Care to the SCR, the concern for and desire to help MZ and FZ as they became parents for the first time and then again with Child Z would be paramount. The focus would not be on controlling them or their behaviour, or on implementing any sanctions, but on being concerned for them and their wellbeing. The following sections consider how Tronto's model could be applied to consider the situation of MZ, for example. The SCR refers to MZ 'disengaging', which was not identified as such at the time of events by the professionals concerned, instead they referred to MZ having *lost contact*.

Caring about – to recognise the need others have for care

The SCR identifies that MZ had just had a baby, had moved house, was attending college, had changed her mobile, had been on holiday and that her nephew had died recently. This information was relayed to a professional who also identified their own concern about the deprived area in which MZ was living. This attention to MZ is important – to recognise needs that could arise that MZ may not necessarily raise herself. However, caution needs to be applied here – the danger in identifying potential needs not specifically raised by MZ herself could manifest as a form of control.

Taking care of – to actually accept the responsibility of care for another

Any professional involved with a service user or carer must take responsibility for the needs identified in relation to them. The professional working directly with MZ must take responsibility – so having identified needs they are then responsible for doing something. As suggested, the concern about social deprivation was raised, therefore, the professional needed to identify how support could be provided to alleviate some of the implications of this.

Care giving – to give care to another

It is important that professionals are competent. Historically, Child in Need cases would be managed by social work practitioners, but due to increasing workloads social work child safeguarding teams now only seem to co-ordinate child protection cases (Children Act 1989), i.e. the more serious cases involving children. With the implementation of the Common Assessment Framework (CWDC, 2009) responsibility is shared across all agencies in contact with children and young people. In giving care to another, it is important that the professional is competent and in possession of the necessary skills. This therefore raises questions about the role of the Family Nurse Partnership (FNP) worker involved with the family – did this person have the necessary skills and training in order to provide appropriate care for MZ?

Care receiving – to receive care from another

In being attentive to how care is received, a practitioner must ensure that any care provided is not oppressive. A difficulty identified in the SCR was that the support provided by FNP was not risk-based and therefore risks were not assessed. This raises questions concerning care giving (above), but how does the concept of risk fit with Ethics of Care? Care and concern and the desire to avoid hurt can be difficult to apply when risks are involved.

Activity 14.4

Now apply Tronto's four ethical elements of care either to the SCR of Child Z (which can be accessed online) or to a case example from your own practice:

- Attentiveness
- Responsibility
- Competence
- Responsiveness

Chapter Summary

This chapter has focused primarily on the seminal work of Carol Gilligan and its implications for social work practice. Her work was further developed by Joan Tronto, who developed the Political Ethics of Care. Both these philosophical perspectives have been considered and applied to social work practice. While the principle of care is intrinsic to social work practice, the concept of control (which may involve some form of risk assessment) raises questions regarding how this is compatible with an Ethic of Care.

Further Reading

Interviews with Carol Gilligan and Joan Tronto are available and are helpful for students/practitioners to read in order to set the context for the theoretical developments.

Carol Gilligan: http://ethicsofcare.org/interviews/carol-gilligan/

Joan Tronto: http://ethicsofcare.org/interviews/joan-tronto/

Featherstone, B (2010) 'Ethic of Care' in M. Gray and S.A. Webb (eds) *Ethics and Value Perspectives in Social Work.* Basingstoke: Palgrave Macmillan.

Chapter 15

Radical ethics

Lesley Deacon

Achieving a Social Work Degree

This chapter will help you meet the following capabilities, to the appropriate level, from the Professional Capabilities Framework:

PCF 1 Professionalism

- Describe the role of a social worker and the importance of personal and professional boundaries and behaviour, demonstrate ability to learn using a range of approaches;

PCF 2 Values and Ethics

- Understand the professional's ethical principles and their relevance to practice, and demonstrate awareness of own personal values and how these can impact on practice;

PCF 3 Diversity

- Recognise the importance of diversity in human identity and experience, and the application of anti-discriminatory and anti-oppressive principles in social work practice;

PCF 4 Rights, Justice and Economic Wellbeing

- Understand the principles of rights, justice and economic wellbeing, and their significance for social work practice;

PCF 6 Critical Reflection and Analysis

- Understand the need to construct hypotheses in social work practice;

PCF 7 Intervention and Skills

- Demonstrate an awareness of a range of frameworks to assess and plan intervention and demonstrate initial awareness of risk and safeguarding;

PCF 8 Context and Organisations

- Demonstrate awareness of the impact of organisational context on social work practice;

PCF 9 Professional Leadership

- Demonstrate awareness of the importance of professional leadership in social work.

Reflection Point

Can morally right decisions be made where there is injustice and discrimination? In other words, how can a social work practitioner act in a way which is morally good, when their actions could in fact be unfair for the service user?

Introduction

The moral philosophies of Deontology and Utilitarianism make a basic presumption about moral decision making: that human beings are free-thinking, i.e. given the opportunity they are free from other influences concerning an understanding of morality. When considering Deontology, for example, it is possible to see influences of religion underpinning morals, i.e. the universal and transcendental nature of moral thinking. However, following the Enlightenment period and certainly today, many people look for more naturalistic explanations and understanding of morals. Utilitarianism can be criticised for its moral justification of using others as a means to an end, and because you cannot foretell the future it is impossible to be sure of the consequences (Anscombe, 1958). This chapter will therefore look at a more current and radical perspective on ethics which is relevant to social work students and practitioners today: Radical Ethics. Its origins can be traced to the political philosophy of John Rawls, and readers should easily be able to see the links between this perspective and Radical Social Work (Chapter 16), therefore connecting with the political philosophies of Marxism and Feminism (see Ethics of Care, Chapter 14 and Feminism, Chapter 9).

John Rawls

There is much debate about the work of John Rawls (1971), which the reader can look at in more depth, but the key principles he raised will be considered here as they are relevant to the application of Radical Ethics in social work practice.

In 1971, John Rawls, an American political and moral philosopher wrote *A Theory of Justice*. He wrote this as an argument against the moral philosophy of Utilitarianism and its popularity. Instead, his intention was to review and reassert a Deontological philosophical basis for the modern age – but his specific focus was on liberalism (Rawls, 1971, 1985). His argument was that even those who held fundamentally different beliefs could (and should) still come together to form a consensus; so he referred to the work of Emmanuel Kant for his philosophical perspective, i.e. that moral goodness lies in the action itself (Bruce Douglass, 2012), (see Chapter 11). As Rawls himself suggested, *justice is the first virtue of social institutions* (1971, p3). So, the first *original agreement* within society is to base it on a principle of justice. He criticises the Utilitarian approach for allowing or condoning the 'loss of freedom' for some in order to enable a greater good to be achieved for others. Justice, he argues, is not *justice* if it allows for such loss of freedom or sacrifice of some. The only reason for a Utilitarian perspective being applied is because of a lack of an alternative which is actually better. He highlighted that instead of a positive approach, Utilitarianism could be argued to be a deficit approach (i.e. starting from a negative) which condones some injustice in order to avoid a greater injustice (Rawls, 1971). The position he argued for was a *Justice as Fairness*. That is, in the status quo (the original position) those in power were responsible for determining fairly the rules and duties which should be applied in order to embrace an equal society. But Rawls later clarified that the principles he espoused were only applicable to democratic societies. Therefore, while a Deontological perspective would be universal, Rawls' political theory was not, and could only be applied to certain societies, such as those in the West. So, as with Virtue Ethics and Ethics of Care, which consider contemporary key concepts, Radical Ethics is a moral philosophical perspective particularly aimed at Western democratic societies. (Rawls (1971) refers to his position as a *theory of justice* but this is not to be confused with Kohlberg's Ethics of Justice, which is discussed in Chapter 14, Ethics of Care.)

Critics suggest, however, that Rawls did not answer, in his work, the questions raised to develop and identify a *true* political philosophy (Bruce Douglass, 2012), i.e. that his perspective therefore effectively leaves everything open to interpretation. For social work, therefore, combining this philosophical position with Radical Social Work practice can help identify key concepts and give it purpose.

Radical ethics and social work

As suggested in Chapter 16, the re-emergence of Marxist theoretical thinking in the 1960s led to questions and scepticisms regarding what can be referred to as a bourgeois illusion of choice and control. That is, that in reality there is no choice for those who do not hold power – they are in fact controlled to stay in their position in society in order to meet the needs of those who own the means of production, i.e. the powerful. This can be seen through the developments of the radical perspective. When a liberalist political philosophy such as that suggested by Rawls (1971) is combined with the principles of Radical Social Work, what emerges is Radical Ethics. It could be argued that this philosophical position is more naturalist than non-naturalist, thus moving a Deontological perspective into everyday life in contemporary society; to be concerned with what is needed for a society to flourish. This refocuses efforts on to the future and how to develop a better society in the long term. The core element and fundamental principle of this moral philosophy is that of social justice. This can be seen from the way in which different philosophical elements can be incorporated and applied. For example, Virtue Ethics – a concern for social justice being a core characteristic – along with Utilitarianism – a concern for what is the right thing for the most people. Applying these together would mean equality for everybody would be better than inequality for anybody.

It also must be noted that Radical Ethics differs from Radical Social Work in two key elements. First, Radical Ethics is a political philosophy and therefore does not just apply to social work but applies to all environments that experience political control, including other public services like health, education, police and social care in general. So, this philosophy looks at wider society and the way in which people are governed and the implications of this. Second, because this is a philosophical position it does not only look at the direct consequences of certain policies but it also looks at the overarching theory concerned with *minimising unequal social powers and their use and abuse in the interests of some but to the disadvantage of dominated individuals and groups* (Clifford and Burke, 2009, p123). So, it could be argued that the philosophical basis of Radical Social Work is in fact Radical Ethics.

Social justice

The concept of social justice is the fundamental principle that underpins the values of social work practice today. Social justice must be concerned with the way in which the societies in which we live are organised and governed, with a particular concern for the fair distribution of resources according to need. The International Federation of Social Workers (2016, website) sets out the key principles of social work as concerned with *human rights and social justice*. As Solas (2008, p125) suggests, the *gap between rich and poor not only persists, but continues to widen*. The social justice that is needed is one that sees *inequality as not only bad, but also avoidable* (ibid., p125). So, what responsibilities do social workers have in relation to this? This is discussed in detail in Chapter 16, Radical Social Work, and raises questions for social workers regarding their moral obligations to social justice. However, for social justice to be effective existing power structures that lead to inequality must be challenged.

> The appropriate response to poverty is OUTRAGE **not** care, comfort or containment.

> (Howe, 2009, p127)

Banks (2012) argues that situating the ethics of social justice in social work means that social work practitioners *need to take seriously the social justice agenda* and in doing so lead to *a commitment to collective action for social change* (pp92–3). While Banks associates this more with an Ethics of Care agenda, it is its key focus on social justice that leads us to also associate this with Radical Ethics.

Application to social work

As suggested by Clifford and Burke (2009), the Codes of Ethics that apply to professional bodies tend to be concerned with *system maintenance, rather than reform or revolution* (p124). Thus, the purpose of practice and its underlying principles have been determined and the Codes are set out in order to maintain this. But what if the application of those Codes or of the assessment and intervention process conflicts with the intended underlying principles?

Case Study

This is an example of a family I worked with which raised some questions about social justice. (The names of the service users have been changed to protect their confidentiality.)

Amy and Carl were both 19 years old and had two children. Their oldest child was three years old and was in the permanent care of Amy's parents. Their second child, Timmy, was three months old. Prior to his birth both Amy and Carl were homeless. They lived on the streets and used different illegal substances. (It was this situation that led to them relinquishing the care of their older child.) On finding out she was pregnant for the second time, Amy and Carl made the decision to get their lives sorted out. They applied for housing and withdrew from taking substances. The home they were given was approximately 15 miles away from Amy's parents. Due to their previous experiences they were on a Child in Need plan (s17, Children Act 1989) when I met them.

The main reason for the Child in Need plan was due to concerns about how Amy and Carl could cope with a new baby and whether they would resort to previous substance use again. At that stage they did not have a good track record of being able to manage. Amy had a medically diagnosed learning disability. Carl had issues with anger management and had a history of petty crime. He was brought up in a number of foster care environments before becoming homeless. So, when considering this situation some issues of social justice need to be considered.

As suggested by Clifford and Burke (2009) the moral dilemma for the child protection social worker can be in knowing that the child's parents, in this case Amy and Carl, are in fact vulnerable themselves. They suggest that a critique of social work concerning safeguarding children can be that much of assessment and intervention concerns *controlling the behaviour of working-class women, rather than trying to change their appalling circumstances* (ibid., p126). (See also Chapter 9.)

(Continued)

(Continued)

Application

When applying a Radical Ethics perspective to this case study it highlights that, in social work practice, sometimes the experiences and vulnerability of a parent, for example, are ignored because the focus is so much on the child. This does not mean to suggest that the focus of safeguarding should not be on the actual service user (the child), but students and social work practitioners need to recognise that sometimes this focus means that parents and carers may be unfairly discriminated against. Another way of looking at this is the fact that by not recognising the lack of social justice, the root causes of the difficulties facing the family are not being addressed. A radical view of social work practice is that it tends to ignore poverty and depression (Clifford and Burke, 2009), and it could be argued that this is particularly the case when considering safeguarding social work.

Further, when considering Radical Ethics in social work, concepts raised by Clifford and Burke (2009, p123) should be considered:

- Social workers must develop a *supporting* relationship with service users whilst planning for child protection.
- The way in which behaviour of the working/benefit class is *controlled* must be considered. When seeking to understand the servicer user has this issue been considered?
- The official ideology of the state tends to ignore deprivation, poverty and powerlessness; a social worker must not.
- The Codes of Ethics that are devised exist to *maintain the system* rather than to promote change for service users.

The application of Radical Ethics therefore places a moral duty on social workers to look at the root causes of difficulties for service users and not the symptoms. A caveat for any kind of radical perspective, however, is to be aware of time, inclination and focus:

> *Time* to be spent by the social worker with the service user in getting to know them and their circumstances in order to understand the root causes of their difficulties rather than just looking at the surface and seeing, for example, child abuse or neglect.
> *Inclination* on the part of both the social worker and the service user to want to understand the complexities of the situation in more depth, or inclination to do something about it.
> *Focus*, as while a radical perspective raises questions about understanding the experiences of a parent, for example, this must not mean that the focus on safeguarding the child is lost.

Reflection Point

Consider a practice example where you have faced a moral dilemma, e.g. the withdrawal of services due to budget cuts, which you assessed were still needed; or the lack of recognition or support of parents in a child protection process. Apply a Radical Ethics position to your example – consider key factors such as social justice.

Case Study: Serious Case Review

Radical Ethics is applied in much the same way as Radical Social Work but with one fundamental difference: Radical Social Work does not set out a moral obligation as such, but Radical Ethics does. Rather than a social work practitioner choosing whether or not to consider the wider implications of policy application, a Radical Ethics philosophical perspective suggests that social work practitioners have a *moral obligation* to consider these factors. So, in order to apply Radical Ethics to moral decision making in the SCR case study, it is important to think about some of the circumstances of the family. From a Radical Social Work perspective the focus is on understanding the impact of social structures on MZ and FZ; however, from a Radical Ethics perspective these need to be considered slightly differently. First, the position of the social worker is different. They must see the human being first of all, so rather than just considering the role of the social work practitioner to the service user or carer, they must see a relationship between two human beings. Then, as with other moral philosophies, they must consider whether the service user or carer has been treated fairly, i.e. social justice. Looking at similar issues as raised in Chapter 16, Radical Social Work, it can be argued that, as human beings, MZ and FZ have not been treated fairly in their lives. The liberal democracy in which they live appears to have treated them unfairly in the following ways, as indicated in the SCR:

the absence of appropriate housing for a significant period of time

the apparent isolation from positive sources of help and support

the age of MZ

substance misuse... some professionals may have taken a tolerant approach to aspects of behaviour that may have been different if it had been exhibited in a different part of the city

both experienced levels of childhood trauma and abuse

MZ was diagnosed with moderate learning difficulties as a child

The probation service and police recognised that FZ had unspecified learning difficulties

FZ has an extensive history of substance misuse and violence and had been unwilling to acknowledge his need for help in regard to mental health and educational or employment support

(SCR Child Z ,pp15–18)

It can be seen that there are similarities between this SCR and the practice example given earlier in this chapter. The outcome of the case example was positive, with Amy and Carl turning their lives around and continuing in their caring role for their child, Timmy. However, the outcome for Child Z, MZ and FZ was not so positive. The list of issues set out above is substantial and those that have been raised, it could be argued, demonstrate a lack of social justice for the family.

Activity 15.1

Consider some of the other issues of concern raised in relation to MZ and FZ above, and apply a Radical Ethics philosophical perspective.

Comment

Housing issue

The absence of appropriate housing for a considerable time for MZ, FZ and their family can be considered from a Radical Ethics perspective. A report by Tuffrey (2010) for the charity Shelter (which works with and supports the homeless) suggests that austerity has led to *affordability pressure* and the rising cost of housing has led to an *affordability crisis*. This means that the cost of housing has risen exponentially and not in relation to wages or benefits, therefore housing has become less affordable. The implications of higher housing costs have not been fully challenged or raised as a concern (Tuffrey, 2010), but just accepted as the norm in our society, which means that the actual unfairness of the situation for families is not something likely to be considered in the course of social work practice – only dealing with the implications of it.

The report by Tuffrey (2010) focused on the *real* impact of this situation on families, i.e. the human cost of a social structure. Her findings suggest that some of the implications concern less money for some to spend on food (28 per cent), a lack of options to relocate for work (12 per cent), and borrowing on credit cards to top up money (13 per cent). Within the rental market, they found that *recent statistics show how the high costs of renting can push households and particularly families with children into poverty* (ibid., 2010, p10).

Affordability has an impact on choices, for example, being able to choose to live nearer to family for support, or to live in areas with better amenities or support services. These undoubtedly impact on families where support, it could be argued, is an absolute necessity. Costs for housing, that must be paid in order to avoid eviction and homelessness, place families in difficult positions so compromises have to made about day-to-day living, e.g. cutting back on food, fuel or house repairs, for example (Tuffrey, 2010). The implications of this situation cannot be ignored as it places pressure on adults to find solutions and manage their situation in order to support their children. As Tuffrey (2010) suggests, *what is clear from our findings, is that housing costs are causing stress for many, which in turn is having a negative impact on people's health, relationships, employment and wellbeing* (p28). So what can be inferred from this knowledge is that due to the current climate in relation to housing it is unlikely that MZ and FZ have been treated *fairly*, instead they will have experienced the pressures associated with this difficulty. This – the implications of social injustice – is something that students and social work practitioners need to consider from a Radical Ethics perspective, not after the fact, but *during* the process of assessment and interventions.

Concluding remarks

Although this book is not focusing on intervention, only understanding, it is clear that much focus of this philosophical position is on moral action. That is, social workers have a moral duty to act against the inequality of opportunity experienced by all service users. They must not sacrifice a service user to achieve a greater good. They must consider the benefit of all.

Critique

A problem in the application of any radical principle is the idea of using people as a means to an end. For example, in considering the application to the case study, how could a social worker have addressed these concerns? Would they have interceded and *advocated* on the part of the family to address any housing issues? This presumes that a social worker was involved at that time, but that was not the case. Therefore, should the housing officer have interceded, recognising the unfairness of the system being imposed, and intervened? But if they had intervened for that family, what about others? As moral outrage is not enough and *action* is required, could individual action be enough, or would more collective action (as suggested by Banks, 2012) be needed? In either case, what does a social worker or housing officer have the power to do, in reality? At the time of writing, junior doctors have just been taking strike action to object to aspects of the government's planned contracts. While it could be argued that this collective action is against inequality, the simple act of striking means that people had non-urgent operations cancelled – so those people were used, in this instance, as a means to an end. When situations like this occur and, in effect, an individual's needs are sacrificed for the collective good, this does not address any immediate problems that person may be dealing with. Thus the options for the application of Radical Ethics can, in reality, be limited.

Rawls (1971, 1985) himself accepted that people have differing opinions and ideologies, so can it really be possible for them to form a consensus? We only have to look at the current disagreements over 'Brexit 2016' to see how people's differing opinions can cause conflict, and some – almost half in this case – will inevitably not get what they were looking for. This brings us back to questions of moral philosophy, and utilitarianism in particular – how can we be sure a decision made for the 'greater good' is not actually doing even greater harm?

Chapter Summary

In this chapter, the political philosophy of Radical Ethics has been set out as inspired by the work of John Rawls and Bailey and Brake's Radical Social Work. Readers have been able to consider a more radical philosophical perspective focusing on the key idea of social justice, i.e. fairness.

Further Reading

The work of Clifford and Burke (2009) has been referred to throughout this chapter. It is recommended that students and social work practitioners read the following chapter from this book: Clifford, D and Burke, B (2009) *Politicising Ethics: Justice, Fairness and Interacting Social Systems*. Basingstoke: Palgrave Macmillan.

Introduction to Part Four – Political Theories and Ideologies

While it is not a professional requirement that social work practitioners be politically motivated, some would certainly argue that they should be. There are concerns from those in and around the profession that by having such prescriptive codes of practice that social work practitioners can become *mindless rule-following {practitioners} at the expense of ethical reflection* (Banks, 2012, p 117). Considering political theories and ideologies, therefore, gives students and practitioners the opportunity to reflect on the *real* impact of certain practice norms and how they may conflict with core social work values. (This is also seen in Part Three Ethics and Moral Philosophies.)

The first chapter in this part concerns Radical Social Work practice by Lesley Deacon – looking at the seminal work of Bailey and Brake (1975) and raises questions regarding the actual impact of social work practice on those it intends to support, specifically concerning poverty. The Five Models of Disability by Stephen J Macdonald sets out the origins and development of disability studies and argues for the identification of five different models in order to understand the different ways in which *disability* can be viewed. Finally, Alan Marshall's chapter on Anti-discriminatory and Anti-Oppressive Practice looks at the specific issue of race in order to understand structural discrimination.

These issues are not the only political ideologies that social work students and practitioners can consider but are helpful in introducing some key concepts and in developing thinking outside of rule-following.

Chapter 16

Radical social work

Lesley Deacon

Achieving a Social Work Degree

This chapter will help you meet the following capabilities, to the appropriate level, from the Professional Capabilities Framework:

PCF 2 Values and Ethics

- Understand the professional's ethical principles and their relevance to practice, and demonstrate awareness of own personal values and how these can impact on practice;

PCF 4 Rights, Justice and Economic Wellbeing

- Understand the principles of rights, justice and economic wellbeing, and their significance for social work practice;

PCF 6 Critical Reflection and Analysis

- Understand the need to construct hypotheses in social work practice;

PCF 8 Context and Organisations

- Demonstrate awareness of the impact of organisational context on social work practice.

Introduction

Radical Social Work was, in some respects, a relatively minor political movement in the UK in the 1970s – being more popular in some regions than others (Lavallette, 2011). So, why raise this as a significant political theory (ideology) in social work practice today? The main reason for the resurgence of a more radical perspective is because of the way in which social workers working at Local Authorities are required to do their job, which suggests they may be required to implement a particular ideology which, when considered in more depth, is in conflict with social work values.

Context

In order to understand the significance of Radical Social Work, the historical context of the profession of social work needs to be considered (see Chapter 1). Why did members of the profession begin to be concerned about the way in which social work practice was being implemented? Thinking back to the origins of social work as a profession and the work of the Charity Organisation Society (COS) it is important to remember that the theoretical basis for assessment and intervention in the profession was *psychological*. For example, as Payne (2014) suggests, taking a behavioural approach enables the use of a 'baseline' for behaviour so that improvements become easier to measure. Using theories concerning personality and behaviour can assist social workers in understanding a service user and their behaviour (Parrish, 2014). While definitely beneficial (as demonstrated in the chapters on psychological theories in social work), there is an inherent problem with the focus of purely psychological theories in social work practice, i.e. that those theories are aimed at understanding the individual and their behaviour, so focusing on them as being solely responsible for their behaviour. The use of these psychological theories to understand individuals and their behaviour suggests that the focus is on *changing* their behaviour, implying that their behaviour *needs* changing so is therefore *wrong* – but wrong from whose perspective? Certainly the work of the COS was concerned with concepts such as the 'deserving' and 'undeserving', as well as what was 'right' behaviour and 'wrong' behaviour (Glasby, 2007; Howe, 2009). However, other perspectives – such as Radical Social Work – look to consider the structural explanations for social problems rather than the individual's behavioural response (Payne, 2014). By structural explanations, this means that in order to understand an individual from this perspective you actually need to understand what they are part of, i.e. society, their place in it and how this impacts on the person (Haslanger, 2016).

Moving on in time, another significant event that is influential in the origins of Radical Social Work is the establishment of the Welfare State and its repercussions. The National Assistance Act 1948 saw the introduction of the Welfare State, following the Beveridge Report in 1942, in which 'five giants' were identified. These 'giants' were viewed as the significant social problems of the time: *want*;

disease; *ignorance*; *squalor*; and *idleness* (Glasby, 2012). To combat these problems, state provision was provided in the form of Social Security, the NHS, Education, Housing and Employment (ibid., 2012). Underpinning these issues was the concept of poverty, which it was hoped would be eradicated by this significant state welfare intervention. However, in the 1960s, confidence in welfare provision began to change due, in part, to the research by Townsend and Abel-Smith (1966) who identified a growth in poverty following the Second World War and the introduction of the Welfare State. Fifty years later, Gazeley et al. (2014) re-examined the research and findings of Townsend and Abel-Smith (1966) and found that it was not poverty of *all* that had risen, but relational-poverty, i.e. that some areas of society were affected more than others. In effect, what had increased was not absolute poverty, but inequality (Gazeley et al., 2014). At the same time as Townsend and Abel-Smith's (1966) research findings, concerns were starting to rise about other influences in society, such as the increasing power of pharmaceutical companies and the way in which post-war migrant populations were being treated (Howe, 2009). These further contributed to the view (suggested by Gazely et al., 2014) of a rise in inequality: the unfair way in which medicine was prioritised for those with the ability to pay, rather than the most in need; and the influx of migrant populations to do more menial tasks in society. The Intellectual Movement of the 1960s started to challenge the function of the Welfare State and the intentions of a Capitalist Society (Howe, 2009). This saw a rise in the number of people studying Sociology and a rise in the popularity of the works of Karl Marx (Howe, 2009), and so concerns began to emerge about what the *social consequences of capitalism* were (Howe, 2009, p124). In a capitalist society, workers are only paid a portion of the value of their work and the capitalists gain the wealth through ownership of the means of production (Marx and Engels, 1848). The concept of the *modern working class developed – as a class of labourers, who live only so long as they find work, and who find work only so long as their labour increases capital* not for themselves but for those that own the means of production, i.e. the bourgeoisie (Marx and Engels, [1848] 2004, p18). According to Lavellette (2011) the problem with the Welfare State was that, in effect, it was devised in order to *meet the functional needs of capitalism* and that it was devised to achieve this through social control (p3). So it can be seen here why structural issues were beginning to be challenged rather than just focusing on individual responsibility.

Origins of radical perspectives in social work

In 1968, the *Seebohm Report* led to integrated social services and social work departments, thus requiring an increase in the number of social workers. This in turn led to an increase in the number of universities offering a qualification in social work (Howe, 2009). So, in the contemporary context set out above, these new social workers entering practice began to question the psychological and medical basis of the profession and brought in sociological and Marxist political questioning to social work practice. In 1975, Bailey and Brake compiled a number of essays challenging the state at the time. They presented radical interpretations of accepted social work theory, practice and intervention, and challenged *state directed bureaucratic welfare* and *public and social causes of private pain* rather than *in terms of individual failing* (Lavalette, 2011, p1). In questioning what in fact social work *was*, this led to questions about its fundamental theoretical basis. They referred to social work practitioners as, in effect, being *trapped* by the organisational and political structure in which they work, which therefore impacted on their power and placed limitations on the scope of their role (Bailey and Brake, 1980). Social work practitioners cannot avoid the simple fact that their actions, whatever they are, have consequences – intended or otherwise. (See Chapter 12, Utilitarianism in particular for a philosophical consideration of consequences.) The problem that arises is the lack of awareness service users may have of their fundamental position in society, something which may in fact be reinforced by the actions of the social work practitioner, intentionally or otherwise. As Bailey and Brake suggest, the *problems and difficulties that are associated with a person becoming a {service user} should be identified and located within some structural and political process* (1980, p8); the same place in which the social work practitioner is placed as an agent. To clarify this, the main question that arose from these essays was: how do the poor become poor? Inequalities were interrogated and challenged due to the control of power, authority and money. The view presented was that in fact capitalism was the cause of deprivation (Bailey and Brake, 1975). This was achieved through using the Welfare State as a tool to ensure that the poor were only provided with enough to keep them as healthy workers but not given too much so that they questioned their position. This approach can be likened to *structural-conflict theory*, which suggests that social order is achieved by socialising people towards the pursuit of rewards, but there is no real equality of opportunity due to the unfair distribution of advantage. Social order is therefore achieved through this domination, and force is only needed if those being disadvantaged actually realise that they are oppressed (Jones, 2002). According to Whitham (2012), *child poverty is driven by a lack of jobs, a lack of full time jobs and a lack of jobs paying a decent wage* (p4). Radical Social Work is an ideological perspective which seeks to draw attention to the disadvantage and oppression caused by authority and power to the oppressed. The focus of Radical Social Work is the fair distribution of goods and services – *social justice* (Ferguson and Woodward, 2009). Poverty is therefore caused by the rich staying rich and powerful and ensuring that the poor stay on their level but do not cause problems. From this perspective, social workers were therefore effectively working as agents of the state to maintain this system; to provide just enough support to their service users but not too much to make those service users question their place in society. The appropriate response to poverty, from a Radical Social Work perspective, should therefore be *outrage*, **not** care, comfort or containment (Howe, 2009, p127). But it is not enough to just be morally outraged – social workers have a responsibility to do something. (This materialist view is also significant in understanding the Five Models of Disability (see Chapter 17).)

From capitalism to neo-liberalism

While it is evident that Radical Social Work emerged from within a capitalist society, students and practitioners must note that today's society (and indeed since the 1980s) onwards is 'neo-liberalist'. (See also Classical Management Theory in Chapter 19.) This saw a significant shift in the Welfare State to 'managerialism', regulation and control. In the 1980s the focus for social work shifted from the *provision* of services to the *justification* of outcomes. This was in the development of the umbrella term of *New Public Management* (NPM) brought in by Margaret Thatcher and her Conservative government, and this refers to the provision of services which are cost-effective, market-friendly and accountable in terms of expenditure and outcomes (Heffernan, 2006). Under this direction, *politicians and policy makers turned to the principles of the market to inform welfare policy and practice* (Hughes and Wearing, 2013, p21). This also guided the way in which social work (as a human service organisation) would be run and the way in which it would have to justify outcomes for the services it provided. As suggested by Mary Langan (in Parton, 1997, pxv) *the result has been a substantial shift in the 'mixed economy' of welfare towards a more market-orientated approach*. The idea of being customer-led and market-driven was to avoid simply providing services for the sake of providing services, and to focus instead on what worked and what did not. According to Dominelli, Britain became focused on *Fordist methods of mass production*, meaning the intention was to make complicated tasks simple by recoding them into key activities and therefore removing the professional authority of the social worker (2005, p13). Thompson refers to this as the socio-technical approach where people (the social work practitioners) and technical (policy) aspects become one (Payne, 2005). Practitioners also became responsible for how resources were being used. However, social work was already an existing profession, and had worked within the classical bureaucratic management framework identified by Max Weber focusing on the *efficient handling of clients... through methods of staffing and structure* rather than on economic efficiency (Weinbach, 2008, p54). (See Chapter 19 regarding classical management theory.) So, NPM, which focused on outcomes and how to achieve them, was introduced onto the existing system with a different focus – clients now became customers, services cost-effective and outcomes measured (Heffernan, 2006).

However, Featherstone et al. (2012) identify how such neo-liberalist policies lead to inequalities by seeking to restore class power – for example, through their lack of recognition of how the gap between the rich and powerful had widened in the 1980s, and through the refocus that took place whereby parents were no longer seen as *subjects* of welfare but as the *means* of welfare for their children. Parenting was thus refocused onto parents' responsibility to effectively parent their children, and the focus on the child within assessments would act to the detriment of parents and their needs. Further to this, evidence in the 1990s and onwards suggests a shift towards rationalisation in terms of thresholds for working with these families, i.e. threshold criteria acts as a *gatekeeper* to determine whether action/resources will be allocated or not.

With this focus in mind, research questions (and continues to do so) how it is possible to measure the outcomes of these services. Deciding what can be considered *evidence* of achieved outcomes *has a highly subjective element to it* (Dominelli, 2005, p5), and whether or not a service has worked depends very much on the perception of the individual service user and their ability to sustain their outcomes. Hughes and Wearing point out that one of the biggest difficulties faced by the change to NPM was the way in which practitioners began to be managed by those without any social work experience, *who may have little affinity with the profession and its values* (2013, p22). However, it is not just practitioners and service users who are concerned with outcomes in social work practice but *a range of people* who may include academics/educators, policy makers, politicians, the wider population, and a variety of professionals including those from health, education, criminal justice and social care, to name but a few.

Application of radical social work to practice

So, from a Radical Social Work perspective, it is not enough to just understand the way in which people are disadvantaged or oppressed economically – a requirement of the application of Radical Social Work is that social workers must do something. Part of this is through awareness-raising with the people they work with and through questioning assumptions about social order (Payne, 2014). So, rather than accepting the implementation of law and policy, Radical Social Workers should challenge these if the implementation would cause disadvantage. For example, consider the following scenario:

> A young couple, aged 19, are living in a one-bedroomed flat and have a six-month-old baby. They have a child protection plan due to neglect. The mother has recently been diagnosed with a learning disability and the usual course of action for the social worker would be to refer the mother to the Learning Disabilities Parenting Programme due to the mother's identified need. However, this programme has just closed down due to welfare cuts, and there is no alternative that the Local Authority can refer to.

From a Radical Social Work perspective several aspects of this scenario can be considered. For example, due to economic reasons a service is no longer available that has been identified as a need for the mother – this is due to structural issues outside of the control of the mother and the Local Authority. So this mother does not get the specific help she needs in order to develop her parenting skills so that she can meet the requirements of the child protection plan. So what does this social worker do? This is an increasing issue for social workers in practice as they come up against the implications of austerity in a capitalist society – where the control of welfare is implemented through social workers who cannot offer appropriate services for the families in their care. Bauer at al. (2015) raised concerns about the lack of advocacy for parents with learning disabilities, yet advocacy would be beneficial not just to the parents but also financially due to the economic implications of continued involvement with Children's Services for these parents. 'Consciousness raising' (Payne, 2014) would involve alerting the mother to the impact on her human rights (Human Rights Act 1998) and those in power about the discrimination that is evident. The HCPC codes advise that social workers must challenge discrimination, so in this it is evident how applicable Radical Social Work is today. However, this is just one voice and Radical Social Work calls for *collective* action. Today, this can be seen being implemented by organisations such as the Social Work Action Network (SWAN) and more generalised organisations such as 38Degrees and Change.org. So perhaps this is an option for the social worker? However, this leads to the most significant critique of applying Radical Social Work to practice – what about now? What can the social worker do immediately for the family who need the help now, not in six months or six years' time, but right now? And what happens to that family if that identified need is not met and their parenting of their child remains a concern, or becomes a more significant concern?

Reflection Point

From a Radical Social Work Perspective, what immediate actions could the social worker take in order to address the structural disadvantage experienced by the family outlined above? What are the possible implications of these actions?

Case Study: Serious Case Review

To apply Radical Social Work to the SCR, the context of the lives of MZ and FZ need to be considered. This enables social workers to more fully understand the impact of structural factors on these parents and just how much 'choice' they actually have regarding their lives and how they live them – and significantly, how they parent. Knowledge of right and wrong parenting is not automatic in contemporary society. While there may be arguments about bonding (Nevid, 2009), a more detailed understanding of 'how to parent' in the modern age is more complex. A significant part of this is determined by the policy and legislation directed by the government onto society – structural factors. So, looking at the SCR, the following structural impacts need to be recognised (NB this is not an exhaustive list):

the absence of appropriate housing for a significant period of time

the apparent isolation from positive sources of help and support

(Continued)

(Continued)

the age of MZ

substance misuse... some professionals may have taken a tolerant approach to aspects of behaviour that may have been different if it had been exhibited in a different part of the city

both experienced levels of childhood trauma and abuse

MZ was diagnosed with moderate learning difficulties as a child

The probation service and police recognised that FZ had unspecified learning difficulties

FZ has an extensive history of substance misuse and violence and had been unwilling to acknowledge his need for help in regard to mental health and educational or employment support

(SCR Child Z, pp15–18)

Looking at one aspect in particular, we can see that the way some professionals may have engaged with this family was to take a 'tolerant' view of the substance use, based on a level of expectation that certain groups within society engage with substance use more than others. So this may not have been identified as concerning – as perhaps it should have been with young children in the house. Both parents were identified with learning difficulties – how much support did they have to redress this? How much *choice* did MZ and FZ have about their parenting style? Both parents had experienced abuse as children themselves so how much choice were they making in their parenting? What was done to help them understand different parenting styles? Thinking from a Radical Social Work perspective, it is not about condoning certain behaviour, but about looking more deeply in order to understand, so to prevent the potential negative outcomes of this.

The legacy of Radical Social Work

Radical Social Work primarily considers *economic* disadvantage, and from a practice perspective this is evident in the way in which certain groups may be viewed by society; for example, lone parents can be viewed by policy as *workless or unemployed rather than legitimately standing outside the labour market as a result of their caring responsibilities* (Davies, 2012, p16). However, further ideologies have developed from the radical perspective in order to consider other factors as important in social work. Critical Social Work, for example, developed from Radical Social Work, and it determined that economics is not the only issue which causes discrimination and oppression – it can also be seen in other forms of 'power' operated daily, and is underpinned by Foucault's power discourse (see Chapter 7, Social Constructionism). Fook (2002) further developed the concept of Structural Social Work which considers other structural factors that cause *problems* such as the social, economic and political (see Chapter 18).

Conclusion

While only a minor political movement in the 1970s, it is evident that Radical Social Work is important for social workers to consider today, especially in relation to identifying discrimination and inequality caused by structural factors, and because of the implementation and impact (at the time of writing) of austerity measures returning the focus of discrimination to an economic perspective. The challenge for social workers in the application of this theory is in the balance of collective action versus individual immediate need, as demonstrated in the debate.

Chapter Summary

This chapter has presented the historical context and key principles of Radical Social Work, demonstrating its theoretical underpinning by Marxism and sociological perspectives. It has been demonstrated how the structural position of social work practitioners has the potential to reinforce discriminatory practice rather than challenge it, so the focus of Radical Social Work is that practitioners should automatically consider the structural position of service users, and the impact their position may have on the reasons for social work involvement. Challenges can then be made against such discrimination by the state.

Legal and Policy Summary

- *The Beveridge Report* 1942 – identification of the Five Giants, i.e. social problems.
- *National Assistance Act* 1948 – origins of the Welfare State.
- *Seebohm Report* 1968 – social work departments set up.

Further Reading

Context is important in order to understand how political theories develop. It would be beneficial for students and practitioners to look back at the origins and intentions of the Welfare State – see Glasby (2012) Chapter 2 *Origins of Community Health and Social Care* in:

Glasby, J (2012) *Understanding Health and Social Care* (2nd edition). Bristol: Policy Press.

While not strictly *reading*, a useful film to watch to understand the context of the changes in society that influenced Radical Social Work is the film *Cathy Come Home* by Ken Loach (1966).

Ferguson and Woodward (2009) give excellent examples of Radical Social Work in Practice, for example to understand the experiences of parents encountering child safeguarding procedures.

Ferguson, I and Woodward, R (2009) *Radical Social Work in Practice: Making a Difference.* Bristol: Policy Press.

Chapter 17

Five models of disability

Stephen J Macdonald

Achieving a Social Work Degree

This chapter will help you meet the following capabilities, to the appropriate level, from the Professional Capabilities Framework:

PCF 1 Professionalism

- Describe the role of a social worker and the importance of personal and professional boundaries and behaviour, demonstrate ability to learn using a range of approaches;

PCF 2 Values and Ethics

- Understand the professional's ethical principles and their relevance to practice, and demonstrate awareness of own personal values and how these can impact on practice;

PCF 3 Diversity

- Recognise the importance of diversity in human identity and experience, and the application of anti-discriminatory and anti-oppressive principles in social work practice;

PCF 4 Rights, Justice and Economic Wellbeing

- Understand the principles of rights, justice and economic wellbeing, and their significance for social work practice;

PCF 5 Knowledge

PCF 5 Knowledge

- Demonstrate an initial understanding of the application of research, theory and knowledge from sociology, social policy, psychology, health and human growth and development to social work;

PCF 6 Critical Reflection and Analysis

- Understand the need to construct hypotheses in social work practice;

PCF 7 Intervention and Skills

- Demonstrate an awareness of a range of frameworks to assess and plan intervention and demonstrate initial awareness of risk and safeguarding;

PCF 8 Context and Organisations

- Demonstrate awareness of the impact of organisational context on social work practice.

Introduction

This chapter will explore the concept of disability and impairment through five identifiable models of disability that are evident in professional health and social care practices. This will commence by exploring a brief history of disability with reference to the rise of clinical medicine. There will be a discussion of how the foundations of clinical medicine were established because of advances in statistical classifications of human physiology, and it is this statistical approach which influenced the formation of the *biomedical model of disability*. During the twentieth century this model became the dominant approach within healthcare and social work practice, but this chapter will describe how in the twenty-first century the model has been redefined as the *biopsychosocial model*, grounded in the work of George Engel.

In conjunction with these medical models of disability, this chapter will examine alternative perspectives and definitions of disability from a sociological perspective, and three versions of the social model will be presented. This will firstly define the Social Model of Disability drawing on the work of Vic Finkelstein on Mike Oliver in order to critique the medical model of disability. The works of Tom Shakespeare and Nick Watson will be considered by examining their criticism of the social model from a critical realist perspective, and examining how this perspective informed the *social relational model of disability*. There will also be a discussion of the work of Maria Corker from a poststructuralist perspective, offering an alternative to the traditional social model perspective. The chapter will then conclude by summarising these five models of disability with reference to social work practice and how applying the different models can significantly transform practitioners' responses to disabled people's abilities, needs, rights and appropriate support packages.

A brief history of disability

Early references to disability pre-date the classical Greek medical Hippocratic texts, which date back to approximately the fourth and third centuries BC. However, it is not until the nineteenth century that the contemporary concept of disability arises out of the formation of clinical medicine and the use of statistics within medical practice. The application of statistical analysis to the practice of medicine results in the establishment of what were considered to be *normative definitions of biological function*, i.e. what is normal for the body and what is not. In nineteenth-century medicine the body was observed, measured and categorised, and this laid the foundation for contemporary medical understandings of the body. From this categorisation individual bodies were constructed through the notion of biological *normality*. That is, the aim of early medical practice was first to understand and categorise human physiology, and second to develop effective treatments and cures to combat disease. By categorising the body through these normative measurements, this resulted in a range of bodies being defined as biologically *abnormal* due to birth defects, disease, injury or ageing, and it is these bodies that are later defined as *disabled*. Although this original definition of disability was established by studies on the physical body, i.e. people with physical impairments, by the end of the 1800s this normative definition was expanded to include abnormal behaviours, i.e. mental health issues, and intellectual ability, i.e. learning disabilities. Emerging from this nineteenth-century definition of disability we can see the development of the biomedical model, which defined professional practice in healthcare and social work throughout the twentieth century.

Medical models of disability and impairment

The biomedical model of disability

The biomedical model can be described as the most recognisable interpretation of disability which influenced professional practice throughout the twentieth century. This model directly developed out of the rise of clinical medicine where disability was defined as a functional limitation resulting from a physical impairment. This directed professional practice, not just within medicine and healthcare services, but also within social work, social care and charity work. The biomedical model is often described as a 'deficit model', whereby human physiology is understood through normative measurements; anything that deviates from medical statistical norms is defined as a biological or neurological deficit. From the biomedical perspective, these biochemical changes are as a result of genetic defects, disease, injury or illness. The biomedical model associates disease with the progression of impairment resulting in disabling factors. As we can see from the model set out below, the biomedical model defines disability as a medical issue, and links disease to the possible onset of disability:

- Disease, illness, impairment and disability are organic conditions: non-organic factors are considered unimportant.

- Disease, illness, impairment and disability are temporary organic states that can be eradicated or cured by medical interventions.

- Disease, illness, impairment and disability are experienced by sick individuals who become the object of treatments.

- Disease, illness, impairment and disability are treated after symptoms appear.

- Disease, illness, impairment and disability are treated in medical environments.

(Adapted from Bilton et al., 2002)

From this perspective, disability is entirely conceptualised in physiological terms, and is motivated by the development of interventions and cures within a medical environment. As disability is defined in medical terms, this model does not acknowledge the social consequences of living with an impairment. In order to understand the biomedical model it is worth examining aspects of the 'International Classification of Disability' developed by the World Health Organisation in the 1980s. Although this has now been revised, it still appears within many key medical textbooks (e.g. Oxford Handbooks of Psychiatry and Clinical Medicine), and it is within this definition that we can view a clear description of the biomedical model. The World Health Organisation defined impairment and disability as follows:

> *Impairment: any loss or abnormality of psychological, physiological or anatomical structure or function.*
>
> - A deviation from a statistical 'norm' in an individual's biomedical status
> - Includes loss/defect of tissue-mechanism-system-function
> - Temporary or permanent
>
> *Disability: any restriction or lack (resulting from impairment) of the ability to perform an activity in the manner or within the range considered normal for a human being.*
>
> - Functional limitation expresses itself as a reality in everyday life
> - Tasks, skills and behaviour
> - Temporary or permanent
>
> (Adapted from Semple et al., 2013, p90)

From a biomedical perspective, in order to understand disability there first needs to be a comprehension of the notion of *impairment*. Thus, the body is defined through a normative measurement, establishing an average baseline of physiological function. Any deviation from this average measurement, through birth defect, accident, injury, illness or ageing, results in the human body being defined as *impaired*. As the model attempts to treat or cure impairment through clinical interventions, these conditions can be regarded as temporary or permanent. From this perspective, disability then results from a person becoming impaired, and thus refers to a *functional limitation* caused by the change in a person's biochemistry. This model suggests that humans have universal functions or abilities; for example, they have the ability to walk, speak, see, hear, etc., and if a person becomes impaired then their normative abilities are directly affected, which restricts their ability to perform tasks. This restriction directly affects how people interact within a social context. From a biomedical perspective, in order to eradicate disability, medicine must treat and cure the physiological aspects of impairment, and so (from the above definition) the biomedical model conceptualises disability entirely within medical terms.

The biopsychosocial model of illness, impairment and disability

The biopsychosocial model developed in response to key criticisms of the biomedical model. It was originally developed by George Engel (1977) as he reasoned that the biomedical model was too reductionist in nature (i.e. too simple) to explain the complexities of illness within a biological and social context. From a biomedical perspective, disease and impairment affect a person's biological function, and this is treated with biochemical responses, i.e. with medication or surgical solutions, suggesting that disease and impairments can be considered objective entities, which affect the body in comparable ways. If we take an example such as pain, from a biomedical model pain is viewed as something objective, i.e. it is experienced in the same way. However, Engel suggests that this is not the case, as people psychologically experience pain in very different ways. For Engel, this reductionist approach to the body oversimplifies the reality of living with an illness or long-term impairment. As illness takes place within a social environment, Engel suggests that the biomedical model must therefore be expanded to include social and psychological factors.

Activity 17.1

Can you think of examples of impairment that may be experienced differently depending on social and psychological factors, for example, not being able to walk? Is this experience different in different cultures? If so, how?

Engel also suggests that a person's lifestyle choices, employment factors or stress levels can result in the onset of disease or impairment. Furthermore, these social issues, resulting in psychological factors, can affect the healing process of illness or the capabilities of people with long-term impairments. Peter White (2005) gives an example of the biopsychosocial model by suggesting that the most common cause of lung cancer is smoking, therefore to eliminate lung cancer people need to stop smoking. However, this is not straightforward as what are the causes of smoking? People's reasons for smoking refer to social and cultural factors, which are not easily overcome. From this perspective, lung cancer is caused through a causal relationship between the social, the psychological and the biological. For Engel, the biopsychosocial model offers a holistic approach, which causally links the biological, psychological and social to comprehend the onset and outcomes of illness and impairment.

It should be noted that the biopsychosocial model does not completely reject the biomedical model as it does accept that disability results from a functional limitation of the body, i.e. impairment. Thus, this model *adds* to the biomedical model by acknowledging that the biological body is affected by the social world, which in turn has psychological consequences for individuals who experience illness or impairment. So, the biopsychosocial model is still classified as a medical model as it individualises disabling factors resulting from a person's impairment, but places these factors within a social context. Hence, the disability is *caused* by a physiological change to a person's body, even though these changes have social and psychological causes and implications.

This is evidenced in the example given in Figure 17.1:

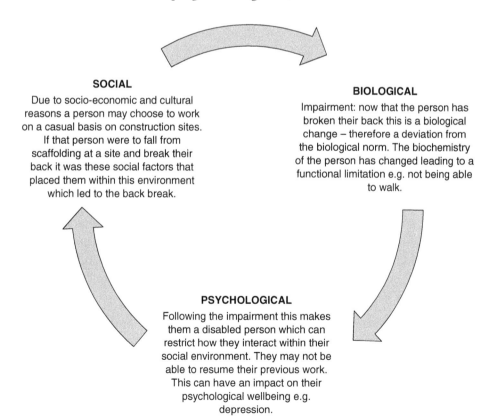

SOCIAL
Due to socio-economic and cultural reasons a person may choose to work on a casual basis on construction sites. If that person were to fall from scaffolding at a site and break their back it was these social factors that placed them within this environment which led to the back break.

BIOLOGICAL
Impairment: now that the person has broken their back this is a biological change – therefore a deviation from the biological norm. The biochemistry of the person has changed leading to a functional limitation e.g. not being able to walk.

PSYCHOLOGICAL
Following the impairment this makes them a disabled person which can restrict how they interact within their social environment. They may not be able to resume their previous work. This can have an impact on their psychological wellbeing e.g. depression.

Figure 17.1 Biopsychosocial model

So, while in this example the social occurred first, the order of these elements should be considered in a circular manner as the biological could come first in other instances due to genetic factors.

The biopsychosocial model can now in fact be described as the dominant perspective to comprehending disability within health and social care, and it currently underpins the recent government strategy to assess disability with reference to out-of-work disability benefits (see Shakespeare et al., 2016).

Social models of disability and impairment

The social model of disability

The social model of disability developed out of the grassroots politics of the 1970s. This model was developed from service user groups, particularly from the Union for Physically Impaired against Segregation (UPIAS). The founders and key contributors to the academic development of the social model were Vic Finkelstein and Paul Hunt – both were wheelchair users. Finkelstein and Hunt were especially critical of healthcare support and rejected the biomedical model that defined disability as a condition resulting from a physiological dysfunction. Both individuals suggested the problems they experienced were not due to the fact that they could not stand up (their functional limitation), but because of *environmental* factors, which prevented them and other wheelchair users from fully participating in social life. These environmental factors included: the way buildings were designed; how public spaces excluded wheelchair users through a lack of adjustments; the way disabled people's voices were ignored by healthcare practitioners; and the stigmatising views of disability prevalent within society, etc.

Hunt and Finkelstein illustrated that medical services offered little support and no cure for their particular conditions. They suggested that their bodies had permanently changed and medical services offered them no interventions or solutions for their conditions. Hunt and Finkelstein established UPIAS, which aimed to represent the voices of disabled people. It was from UPIAS that we see the first definition of the social model of disability in a document entitled the 'Fundamental Principles of Disability'. This stated that:

> *In our view, it is society which disables physically impaired people. Disability is something imposed on top of impairments by the way we are unnecessarily isolated and excluded from full participation in society.*

> (Oliver, 1996, p33)

This new definition of disability was defined within academia by the work of Mike Oliver. Oliver was also a wheelchair user and a disability activist, and he suggested that disability was created because of *disabling barriers,* which related to social inequalities and structural exclusion of disabled people. He also stated that the biomedical model focuses on eradicating impairment, but in reality very few impairments have been cured by medicine. Oliver claimed that *{e}nvironments are often designed to exclude us, transport systems that claim to be* public *continue to deny us access and when we protest, we are told there is no money* (Oliver, 1993, p24, own emphasis). Oliver defines the social model as:

- *Disability* – referring to how disabled people are excluded from contemporary society;

- *Impairment* – referring to a physiological or neurological variation resulting from birth or a life course transition.

To demonstrate how the social model conceptualises disability in a different way to the medical model, Oliver presents an analysis based on the Office of Population Censuses Survey. He suggests this survey is underpinned by an individualised (medical) model ideology:

- *Medical model:* Are your difficulties in understanding people mainly due to a hearing problem?

- *Social model:* Are your difficulties in understanding people mainly due to their inability to communicate with you?

- *Medical model:* Does your health problem/disability affect your work in any way at present?

- *Social model:* Do you have problems at work because of the physical environment or attitudes of others?

- *Medical model:* Does your health problem/disability mean that you need to live with relatives or someone else who can help or look after you?

- *Social model:* Are community services so poor that you need to rely on relatives or someone else to provide you with the right level of personal assistants?

- *Medical model:* Does your health problem/disability prevent you from going out as often or as far as you would like?

- *Social model:* What is it about the local environment that makes it difficult for you to get about in your neighbourhood?

Reflection Point

- Consider the way in which the questions are posed from a medical model perspective – how might this make a person feel about themselves and their position in society?
- Think of examples where you or a friend or family member has experienced the medical model.

Oliver suggests that, from a social model perspective, the key focus is on how disabled people experience universal structural barriers. These barriers exclude disabled people from social participation, and so the concept of disability becomes the fundamental concern and impairment becomes a less important factor. This is of particular importance to social work practice, which takes a more social focus. Oliver states that people with the same impairment can experience different disabling barriers due to their social circumstances. From this perspective, professional practice should focus on removal of the barriers that exclude service users, rather than focusing on impairment-related interventions. This then transforms social work practice from a discipline that works alongside medicine to access impairment-related services, to a service that removes disabling barriers within people's homes, communities, working environments and society as a whole. The social model is an approach grounded in social inclusion, rather than one based on cure or exclusion, and it can be used in contemporary practice to support disabled people in a social context.

Critical realism and the social relational model of disability

At the turn of the twenty-first century, although the social model has been implemented in social work and social care practices, a number of criticisms have emerged concerning its lack of recognition of the impact of impairments. As the social model focuses exclusively on removing disabling barriers, impairment-related issues are viewed as insignificant. One of the initial critiques of the social model came from the activist Liz Crow, who stated that the social model transformed her life, as it illustrated how structural disabling barriers affected her day-to-day experiences. Furthermore, the social model empowered her to challenge professional practices and social institutions. But Crow (1996) also illustrates how impairment-related issues, i.e. physical pain, did cause her problems in *conjunction* with disabling barriers, and thus Crow argued that the social model of disability must acknowledge issues of impairment in order to construct an authentic account of disability. Crow stated that:

> In fact, impairment, at its most basic level, is a purely objective concept which carries no intrinsic meaning. Impairment simply means that aspects of a person's body do not function or they function with difficulty. Frequently this has taken a stage further to imply that a person's body, and ultimately the person, is inferior. However, the first is fact; the second is an interpretation.

> (Crow, 1996, p211)

Crow suggested that the social model needs to be extended to incorporate the concepts of disability – structural disabling barriers – and impairment – functional difficulties or variations. Similar to Crow, Tom Shakespeare and Nick Watson (2001) applied a parallel critique of the social model of disability. In a paper entitled 'The Social Model: an Outdated Ideology ', Shakespeare and Watson argued that in order to develop a theory of disability there must be an acknowledgement of the impact of impairment. They suggest that both the biomedical model and the social model are over-simplistic, with one focusing entirely on impairment and the other entirely on disability. They suggest that in order to accurately comprehend disabled people's experiences there needs to be a focus on how both disabling barriers and impairment interact with one another. Shakespeare (2013) suggests that disability is produced entirely within a social context, yet disabling factors cannot be recognised until there is an acknowledgement of a person's impairment. Shakespeare and Watson suggest that:

> People are disabled both by social barriers and by their bodies. This is straightforward and uncontroversial. The British social model approach, because it 'over-eggs the pudding', risks discrediting the entire dish.

(Shakespeare and Watson, 2001, p17)

Shakespeare (2013) illustrates the impact that pain has on people's lives, which is comparable to structural factors such as stigmatisation, employment and environmental barriers. He also asserts the importance of impairment types by suggesting that a person with schizophrenia experiences very different disabling barriers to someone with a visual impairment or someone with dyslexia. Shakespeare's approach is entrenched within a *critical realist* theoretical framework, illustrating that critical realism incorporates how we construct realities within a social context and how reality transpires independently from human perception. Shakespeare goes on to suggest that reality exists in four different domains consisting of the *sociological*, the *psychological*, the *biological* and the *molecular*, and to develop a theory of disability, researchers must acknowledge all four domains. Carol Thomas (2007) was the first to actually refer to the social relational model of disability and while Shakespeare and Watson do not directly refer to this model, recent writers have integrated their critical realist approach within this framework (See Shakespeare, 2015).

So, the *social relational model of disability* refers to: disabling barriers in the form of structural exclusion; psychological factors resulting from social oppression; and impairment-related issues which, due to a biological/neurological variation, affect a person's life course. Although this approach is grounded in a social model ideology through the notion of disabling barriers, this model attempts to develop an *interactionist* perspective to conceptualise disability and impairment within a social context, as disability interacts with impairment.

Post-structuralism and the affirmation model of disability

In response to previous critiques of the social model an alternative account, which includes impairment, arises from post-structural theory (see Chapter 7 on Foucault and Chapter 2 on Lacan). This perspective develops from the work of Maria Corker (1999) who was influenced by the philosophical writings of Michel Foucault (see also Chapter 7). Corker draws on a linguistic perspective to conceptualise disability and impairment and, similar to critical realism, argues to bring back impairment into the model. However, her definition of impairment is radically different from that of Shakespeare and Watson. Corker argues that not only is disability constructed within a social context but so is impairment. Therefore, concepts like disability and impairment are constructed within a medical environment, in which bodies are defined by discourses (language) and conceptualised through notions of normality. For Corker, medical labels that are attached to bodies are created in a socio-cultural context; hence, disability is a generic label, which situates a person outside established social and cultural norms. The 'disabled' label is justified by the medical concept of impairment types. Medicine presents these labels as scientific and objective, i.e. outside of human interpretation, but Corker proposes that these labels are products of the socio-cultural and political landscape. Therefore, impairment and disability are linguistically constructed within a cultural context.

From this perspective, impairment types only come into existence because there is a political, cultural and economic need for a label. Within society labels are created and attached to individuals as a system of control – they are politically motivated and used as a system of organising and controlling populations. Therefore, if a person is diagnosed with paranoid schizophrenia, they might receive treatment in a psychiatric unit. If their 'negative' behaviours persist they might be supported and housed in a residential care unit. From a poststructural perspective, this medicalises and disciplines a person's behaviour within an institutional setting. This process stigmatises the labelled person and cultivates a social narrative that diverts mass culture away from exhibiting similar undesirable behaviours. Therefore, not only does a label regulate an individual's actions, but it is employed as a technique of social and cultural control. For Corker, the biomedical model constructs labels of impairment in order to control disabled bodies within society. Paradoxically, the social model develops an oppositional approach to the biomedical model, which defines disabled people in sociological, rather than medical terms. Yet, for Corker, neither model is entrenched in reality as both create linguistic techniques and practices that operate to control populations.

Influenced by this cultural perspective, disability scholars have applied the social model as a confrontational discourse to redefine disability and impairment. Alongside post-structuralism is the development of the *affirmation model of disability* defined by Swain and French (2000). This considers both disability and impairment as constructed categories; from this perspective, the concept of normality is constructed within a cultural environment. Hence, to be normal requires a particular performance, which relates to social norms, and these norms are attached, through labelling, to individuals whose bodies are considered as acceptable or unacceptable within a cultural context. For Cameron:

> *Disability [refers to] a personal and social role which simultaneously invalidates the subject position of people with impairments and validates the subject position of those identified as normal.*

> (Cameron, 2011, p20)

Thus, the disabled body is constructed as abnormal, and this validates the importance of *normality* in society, and so produces a performance of normality (i.e. what it looks like) constructed in a historically specific cultural setting. From this perspective, if disability and impairment are culturally and historically constructed then, it is argued, that understanding of these can be changed. Therefore, from a biomedical perspective, disability and impairment are universally constructed in negative terms (negative deficit ideology). If we accept that disability and impairment are culturally constructed through this ideology, then it follows that we can amend this construct into a positive and empowering ideology instead. For Cameron, impairment should really be understood as *difference* rather than viewed as a *tragedy* – tragedy brings with it a vision of negative events and a negative impact, difference however does not. Therefore, if this transition in understanding can occur then the notion of disability can and should be celebrated.

Application to social work practice

By applying a medical model approach, disability is conceptualised as a biological deficit which affects social interaction, and to overcome the disability there needs to be an intervention which can successfully treat or cure an impairment. From a social model perspective the focus is on barrier removal. Yet, the version of the social model chosen by practitioners will again transform how they respond to people with disabilities. From the traditional social model perspective, a social work practitioner would focus entirely on addressing the disabling barriers experienced by the person rather than the impairment of the individual. From a social relational model perspective, they would focus on both – the disabling barriers and impairment-related issues experienced. From an affirmation model perspective, social workers would assist in transforming understanding of disability and impairment to a more positive perspective in order to empower individuals and communities who are excluded within society. This illustrates the importance, in social work, of the five models of disability as it guides practitioners towards support of service users experiencing impairments or disabling factors.

Activity 17.2

1. Consider the five models of disability and think about examples of where you may have applied these different approaches. Consider which approach you have tended to follow and identify both advantages and disadvantages to these.
2. Consider also the five models and social work values. Which do you argue are the best fit?

Case Study: Serious Case Review

Within the SCR of Child Z (2013), it was revealed that both parents have an unspecified learning disability. Although they had visits from a health professional, at no point did the health

(Continued)

(Continued)

visitor highlight any concerns about the family environment or risk to the children. From a social model perspective, it becomes clear in the SCR that neither parents had access to support in relation to their impairments. Furthermore, there is no information to suggest that the health practitioner attempted to access additional services to support the family preceding Child Z's death.

Thus, we can observe in the SCR that there were barriers which both parents were experiencing, and which were relevant to their parenting roles. From this perspective, it could be argued that neither FZ nor MZ were supported with their parenting roles. From a social model perspective, there is evidence of multiple barriers both within the family home and wider social issues concerning long-term unemployment and deprivation. The family was living within very restricted means due to the fact that neither could gain employment. If wider structural barriers were removed, providing disabled people with equal access to work, then either parent might have had access to employment and their living conditions could have been significantly improved. From a social model perspective, the SCR reveals potential barriers of a lack of support from professional services. It must be noted that this analysis from a social model perspective is not necessarily one that the panel of the SCR would apply, so from this perspective, however, some interesting questions and concerns are raised about how people with impairments and disabling environments are supported.

Chapter Summary

As indicated, the concept of disability has multiple meanings depending on the model that is applied in professional practice. Depending on whether a practitioner applies a medical model approach or a social model perspective, they may consider disabled people as patients, who need access to medical interventions, or as service users that require barrier removal to enable full participation in their communities. For social workers, knowledge of these models is vital in guiding professional practice and service provision. The choice of which model is used within health and social care services will directly relate to the type of services a person will gain access too, and therefore it is important for a social worker to have a wide-ranging knowledge on these debates concerning disability and impairment.

Further Reading

Corker, M and French, S (1999) *Disability Discourse*. Buckingham: Open University Press.

Oliver, M (1996) *Understanding Disability from Theory to Practice*. Basingstoke: Palgrave.

Shakespeare, T (2013) *Disability Rights and Wrongs* (2nd edition). London: Routledge.

White, P (Ed) (2005) *Biopsychosocial Medicine*. Oxford: Oxford University Press.

Chapter 18

Anti-discriminatory practice

Alan Marshall

Achieving a Social Work Degree

This chapter will help you meet the following capabilities, to the appropriate level, from the Professional Capabilities Framework:

PCF 1 Professionalism

- Describe the role of a social worker and the importance of personal and professional boundaries and behaviour, demonstrate ability to learn using a range of approaches;

PCF 2 Values and Ethics

- Understand the professional's ethical principles and their relevance to practice, and demonstrate awareness of own personal values and how these can impact on practice;

PCF 3 Diversity

- Recognise the importance of diversity in human identity and experience, and the application of anti-discriminatory and anti-oppressive principles in social work practice;

PCF 4 Rights, Justice and Economic Wellbeing

- Understand the principles of rights, justice and economic wellbeing, and their significance for social work practice;

PCF 6 Critical Reflection and Analysis

- Understand the need to construct hypotheses in social work practice;

PCF 7 Intervention and Skills

- Demonstrate an awareness of a range of frameworks to assess and plan intervention and demonstrate initial awareness of risk and safeguarding;

PCF 8 Context and Organisations

- Demonstrate awareness of the impact of organisational context on social work practice; and

PCF 9 Professional Leadership

- Demonstrate awareness of the importance of professional leadership in social work.

Introduction

Social work is a profession and range of interventions that endeavours to improve the welfare of the individual or group, but also to promote social justice for the wider society we live in (Thompson, 2012). It is a profession steeped in debates about values and morality. One of the core ideas within this value framework is that of anti-discriminatory practice (ADP) as a way of both reducing the harm social work interventions may inadvertently cause and improving the situation of disadvantaged groups (Thompson, 2012).

As a group of professionals working as mediators between service users and service providers, social workers have a pivotal role in tackling discrimination and disadvantage (Payne, 2014). Because social workers often intervene at moments of crisis or with people who are vulnerable at that point in life, our actions become more powerful and critical to people's lives. ADP is widely seen not just as a bolt-on optional idea, but a crucial element of the work and philosophy of social work practice:

> *There is no middle ground; intervention either adds to oppression (or at least condones it) or goes some small way towards easing or breaking such oppression... If you are not part of the solution you must be part of the problem... An awareness of the socio-political context is necessary in order to prevent becoming (or remaining) part of the problem.*

> (Thompson, 2006, p15)

The importance of ADP is sewn into the fabric of the social work profession not just in the Professional Capabilities Framework (PCF 3), but the core definition of social work itself, which is to:

*liberate vulnerable and oppressed people with the ultimate aim to promote
social inclusion*

(International Federation of Social Workers, 2012)

Key concepts

In order to understand ADP, it is beneficial to first of all consider the meaning of some
key concepts.

Discrimination

Thompson (2011) suggests that discrimination first begins when a particular
characteristic of a group of people is seen as significant, and that it becomes the basis
on which to treat people in that group differently. This can theoretically mean treating
some people more favourably, but predominantly in social sciences we use the term
discriminate to mean the *unfair* and *unfavourable* treatment of one group over another.
This may give rise to specific terms for types of discrimination such as racism, for the
unfair treatment of people based on ethnicity; or sexism for the same discrimination
against one gender (Thompson, 2011).

Discrimination can be direct or indirect (Howe, 2009) – direct (or explicit) being the
clear, overt discrimination that impacts on a group first hand. For instance, racist or
insensitive language used when talking to someone from a minority ethnic group, or
banning women from a shop or club. Indirect (or implicit) discrimination is an action,
policy or law that unfairly impacts on a particular group, while at first sight appearing
to apply to everyone equally. This could be, for example, a work policy that states that
employees pay for their own disability adaptations such as glasses or orthopaedic chairs.

Oppression

This can be seen as the deliberate (on some level) degradation and discrimination of
one particular group of people, with a set of characteristics, over time (Dominelli,
2002). The discourses of much of society uphold this discrimination, reducing the
opportunities and life chances for this group of people. These differences are usually
seen to be upheld and maintained by the high levels of power held by those in the
majority or at the top of a society's hierarchy.

One example of oppression could be the inequalities that women have been subjected
to in British society for centuries (see Chapter 9). For much of history in the UK, as
a nation, women were treated unfavourably compared to men and this was backed
up by law. In previous centuries, for example, women were unable to own their own
property and they did not get an equal right to vote until the Equal Franchise Act
1928 (Warwick-Booth, 2013). Currently in the UK there are few if any legal forms of
discrimination surviving, yet discrimination still exists in one form or another. Women

tend to have lower wages than men on average, have poorer employment conditions and consistently as a group carry out a larger proportion of childcare and domestic cleaning than men (Thompson, 2012).

Origins of ADP

Anti-discriminatory practice as it is known today arose in the 1970s from concerns about how ineffective social work was in delivering social justice (Okitikpi and Aymer, 2010). (See Chapter 16.) The core goals of the profession and cause were to help the vulnerable and to prevent suffering, and fighting discrimination has been part of social care and charitable organisations for much longer (Okitikpi and Aymer, 2010). However, it was becoming evident in the 1970s that despite much determination and hard work, inequalities and injustices were visible in many areas of British life.

This decade (1970s) had seen the introduction of legal protections to groups of people who were seen as being unfairly treated on a regular basis (Bartoli, 2013). But discrimination in the field still persisted. Okitiki and Aymer (2010) highlight several key areas that helped to change how social workers thought about their profession and its ability to affect social change during this formative period of the 1970s.

When considering the concept of race, discrimination was evidenced in particular areas of social work practice, for example, concerning the care of vulnerable neglected and abused children (Okitikpi and Aymer, 2010). Social workers were seeing high numbers of children from black and minority ethnic (BME) backgrounds taken into care. In the mental health system the over-representation of young African-Caribbean men in hospitals was persistent and worrying (Fernando, 2010). Psychiatric beliefs that promoted ideas of a mental deficiency in people with non-European ethnicities were fading quickly from official discourses and psychiatry (Fernando, 2010). The profession was seeing an increase in the proportion of black men in particular, who were over-medicated, spent longer time in hospital wards against their will and were more likely to be put in isolation rooms, compared to their white counter-parts. This was occurring despite the increase in numbers of psychiatrists from BME communities (Karban, 2011), so some began to criticise psychiatry as being too Western and Eurocentric (Fernando, 2010). The nature of police racism was starting to become public too, with people from ethnic minority groups being greatly over-represented by stop and search figures and treated harshly (Okitikpi and Aymer, 2010). Professionals were also seeing the engrained nature of poor school results for poorer families (of which a disproportionate number were from BME communities) that impacted on social mobility (Okitikpi and Aymer, 2010).

At the same time, the increasing growth of civil rights activism and awareness was evident in the form of lesbian and gay rights campaigns and the moves to give people with disabilities more control over their lives and services (Thompson, 2011). Prior to 1994 the age of consent for gay men was 21 and it had in fact been illegal until a few decades previously (Thompson, 2011). Gay couples were often banned by local authorities from adopting children and overt discrimination was evident (Okitikpi and Aymer, 2010).

Within the social sciences there developed a greater understanding that the disadvantages experienced by some groups were embedded in the processes and structures of our society (Smith, 2008). Previously dominant views of the reasons for income and power inequality between BME groups and white people, or between men and women, suggested that this was mainly due to the inherent superiority of one group over another and part of the natural order of the world (Okitikpi and Aymer, 2010). Research and academic thinking was highlighting that this was not the case, but that dominant groups in society were entrenching privilege, directly and indirectly, by their creation and maintenance of their own culture, economy and values that served to keep some people poorer (Warwick-Booth, 2013).

There were increasing calls for social work to be more radical in its fight for social justice and to do more to challenge the triggers for discrimination and disadvantage at its roots (Okitikpi and Aymer, 2010). (See Chapter 16, Radical Social Work.) Social work's contribution to fighting discrimination could be seen at that time to be moving from what Payne (2014) calls Individualist/Reformist or Reflexive/Therapeutic approaches to what he sees as a Socialist/Collectivist philosophy. (This can be seen in Chapter 1.) The first approach was described by Payne (2014) as primarily a problem-solving framework that stuck a plaster on society's ills, without necessarily fixing some of the long-term causes of these problems. The reflexive/therapeutic method was orientated around creating a helping relationship with vulnerable and disadvantaged people with a mind to helping them to come to terms with previous trauma or hurt, and teaching them new skills, thus enabling them to get on with their life themselves. Again, however, this did not attempt to address the underlying societal triggers. Payne (2014) describes the Socialist/Collectivist approach to social work as a way of raising awareness in disadvantaged groups of how to change their position in society and to campaign for social change. This type of social work intended to challenge the root causes and to change society. Whether social work in practice ever fits easily into his three categories is a difficult question, but the addition of this radical and transformative philosophy has shaped modern social work.

Activity 18.1

Consider people with disabilities in the UK. Do you think that this group of people experience discrimination in this country and, if so, how? What evidence is there to show this? Does this group experience oppression? What power structures and aspects of society contribute to this state of affairs?

Understanding how discrimination and oppression perpetuate

That unfair treatment of minority groups has historically been part of our society, and that unjust discrimination still exists today is not so controversial (Payne, 2014). How discrimination continues over the generations and how to combat the injustice is more debateable. Sociological disciplines have pointed to the impact of poverty, education, the media and political discourse on how different groups are seen and treated within society (Thompson, 2012). Psychological studies point to the use of language and experience impacting on marginalised groups' perceived identity, promoting their relative isolation, while simultaneously encouraging others to reinforce the view that some groups are materially different from the majority in some way (Dominelli, 2002). For example, when a young person from a BME group sees few BME people on TV in positive role-model positions they may feel that the media and public life is not for people like themselves and may therefore consider themselves *second-class citizens*.

Okitiki and Aymer (2010) use discrimination against BME groups (commonly known as racism) as a way of demonstrating different approaches to understanding and combating discrimination (Okitikpi and Aymer, 2010). From their identified approaches concepts of assimilation, multi-culturalism, black perspectives and anti-racist social work will be considered in order to understand some of the competing ideas and values within the fields of equality and discrimination.

Assimilation

This approach suggests that the key driver for racist views and actions in society is that first-generation immigrants, and their descendants, do not fully fit into the mainstream culture or expectations. This creates division, suspicion and possibly misunderstandings between groups. Advocates for this kind of approach say that to tackle racism more educational opportunities need to be provided for immigrants to learn about the mainstream culture and to encourage them to become assimilated into the population (Okitikpi and Aymer, 2010). Critics of this kind of thinking point to various studies that show racism can also be endemic for British-born BME people who are born within British culture. In fact, there is evidence that African-Caribbean men are more discriminated against within the psychiatric system (longer hospital stays, higher doses of medication and many other aspects of control) as time goes on, which appears to contradict the predictions (Fernando, 2010).

It can also be said that this approach appears to put the blame for racism on immigrant communities for not fitting in well enough, rather than those who are part of the oppression (Okitikpi and Aymer, 2010). Some commentators suggest that this is a by-product of the social construction (see Chapter 7) of concepts such as race and nations (Dunk-West, 2014). Rather than assume that ethnicity is a real-world characteristic (i.e. that it exists), the idea is that they are in fact just categories *created* by those in power, via the language they use. If sub-groups in humankind are created then the concept of people who are *different* to you are also created. Creating the idea of a *nation* in effect introduces the concept of the *foreigner*, i.e. the other (Dominelli, 2002).

It may also lead to a cultural deficit model, which can support ideas that some cultures are, by their very nature, inferior (Payne, 2014). For example, this suggests those not born, but living, in the UK are inferior to those who were born here. Those opposed to this approach argue that it seems to work on the idea that less diversity of culture is a good thing to strive for, which is the opposite of what modern social work believes, and that changing culture (i.e. becoming assimilated) is an easy thing to do (Payne, 2014).

Multi-culturalism

Also known as Liberal Pluralism, multi-culturalism has been part of the dominant political discourse on fighting discrimination in the UK since at least the 1990s (Okitikpi and Aymer, 2010). This set of ideas suggests that discrimination largely arises through a lack of understanding of minority cultures and that respect and knowledge of others needs to be promoted; pushing for the idea of co-existence and legal equality are the main strands of attack (Payne, 2014). If a person is made equal in law, then it is suggested that everything will settle into a calm and understanding equilibrium.

Those who oppose this philosophy argue that it can lead to a separate, but equal society where different communities survive as largely non-interacting parts (Okitikpi and Aymer, 2010). Some suggest that it ignores the economic, political and social structures that perpetuate racism and operates on a colour-blind basis – that sorting out equality is something to do with law and that issues of ethnicity or race should be ignored (Bartoli, 2013). Furthermore, it makes a worrying claim that education alone can resolve the problems:

> *Making racism in social work practice a matter of individual import ignores the role of institutionalised racism and discounts the significance of direct or unintentional racism. It pathologises the overtly racist few. Ignores the subtle racism of the majority, and obscures the interconnections between structural forces and personal behaviour. Moreover, it converts racism into a matter which can be educated away, thereby ignoring the link between its eradication and the transformation of our socio-economic and political structures.*
>
> (Dominelli, 1988, p21)

Black perspectives

This way of seeing racism is based on strengthening the views and ideas of BME groups and getting them more widely known (Okitikpi and Aymer, 2010). At its core is a belief that mainstream British culture is very Eurocentric, revolving around long-established norms, expectations and histories. British culture did not develop in a neutral and haphazard manner. Dominant groups in society influence the laws, media and politics of this society, and usually, directly or indirectly, reinforce their own views about what is good, morally right and ideal (Smith, 2008). As white males have for centuries been predominantly holding the reins of power in this country, UK culture and expectations tend to be based on their outlook and value system. Promoting a more Afrocentric world view, as well as other ways of knowing and understanding the world, is meant to help create a more positive and confident set of identities around BME groups, allowing them to play a more confident and equal role in society (Dominelli, 1988).

One line of criticism against this type of argument is that there are as many black perspectives as there are BME people (Payne, 2014). (This can also be seen in Chapter 9 in relation to different forms of feminism.) Putting all people from BME backgrounds in one group could be seen as racist in itself. Does it lead to possible charges of increasing cultural relativism where morals and values are seen as different across cultures, or are there shared rights and wrongs that we either agree on or enforce (Okitikpi and Aymer, 2010)? This approach also emphasises cultural issues again, leading to charges that it again sets aside economic or structural problems (Payne, 2014).

Anti-racist social work

This approach to social workers tackling discrimination experienced by people from BME backgrounds developed in the 1970s and suggested that this was an individual and professional task that needed more than government intervention (Dominelli, 1988). Social work and its interactions with people in need, was seen as part of the system that could perpetuate racism knowingly or unknowingly. Every time a social worker dealt with casework, assessed a family or spoke to a service user they were making a political statement of some kind (Bartoli, 2013). A key feature of the anti-racist social worker was the requirement to help non-BME social workers recognise their own in-built racism and to tackle their own discriminatory ideas and actions. However, in doing so, it suggested that all white social workers were racist in nature (Okitikpi and Aymer, 2010). This could be difficult to accept as social workers enter the profession to help people and fight for social justice. To be told that they are acting in a discriminatory manner can be challenging for them to take on board and may also be met with charges that it is itself a racist idea.

Some commentators on this approach warn that it frames the experiences of people from BME groups in a confrontational approach with those of white people, whereas this may not be their own perspective or how they see the narrative (Payne, 2014). Its emphasis on ethnicity can ignore the areas of gender and class that may be more important or inter-connect with this area (Bartoli, 2013).

Anti-discriminatory practice

In the 1980s, ADP began to grow from the debates over equality, discrimination and the role of social workers in tackling it that were seen in the previous decade (Okitikpi and Aymer, 2010). This development of ideas was created from a fusion of the knowledge base of structuralism, the need for self-awareness and reflection from anti-racist social work and the need not to replace one kind of deterministic prejudice with another (Payne, 2014). Moving from racist views that people from BME groups were more criminally inclined, to the understanding that poverty is a much bigger influence in criminality, could again stereotype BME communities as being poor and therefore criminal.

ADP saw a move from the previous emphasis on individual actions in perpetuating discriminatory situations, to the addition of sociological triggers in changing life chances and how discrimination can emerge from indirect prejudice. Another key aspect was the idea that one disadvantage did not trump all others (Okitikpi and Aymer, 2010) and that all aspects of an individual's experience in life needed to be carefully analysed. This developed the idea of social justice being an overall umbrella term for the ideas rather than individual threads such as anti-racism or feminism.

Thompson (2012, p33) developed the PCS model of understanding discrimination and how different aspects help to create such disadvantage. P is the Personal or Psychological factors that occur on an individual level. This could be our own biases, our emotions or approaches to particular groups, moulded by our own interactions. C stands for the Culture we live in, how it creates different kinds of worth in certain characteristics and creates narratives about differences and social norms. This covers the role of language in shaping discussions and the way that the media portrays groups. S is the Structure of Society and government. The way services are set up and the processes they use all impact on discrimination.

Case Study: Serious Case Review

In the report on the death of Child Z (Manchester Safeguarding Children Board, 2013, p68) the analysis found that the family nurse (FN1), amongst other professionals, had not noticed some warning signs about the poor quality of care Child Z was receiving. This included the very dirty state of the highchair as well as general dirt and chaos in the house. The report mentioned that the professionals involved in the child's care tried to interact in a caring way with the family and reported that the mother was engaging well with their work.

This may relate to ADP and the innate preconceptions that professionals have about people from working-class backgrounds and social workers need to be aware of their biases. Could it be that the professionals involved accepted the chaos and dirt mentioned in the report

(Continued)

(Continued)

as part of the reality of families in areas of multiple deprivation? The messages we receive from the media regarding people in areas of poverty are often quite negative, with stereotypes from programmes like *The Royle Family* and *Benefit Street*. This could correspond to Thompson's (2012) Cultural contribution of discrimination. The nurse and other workers may have accepted a poorer quality of domestic hygiene than they would have from families with more money. Does this mean that the professionals involved in her care offered Child Z a poorer service because of innate prejudices?

Activity 18.1

The father of Child Z (FZ) in the Serious Case Review is reported to have had a history of depression (that led to at least one suicide attempt) and alcohol abuse. Do people with mental health problems suffer from discrimination in Britain and how does this manifest itself? What factors influence this? Think about the same questions with regard to alcohol misuse. Are there any differences in the levels of discrimination?

Chapter Summary

Social work is a profession that strives for social justice and equality. However, the causes of discrimination and how to intervene to make a difference in the lives of those disadvantaged by society is a contested topic. Anti-discriminatory practice involves analysing not only the service users we work with and the society that impacts on them, but our own assumptions and realities.

Reflection Point

- Every social worker will bring their own preconceptions and personal biases to their practice.
- It is only by being aware of our place in society and the preconceptions we hold that we can challenge them.

Further Reading

Thompson, N (2012) *Anti-discriminatory Practice* (5th edition). Basingstoke: Palgrave Macmillan, pp32–6.

The PCS model is widely used in social work to examine the causes of oppression and discrimination in a systematic manner. Read about the model in more depth and consider how this might influence your practice as a social worker and how it may influence social work in the real world.

Introduction to Part Five – Organisational Theories

It would be fair to say that all professionals (to a greater or lesser extent) involved in any kind of safeguarding practice understand that they need to work effectively in partnership with other professionals **and** to communicate effectively. However, SCRs often identify problems in partnership working where a child or adult has been seriously harmed or died; where information was not shared as it should have been; where information was shared but not understood or where policies were not in place. So what is going wrong? How can there still be mistakes made, intentionally or otherwise, in effective partnership working when practitioners know they need to work together? Rather than taking a focus on individuals, the next two chapters on Classical and Modern Management Theory and Organisational Theory will look at some of the potential reasons for these complications. Looking at the way organisations operate – and indeed the specific focus of different groups of professionals – can help to identify some of the crossed lines of communications and understanding that occurs and therefore the implications for service users and carers.

Chapter 19

Classical and modern management theories

Lesley Deacon

Achieving a Social Work Degree

This chapter will help you meet the following capabilities, to the appropriate level, from the Professional Capabilities Framework:

> ### PCF 1 Professionalism

- Describe the role of a social worker and the importance of personal and professional boundaries and behaviour, demonstrate ability to learn using a range of approaches;

> ### PCF 8 Context and Organisations

- Demonstrate awareness of the impact of organisational context on social work practice;

> ### PCF 9 Professional Leadership

- Demonstrate awareness of the importance of professional leadership in social work.

Introduction

In this chapter, social work students and practitioners will be introduced to different management theories that can help in understanding how organisations, and people in organisations, work. While many students, and indeed practitioners, may feel as though this is less relevant because they do not intend to become a manager, that is not in fact the purpose of this chapter. It is not about setting out management skills and knowledge in order to develop into, and within, management, but to address the danger that *{p}eople who do not perceive themselves as managers {may} not bother to understand what managers do or why they do it* (Weinbach, 2008, p13). It is important to understand management in social work practice as this directly impacts on the way social work practitioners work and the way services are provided. The focus of this chapter is therefore really on the managed, i.e. the way in which practitioners and partnership professionals may be managed. Understanding the ways in which this occurs can help to understand why successful partnership working, while intended, may sometimes not be effective. This chapter will begin by looking in more depth at classical management theories that still underpin and have *an enduring and worldwide impact* on the way in which organisations work today (Hafford-Letchfield, 2009, p6). Following this, modern management theories will be considered which, it could be argued, are key to understanding social work practice today. This chapter is intended to be read alongside Chapter 20 (and parts of Chapter 16) in order to fully understand the role environments play on the way in which social work practitioners work.

What is management?

According to Weinbach (2008) the concept of management is ways of *shaping and exerting an influence over the work environment* (p5). Managers are those who are viewed as organising and overseeing the day-to-day requirements of a team; whereas leaders are often those who are seen to have certain attributes (in their personality) to bring about change and development within an organisation (Gray, 2010). This does not mean that managers cannot be innovative and lead change, but their main focus is the running of day-to-day practice – in essence, management tends to be a *practical activity* concerning *planning and organising* (Hafford-Letchfield, 2009, pp23–5). There can also be different levels of managers, for example, in social work practice – a team manager, a department manager, a service manager. Management itself is both a science and an art, as while knowledge is used to make decisions the actual decisions themselves cannot be determined to be right or wrong, so managers use the best available knowledge on which to base these decisions. Complexity is added to this by the human element, which creates complexity and uncertainty because of the nature of human beings. This is particularly an issue in human service organisations, which is where social work and its partner agencies are placed.

There are various aspects within organisations that can impact on a manager's decision making. For example: policy and legislation; attitudes; resources; prioritising need; and stakeholders. In social work environments these are evident in a variety of policy and legislation that legitimises practice and sets out clear duties, rights and responsibilities. Attitudes refer to the people themselves, be that the manager, social work practitioner, colleagues, service users, carers, partnership agencies, etc. An attitude *is something that is a feature of our internal world... that is acquired and shaped by our experiences and which actively and directly influences what we do and how we behave towards the 'thing' our attitude is about* (Callaghan and Lazard, 2011, p3). These are therefore the predispositions that we have to respond to certain stimuli and help make sense of our social world. So each individual, from a psychological perspective, is subject to certain attitudes, beliefs and behaviour which, when acted out, can impact on decision making and the way in which staff are managed, and conversely on the way in which staff respond to being managed. Resources are a key, significant issue at the time of writing this chapter, as the UK is experiencing a time of austerity, so the impact of this on the way in which social work is managed is important, in respect to staff levels and workload, service provision, etc.

This chapter will now look at how the concept of the *manager* emerged, and from this how different theoretical perspectives developed to explain the role.

The emergence of the manager

The introduction to how theory developed in social work was set out in Chapter 1; the Industrial Revolution was a pivotal event in this development, and is also intrinsic to understanding the development of the concept of management and of different theoretical perspectives on how management works. The birth of the factory led to a requirement for a different style of operation. The owners of the factories did not work in them, so instead hired someone to oversee these operations. This became the 'manager'. This role was new and led to the emergence of different theoretical perspectives as to how this role could function effectively. The manager was, in essence, in the middle between the owners and the workers. Their role was to manage the workers effectively in order to bring about the best productivity and therefore profit for the owners. It is understandable that it was during this emergence that the theories of Karl Marx were also developed (see Chapter 16) (Weinbach, 2008).

Scientific management theory

Thinking back to aspects of the Industrial Revolution a shift occurred in terms of the way in which jobs were performed and overseen. Factories introduced the idea of the 'production line' whereby workers had a specific job to do in that line, then the next worker did their job and so on. It is helpful to visualise this process to understand the way in which work was therefore perceived. Repetition was the key concept, i.e. an individual worker would do the same thing hour after hour, day after day, week after week, and so on. When considering a psychological perspective on this and attempting to understand the human psyche it can be seen that workers would be unlikely to be motivated by this – so what was their source of motivation? The answer would be money – to be paid for this work in order to be able to afford to live. This is the principle of the *economic man* – the rational being who slots themselves into the wheel of the *organisational machine* (Hughes and Wearing, 2013).

The engineer Frederick Taylor (1856–1915) is the person associated with this perspective, and assumptions were made regarding this motivation, as set out in Table 19.1, below.

Table 19.1 Assumptions regarding motivation

Workers are motivated by economics, i.e. pay and financial security
Workers act rationally
Workers prefer simple tasks
Workers require and seek out supervision guidance
Workers seek out a stable work environment
(Weinbach, 2008)

As suggested in the introduction, management is not just about the manager but how the employee responds to and what they seek from their manager. So, these suggestions from Taylor would suggest that certain types of management would work better than others to achieve a motivated workforce. So, the focus here would be on the manager to devise and implement different types of management that would improve productivity – to keep the workers satisfied and motivated while maximising profits for the owners. In theory this means that if more money is offered, e.g. in the form of *bonuses*, then the worker would work harder to achieve this. But this presumes that money, and rational acceptance of the existing order, is indeed their motivating factor for work.

With the emergence of the information age in contemporary society it may be that some would argue that this management theory is largely redundant, especially when considering the reduction of industry in the UK since the 1980s in particular. However, it could also be argued that a modern example of this type of work environment, and Scientific Management theory in practice, is the *call centre*. Doxford International Business Park in Sunderland *is one of the region's key locations for corporate headquarters and financial and customer services centres* (Regus website). In this location there are a number of call centres, and recruitment companies regularly advertise jobs for workers. A number of recent adverts accessed used the term 'benefits' as motivation to attract potential employees (Reed website). In addition, the roles in these organisations refer to answering calls and dealing effectively with difficult customers. So, while training is offered in how to do this, the work effectively remains the same – answering calls and following fixed procedures. Employees will be allocated to specific teams so will deal with the same types of calls. Because of the level of simplicity in the work, employees can become productive more quickly as they learn how to do the work. So, in this, the similarity to a scientific management process can be seen. Motivation is likely to be financial rather than job satisfaction. The question arises, however, whether this type of management theory can relate to social work practice today: a profession that certainly cannot be referred to as 'simplistic'? It could be argued that there are two significant relationships between this theory to social work practice: the concept of the *evidence base*, and the idea of *cost-effectiveness*.

Evidence-based social work

There is no doubt that social work practice requires an evidence base – looking at the PCFs alone identifies the need for knowledge at different levels in practice. However, there is a conflict in practice between those that see it as *common sense* and those that take a theoretical approach.

A conflict arising from the scientific approach to an evidence base is that it removes decision making away from *'art' factors such as instinct {and} experience* (Weinbach, 2008, p49). From a social work perspective this could be referred to as professional judgement. Eileen Munro criticised some of the processes imposed on social work for taking away social work practitioners' ability to make professional judgements (2010a, b and 2011). This does not suggest that social work practitioners should not be evidence based, but there needs to be a balance with regard to what can be evidenced while using professional knowledge and experience in order to make decisions. Human beings are complex, and no amount of an evidence base can be 100 per cent accurate, and nor is the concept of 'common sense'. What social work practice is, is a complicated area of work – it is both an art and a science.

Reflection Point

In what ways is social work practice required to be cost effective? Why is this important?

Administrative management

Henri Fayol (1841–1925) was a French engineer who theorised about how management should take place (Shafritz et al., 2015). It was his perception that there were certain patterns to good management, which were in fact universal, i.e. they transcended different cultures and could be applied to any situation (Weinbach, 2008). While Fayol was writing before Taylor, his work only really became recognised in the mid-twentieth century. His focus was not so much on the actual work tasks involved, but on the efficiency of an organisation. Fayol set out key principles regarding management with the main assertion being that *good management could be taught* (Weinbach, 2008, p51).

These principles are not meant as rigid or prescriptive rules, but as guidance. Fayol also suggested that management was not just specific to work places but also to different aspects of life – any aspect where organising and control took place; for example, running a home, managing the family, organising social events. The table on page 204 also indicates how the principles might be applied to social work practice. There is some indication of good examples of management in social work (taken from a generic and personal perspective) but there are also immediate concerns for the

Table 19.2   Fayol's 14 Principles of Management

	Principle	Explanation	Application to Social Work
1	Division of Work	Specialisations	Having job roles that are specialised is significant in social work practice, especially when considered in the context of safeguarding both children and vulnerable adults.
2	Authority and Responsibility	A manager has authority over others and with this comes responsibility.	This is evident in supervision in social work practice – managers also take on responsibility for decisions.
3	Discipline	There is an agreement between employees and employers when they agree to work there.	As professionals social workers agree to adhere to this when registering with the HCPC.
4	Unity of Command	Accountable only to one boss.	Social work practitioners are directly accountable to their team manager first and foremost.
5	Unity of Direction	One plan for a group of activities that have the same purpose.	Chief social workers were appointed in 2013 in order to lead the direction of social work practice.
6	Subordination of individual interest to the general interest	Self-interest should be discouraged in favour of the benefits of the organisations as a whole.	The focus of social work practice should be, and is, on the service users and carers.
7	Remuneration	Employees should be paid fairly.	Social Work practitioners have a clear pay scale. But does it fairly reflect the complexity of the work in practice?
8	Centralization	A balance is needed between centralizing and decentralizing processes. Some centralization however is always needed.	There has been increasing centralization of administrative functions within social work.
9	Scalar chain	For emergency situations a communication procedure should be in place so information does not have to go one step at a time up the chain of command.	Emergency practice takes place in safeguarding in particular where lines of communication can change when there is an emergency.
10	Order	Employees should be placed where they work best so they can make the best contribution.	Allowing movement of staff to different areas is important, for example how long can practitioners continue to work effectively in frontline safeguarding without a break?
11	Equity	Fairness is needed in the application of a common sense approach, not just through regulations.	To apply social work values sometimes managers and practitioners need to think outside of the box.
12	Stability	Successful companies tend to be more stable with less staff turnover.	This is a problem in contemporary social work due to changes in governance and high workloads leading to high staff turnover particularly in safeguarding children.
13	Initiative	Manager should encourage initiative from employees.	Practice changes over time so new practitioners can bring new ideas.
14	Esprit de corps	Harmony is important.	Social work practice can be stressful so harmony and support in teams is essential.

(Adapted from Weinbach, 2008)

profession, e.g. around stability in particular. It can certainly be argued that social work is not stable – as a public service, its focus, governance and procedures shift depending on the ethos of the government in power.

We can see the theory of Administrative Management in general in social work practice, for example, in the implementation of the NHS and Community Care Act 1990. This Act was based on the Griffiths report (1988) by Sir Roy Griffiths, the former Managing Director of the supermarket chain, Sainsbury's. The view of public services at this time was of a lack of effective management; that public services were not working properly. The use of Griffiths was to imply that management, regardless of the environment in which it is experienced, is the same. The process and skills necessary for good management are the same across the public and private sectors, so suggesting, as Fayol did, that good management can be taught. There are certainly concerns about the way in which this *managerialism* focuses on a narrow range of performance indicators and management control, thus reducing the need for critical thinking on the part of the social work practitioner (Hafford-Letchfield, 2009). There is also concern that more recently the shift in this managerialism has led to more defensive practice as practitioners use processes to defend their actions against negative public perceptions (Hafford-Letchfield, 2009). However, its principle concerning the ability of good management to be taught is certainly something that is applied to social work organisations. For example, to be promoted to be a team manager, social work practitioners do not need previous management experience, as they will receive training, so it effectively opens up management to everyone.

Bureaucratic management

Bureaucratic management theory was first identified by Max Weber, but while he identified it, this did not mean he espoused it as the best and most effective management theory, as he also referred to it as dehumanising (Hughes and Wearing, 2013). Bureaucratic organisations focus on the *efficient handling of clients... through methods of staffing and structure* rather than on economic efficiency (Weinbach, 2008, p54). The key principle that underpins a bureaucratic organisation is the concept of 'rules' – the organisation is based on these and functions within these. These rules clearly set out a hierarchical structure in which levels of the organisations are governed by those above and so on. Each role within the organisation is clearly defined through these rules and the roles exist in their own right, employees do not have a right to them or a hold over these – the roles themselves take precedent. Authority in such organisations therefore comes from the rules set out by the organisation and it is these that must be followed. It is due to this complete emphasis on the following of rules that leads to the identification of bureaucratic organisations being focused on *efficiency* (Cole and Kelly, 2011).

In social work practice, this can be seen as a clear set of rules and regulations with a focus on everyone being treated the same. In this way, there is a set of *clearly defined and procedurally determined rules and regulations* that are known and understood by the people working under them, and it is through this that efficiency is achieved (Hughes and Wearing, 2013, p35). For example, service users and carers are entitled to the same level of assessment according to needs – the rules are set out to be fair and equitable. In the organisations themselves, however, promotion would be based on an employee's success at the current job they were doing rather than any proven ability to do a more senior role (Weinbach, 2008, p56). As suggested, the roles exist already and competency is established in previous roles further down in the organisation's hierarchical structure (Cole and Kelly, 2011). In terms of social work this means that a social worker could be promoted to manager based on their abilities as a social worker rather than on any management experience or skills. The authority comes from the role the person fills rather than from the person themselves (Hughes and Wearing, 2013, p35). This leads to some questions regarding the effectiveness of bureaucratic organisations. Other skills and experience of an individual may not be considered; instead, it would only be their perceived success in the role they are applying *from*, meaning they are not necessarily assessed for suitability for the job they are applying *for*. Additionally, a significant concern is that the bureaucracy itself can grow out of control and lose its effectiveness – rules and regulations can be developed for the sake of the rules themselves rather than the purpose of the work.

Example of out of control bureaucracy

I needed a new eraser for work and there was no longer a stationery cupboard, due to the cost concern of people helping themselves, so I requested a new eraser from the administrative person responsible for stationery orders. However, the rules stated that I could not go direct to that person – instead I had to contact my team leader to request the eraser and, if approved, she had to contact the administrator directly. Then only boxes of a large number of erasers could be ordered, so the request was held until the cost could be justified, i.e. more people needing a new eraser. The process to get the new eraser took so long that I gave up and bought one myself...

While this may appear to be a frivolous example in a social work theory book, it helps to illustrate the point effectively. What if it was not an eraser, what if it was an essential service or equipment for someone? For example, Panel Processes leading to delays in service provision to people in need, or leaving people in expensive hospital beds or re-ablement provisions? The principle would remain the same because bureaucracy attempts to promote fairness by being free of the 'human element', i.e. professional judgement.

Activity 19.1

Think of examples from your own practice when bureaucracy appears to be overly controlled, i.e. it appears to cause more problems than it solves.

Despite changes and development in management theory, the *archetypical human service organisation remains the bureaucracy* (Hughes and Wearing, 2013, p31). So, it is likely that anyone entering social work practice will experience bureaucratic management in some form at some point in their career.

Case Study: Serious Case Review

The first point in the application of classical management theory to the SCR of Child Z is the immediate recognition that a SCR functions within a bureaucratic structure. This is evident in statements made such as:

> *Regulation 5 of the Local Safeguarding Children Board Regulations 2006 requires a Local Safeguarding Children Board (LSCB) to undertake a review of a serious case in accordance with the procedures that were set out in chapter 8 of Working Together to Safeguard Children (2010) but now amended and found in chapter four of Working Together to Safeguard Children (2013) issued in April 2013.*
>
> (p4)

> *The Serious Case Review panel at their first meeting on the 12th February 2013 confirmed the scope and terms of reference for the SCR...*
>
> (p6)

> *Individual management reviews were completed using the template provided by the Manchester Safeguarding Children Board (MSCB), and were quality assured and approved by the most senior officer of the reviewing agency*
>
> (p7)

These extracts demonstrate clearly the rules and regulations followed by the SCR and its purpose – terms such as 'in accordance', 'procedures', 'terms of reference', 'template' and 'quality assured' are indicators of these.

The SCR also identifies issues of rules and regulations that did not work effectively in the case of Child Z, and which needed to be addressed. For example, the ambulance service was recommended to update their *Sudden Unexpected Death of Children Procedures* to ensure that police were automatically informed.

(Continued)

(Continued)

What is also evident from the SCR is where bureaucratic management structures may have interfered with the process of information sharing:

> *The IMR author is unsure of why the CIN flag was inserted and identifies some confusion in regard to the Trainee Probation Officer's understanding about the process. This is explored in later sections of the report; the significance here is not so much whether a procedure was sufficiently understood and complied with but rather the degree of insight and understanding about the significance of CIN indicating a child who may be prevented from appropriate development as a precursor to more serious concerns about significant harm; in this case Child Z had yet to be born and therefore there was no child to be the subject of any process*
>
> (p29)

The above example demonstrates concerns regarding bureaucratic processes and whether they are in fact understood. The issue of the CIN (Child in Need) flag is raised. A flag was added to an electronic system but it is not clear how much the concept of a child in need was understood and what could be done in the case of Child Z at that point as she was not born. This creates a problem where employees use systems and processes without necessarily fully being able to understand them. Wastell and White (2014) suggest that there has been (and remains) a focus and increasing shift towards conformance and standardisation and specifically through the use of electronic documentation within professional practice. The Integrated Children's System (ICS) has been used in social work practice since 2007 as it was set up to provide *a framework for the development of electronic recording systems for CSCS in accordance with the assessment framework and other guidance and regulation* (DoE, 2011, website). However, a review by Bell et al. in 2007 found serious flaws in the system. Practitioners and their managers found it too prescriptive, long, repetitive and focused on tick boxes. The complex needs of specific children could not easily be slotted into the system, and it was not clear in the system where risk assessments should be completed. (Similar experiences were found by Deacon (2015)).

This demonstrates two major problems with a bureaucratic structure: first, if a system is too reliant on ticking boxes it *allows* its users to get by without developing any understanding of the reasons behind each box; second, when there is complexity and people and interactions they do not fit easily into the boxes provided...

Modern management theory

Whilst classical management theories have been explored so far, their application has been made to modern practice thus indicating their continuing importance. There are also a number of theories in modern management theory that are particularly significant today. Psychological theories regarding personality and motivation have not been explored here – it is recommended that readers read the Psychology chapters in this book and then access managerial texts concerning these, which will help in understanding people; and how people work within these organisational contexts.

In terms of modern management, the focus on managerialism in the UK from the 1980s onwards (New Public Management) led to a shift in how public services were (and are) managed (Hughes and Wearing, 2013). This is set out in detail in Chapter 16 *Radical Social Work*. In this, and earlier in this chapter, the underpinning reasons for this managerial development were explored, with reference to the Griffiths Report (1988) where the concerns about the potential for public money to be wasted or mismanaged were pervasive and so the decision to implement private sector strategies onto the public sector was made (Hughes and Wearing, 2007). This, in turn led towards the neo-liberalist management focus that is evident today in the public services, as set out in the section *From capitalism to neo-liberalism* in Chapter 16, Radical Social Work. What this means is that power is exerted in services in order to ensure that personal, individual, responsibility is taken. As suggested by Featherstone et al. (2012) for example, this refocus in safeguarding children placed the focus firmly on the parent as being responsible for their child and what was happening to them. It could therefore be argued that this has led to a return to a more psychological focus for social work – the focus on the individual, rather than on the impact of structural factors.

Chapter Summary

It is important for students and social work practitioners to understand the foundations of management and management theory relevant to social work practice today, which is what this chapter has demonstrated. All work takes place within organisations and within management structures; therefore, students and practitioners must understand the way in which these structures influence their work and the way in which service users and carers are treated, and how services are provided.

Further Reading

This chapter, and the author's understanding of management in social work organisations, has been largely influenced by the work of Robert Weinbach.

Weinbach, R (2008) *The Social Worker as Manager: A Practical Guide to Success* (5th edition). Boston, MA: Pearson. (A sixth edition with L.M. Taylor is now available.)

The text is clearly written and demonstrates effectively different concepts of management-related social work practice.

Chapter 20

Organisational culture

Lesley Deacon

Achieving a Social Work Degree

This chapter will help you meet the following capabilities, to the appropriate level, from the Professional Capabilities Framework:

PCF 1 Professionalism

- Describe the role of a social worker and the importance of personal and professional boundaries and behaviour, demonstrate ability to learn using a range of approaches;

PCF 8 Context and Organisations

- Demonstrate awareness of the impact of organisational context on social work practice;

PCF 9 Professional Leadership

- Demonstrate awareness of the importance of professional leadership in social work.

Reflection Point

Before reading this chapter, consider how much knowledge of the theories underpinning organisational culture do you think you would need in order to be an effective social worker? In which areas do you think it would be particularly important, if any?

Introduction

This chapter will specifically focus on the seminal work of Charles Handy, an Irish businessman and philosopher, who wrote *Understanding Organisations* (1976, first edition). The concepts Handy identified in this book in relation to organisational culture are as relevant today as to when they were written, and are beneficial for social work students and practitioners in understanding the impact of organisational culture on social work practice and, in particular, on working together. Throughout this chapter Reflection Points will be raised to help the reader understand the importance of organisational culture and to evaluate their own experiences.

Organisational environments

There is no one definition of what an organisation is or how it is structured; the main purpose of an organisation is to work towards a collective goal in an environment where different necessary activities are identified and sub-units created in order to focus on specific activities – these activities then need to be organised and directed (Hafford-Letchfield, 2009). The work conducted by Charles Handy attempted to conceptualise and understand the shared values, beliefs, norms and attitudes behind the way organisations work, as it is evident that all organisations work differently – there is no one way of working or running an organisation. As societies have different cultures that can be unique, so do organisations (Weinbach, 2008). It does not matter whether organisations may, on the surface, appear to have the same purpose or motivations (for example Children's and Adult's Social Care Services); there are underpinning beliefs and foci unique to each organisation that influence the way in which that organisation is run and the way in which its services are provided. In fact, the culture that exists within an organisation can be *subtle* and *imperceptible*, and staff who have worked in the same environment for a long time can often view the culture as *natural and inevitable* (Thompson, 2015, p51). Organisations are, therefore, often underpinned by *tacit* rather than explicit rules, i.e. expectations regarding the correct focus and the correct action are unspoken. While many qualified social workers will work in large bureaucratic organisations such as Local Authorities (see Chapter 19, p205 regarding bureaucratic management), others will work in smaller charitable or private organisations that still rely on government funding and so are also guided by the same rules. While there are similarities the actual organisational contexts will be different, and therefore it is important for students and social work practitioners to have an understanding of the theory underpinning these (Hughes and Wearing, 2013). This is especially important as there is no official rule book to follow, but the actions of employees are expected to fit with the unspoken rules (Deacon, 2015); new employees tend to learn through observation of others. (Social Learning Theory, identified by Albert Bandura, sets out a psychological theory as to how behaviour is learned from the observation of others, see p31)

Reflection Point

Can you think of examples from a place where you have worked where you were expected to know how to do something but it was not something that had been explained in detail?

Charles Handy's four organisational cultures

According to Handy (1976), there is no one right culture that should be followed; the best organisational culture is the one that suits the needs of the organisation to meet its purpose. The culture could therefore shift and change depending on the organisation's needs. He identified four different types of culture that he observed to exist within organisations.

Power Culture

What can be seen from a Power Culture is the idea of a central person, a central figure who has the power; that person is in control. The way in which the organisation is structured is pointing towards that person, and therefore that person would have all the power in that organisation. An example of this might be a family business where the main person or a few individuals have complete control over that organisation and how it runs. An advantage of having a Power Culture is the ability of the organisation to change. So, if external factors lead to a requirement for change this can be achieved very quickly by the person at the centre, with the power, deciding on the changes needed and implementing these. However, the nature of such organisations is that they do not encourage teamwork, as if an employee wants to succeed then they need to try and anticipate what the person in the power wants or needs. So, employees will be inward-looking towards that person and what they want. Rewards for the employees will be based on results; on achieving what the person in power wants the organisation to do. The culture is therefore very individualistic (Handy, 1976).

An example of this kind of culture within a health and social care environment, it could be argued, would be a GP surgery. There may be one or more GPs who work together in a partnership and they have the power within that organisation. The formation of Clinical Commissioning Groups (CCGs) following the Health and Social Care Act (2012) is an example of this power, as GPs now sit on CCGs and can focus on the needs of their particular area. If they do not identify those needs then they will not necessarily be addressed within their practice.

From a social work perspective this could manifest as powerful leadership (Hughes and Wearing, 2013); for example, this could be an organisation where a significant leader is driving the focus and ethos of the organisation. A strategic leader could provide *the overall vision… that drives the organisation forward* in that they can be inspiring, driving the motivation of employees within the organisation (Hafford-Letchfield, 2009, p27).

Reflection Point

In your working life have you had experience of a powerful and motivational leader? What were the benefits and what were the adverse effects?

Role Culture

There is a clear and distinct similarity between organisations that are underpinned by the classical management theory of 'Bureaucratic Management', and those that have a Role Culture (see Chapter 19). Role Culture is similar because it is underpinned by adherence to rules and regulations (Hughes and Wearing, 2013). Within a Role Culture, there are straight and narrow lines indicating specialisms of employees. Lines are only vertical and not horizontal, so there is a significant focus in these organisations on standardisation and clarity regarding employees' roles and expectations. So, even if there is no one there to fill it at a given moment in time, the role still exists and can be understood (Handy, 1976). For example, a social worker is a role within an organisation and there are clear expectations regarding that role within that organisation, as well as expectations due to the professional nature of the role (e.g. HCPC underpinning guidance). Other such examples are nurses, police officers, probation officers, etc.; the individuals filling these roles have expectations of the role, as do the management of the organisation and the customers or service users.

Change in organisations that have a Role Culture can be very difficult and very slow (Handy, 1976). These roles do not just exist in one organisation but in many, and such professional roles usually have regulatory bodies (e.g. HCPC, as suggested) so change is slow because there are many levels to filter through before anything can be implemented. This culture is particularly dominant in health and social care environments due to the professional nature of many of the roles within these organisations. Because of this difficulty with implementing change, organisations with a Role Culture ideally need stable environments in order for them to work effectively. At the time of writing the impact of austerity measures particularly focusing on health and social care environments can have a detrimental effect on these organisations and, as suggested in the previous chapter, high workloads and staff turnover rates do not indicate a stable environment.

The clear links between Role Culture and Bureaucratic Management are evident in the focus on clear job descriptions and role definitions; rules for advancement are based on success in previous roles rather than on other experience (Handy, 1976). In applying for a job as a social worker one of the first pieces of information potential employees will be given is a job description of the expectations of that role. These are set out in a clear but prescriptive way, so that each employee hired into that role has the same expectations placed upon them.

Task Culture

In a Task Culture the focus of the organisation is around specific projects. Employees may be drawn together at certain points in time to complete a particular project with a particular focus – this can often be referred to as Project Management. This can be used within particular organisations even where that organisation is underpinned by a different kind of organisational culture (Handy, 1976). Task Cultures can be particularly beneficial in health and social care environments as they can be set up and employees moved to focus on a particular task, and then moved back as needed. For example, in a social work environment a particular project could be identified, such as implementing Motivational Interviewing or CBT with a particular service user group. Often in Local Authorities, these are referred to as 'secondments' so the employees move into the new roles only temporarily while the need is present. When that need is fulfilled (or no longer required) the Task Culture can be disbanded and employees returned to their previous roles.

A Task Culture is very different from a Power Culture as the focus is primarily on *teamwork*; on employees working together towards a shared task or focus. Teamwork, and indeed partnership working, is pivotal in social work especially in relation to multi-agency working (this is addressed on page 215). For a Task Culture to be effective, the team members *must* work together because the primary focus is the task. The focus cannot lie with an individual, and there cannot be too many rules and regulations to follow as they can distract from the focus on the task, they may not be applicable or helpful in that particular situation, and they may even hinder the completion of the task. The flexibility of these types of organisation means they can manage change quickly and effectively. This also means that decisions can be made to disband a Task Culture if and when it is identified that a different culture may be more beneficial, e.g. with the clear identification of roles, responsibilities and chains of command (role) or the implementation of an overall decision-maker (power) or collaborative decision-making (person). Once the situation has stabilised, a Task Culture can then be reformed as necessary (Handy, 1976).

Person Culture

The focus of a Person Culture is that no member is more important than any other. The idea of this is consensus management; that decisions are made by agreement. These could be service user-led organisations, where service users set up and run their own organisations, giving everyone a voice. Co-operatives are examples of person cultures, where every employee has a say, and everyone has *equal* say. The problem with these cultures is in agreeing action, as this can only be achieved by consensus – what if that is not achieved? (Handy, 1976) Person Cultures, therefore, do not tend to dominate social work practice, but as noted they can be common in service user-led organisations. As Handy suggests, *[i}f there is a structure or an organization it exists only to serve and assist the individuals within it* (1976, p189). So, a service user-led organisation would be *set up* by service users, *for* service users and is *run* by service users. There would be no other *super-ordinate objective* to the existence of the organisation (ibid., p190). While this is not the dominant culture of all the organisational cultures, it is possible that certain individuals are more drawn to this perspective and way of working even if, by necessity, they are working in a different cultural environment. For example, a university lecturer may perceive themself in this way – operating from their own perspective as a Person Culture but *within* a Role Culture environment. The lecturer's focus is to use the university as a base in which their own career can be built (Handy, 1976).

A more recent alternative perspective, however, is a Person Culture in which tasks are matched to specific people (Hughes and Wearing, 2013). So, if considered on a micro level, it could be argued that aspects of Person Culture from this perspective can take place in any organisation. In social work, for example, it could be where a specific case is given to a practitioner because of their specific knowledge and experience. In the example of the task culture given earlier, it could be argued that if decisions in that environment were conducted by consensus then this would be demonstrating aspects of a Person Culture.

Partnership working

When considering any organisational culture in social work, the concept of partnership working must also be considered as this is a key element of all work that takes place. *The essence of partnership is sharing. It is marked by respect for one another, role divisions, rights to information, accountability, competence, and value accorded to individual input* (SCIE, 2008, p12). Social work as a practice does not take place in isolation or in a silo. Social work practitioners work in partnership in a variety of different ways, for example:

- with service users and carers;

- with other social work practitioners;

- with other professionals;

- with other agencies;

- with the public.

The service users and carers that practitioners tend to work with are those often with *complex, cross-cutting needs, typically requiring a more coherent and 'joined-up' response from a range of agencies* (Glasby, 2012, p73). In working with adults, for example, the Care Act (2014) emphasises the need for partnership working between professionals and agencies, and SCIE (2008) identifies different types of partnership working:

- shared learning;

- cooperation;

- collaboration;

- teamwork;

- joint education/practice;

- interdisciplinary partnership working;

- multi-disciplinary working;

- participation.

Partnership working is, therefore, focused on the idea of collaboration and, as already indicated, sharing. This is a significant value in social work practice and is at the core of effective working (Thompson, 2015). However, experience of partnership work is inconsistent and there is no 'one clear way' to do it (as is the norm for all aspects of social work practice, knowledge and skills). So, while the principle of partnership is essential to social work practice there are external factors that can impact on its effectiveness.

The task environment

In addition to understanding the concept and importance of partnership in social work practice, it is also imperative to understand that human service organisations and the way they operate are impacted upon by the external environment, e.g. law, policy, austerity, etc. A task environment *consists of any persons, organizations or groups on whom it is dependent for goal achievement and who have the potential to support or interfere with its efforts* (Weinbach, 2008, p21). The external factors which impact on social work practice are therefore all stakeholders in the practice, such as:

- current and past service users and carers;

- potential new service users in the general public;

- other people who are affected by services, e.g. neighbours;

- taxpayers/voters and charitable donors;

- the government;

- the media;

- workers, unions and professional bodies;

- suppliers and partner agencies;

- agencies who buy services and internal 'customers'.

(Adapted from Weinbach, 2008)

Task environments are becoming more complicated for public sector organisations and more like the culture of private businesses due to the neo-liberalist agenda currently in place (see Chapters 16 and 19). Health Trusts, for example, can describe themselves as 'health care businesses' rather than public services, a distinction that has implications for how they go about providing services and prioritising their work. An increasing number of health and social care environments are becoming privatised as employees become employed, for example, by Virgin to carry out health care tasks. Fostering and Adoption agencies in children's social care services are also increasingly private companies.

Operating within task environments also increases potential sources of hostility for social work practice. For example, they often deal with involuntary service users, especially in child protection and mental health services. Hostile environments and negative public image can impact on the actual practice taking place and potentially lead to defensive practice and avoidance of risks. This can then result in shifting the practice to a bureaucratic focus rather than a service user focus, as practitioners concentrate on the recording of decisions and increased bureaucracy to protect themselves (Weinbach, 2008). Such environments can also lead to staff groups who want to privilege their professional group over staff with other (or no) qualifications. Stress in the workforce can increase for those who feel under attack, e.g. the perceived 'hostility' towards public services from the government through cutbacks, job cuts, pay cuts, etc. As well as this there are justified anxieties about the ability of agencies to go on providing services to vulnerable people in an adverse funding climate.

All of these issues need to be taken into account when considering how partnership working takes place. Social work practice is not the only professional body to experience this – any human service organisation is beholden to the task environment which therefore impacts on practice.

Application to social work

It is evident from the information provided on Handy's Organisational Cultures that any and all of the cultures he identified can be found within health and social care environments. Particularly when considering multi-agency working, however, Role and Task cultures are predominantly evident, and this can be illustrated with the following example.

Example: Community Mental Health Service

An example of a Task Culture could be a multi-disciplinary team (i.e. a team set up with professionals from different disciplines) that has been set up with a particular focus, such as a community mental health service. This environment may have a number of different professionals brought together – either employed directly by the organisation or on secondment from other teams within a Local Authority or the NHS. The aim of the organisation would be to provide a 'one stop shop' for service users who have mental health concerns. Possible professionals involved could be:

(Continued)

(Continued)

- *mental health nurses;*
- *social workers;*
- *occupational therapists;*
- *physiotherapists;*
- *cognitive therapists.*

While these professionals come together to provide mental health services in a holistic fashion, this does not necessarily mean they will all have the same focus and all be able to work together well, as they first need to put aside individual professional priorities and focus on the holistic view. When considering the predominant culture these professionals are likely to have come from, i.e. Role Culture, it is likely that they will be used to having specific roles and responsibilities with a clear chain of command. However, there could be inherent and fundamental differences in the way each of these professionals will focus on the service user and how they will prioritise. The relationship between social work and health care is often complex and sometimes fraught with difficulties (Thompson, 2015, p48), and this is an important explanation as to why working in partnership with others can be problematic. This can be illustrated by looking at the stick person in the Activity below.

Activity 20.1

Using the stick figure below, indicate what the focus of each professional is likely to be when dealing with a service user with mental health concerns. (*Prospects* have examples of the job profiles for all the above roles, and these can be found at www.prospects.ac.uk/job-profiles.)

What becomes evident is the different main focus of each professional, as illustrated below. This does not mean that these professionals are not capable of taking a more holistic view, and indeed many do, but it does go some way to identifying why there may be problems in working in partnership across different professions.

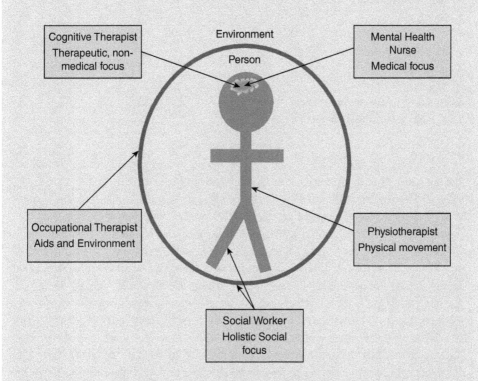

What is shown here is how different roles can look at the same issue but in different ways; for example, a Mental Health Nurse may support a medicalised view of a service user as being in need of medical treatment for their condition, whereas a Cognitive Therapist will focus on talking therapies. There will be times when these professionals are in agreement and co-ordinate their response, but there will also be times when these professionals disagree and see different priorities in understanding and treating the service user. The problem in specialist professionals coming together is that it can be difficult to control them and focus them on the particular task. Going back to the beginning of this chapter and considering what Handy's intentions were, i.e. shared values, beliefs, norms and attitudes (1976), it is this basis, it could be argued, which creates the most significant barrier to effective partnership working. As referred to earlier, the existence of tacit rules in organisations means that perceptions and ways of working are seen as normal (Deacon, 2015), so it could be suggested that this makes it difficult for some practitioners to articulate why a particular focus is more important than another – *because it just is...*

Case Study: Serious Case Review

Looking at the SCR, the first evidence of the need for partnership working can be found in the number of agencies identified as being involved with Child Z and her family to a greater or lesser extent:

- six different health services;
- police;
- children's social care;
- housing;
- probation;
- SureStart;
- education and employment service;
- a charity supporting children and families;
- a college;
- housing.

This list alone significantly demonstrates the complexity of people's lives and the number of agencies involved, especially when they are identified as vulnerable. The risks and vulnerabilities identified were: teenaged parents; parents with learning difficulties; offending history; domestic abuse; self-harm; housing; substance misuse; mental health; and engagement with services (p9). Looking at the information provided, some examples of a specific professional focus are evident. One such example is that of the family nurse whose work focused on strengths and positives. The SCR refers to a visit in which Child Z was seen; the recordings reported that *Child Z was feeding well and putting on weight*, there was however *no reference to clutter* (p38). An analysis must be taken in the context of these recordings being based on minimal information and a basic example, but it does raise some questions when applying an organisational theoretical perspective – concerning the focus of the family nurse. The SCR's reference to clutter not being mentioned either suggests that there was no clutter or that it was not observed or deemed to be relevant. Either way, information about the home environment (i.e. concerns regarding social or emotional neglect) was not observed, the focus instead was on the health and physical needs of the child. This suggests, from the perspective of Role Culture, a particular professional focus. This is also evident from children's social care (CSC) services as well, where the report suggests that *[t]here may have been a misunderstanding in CSC about the VBS [Vulnerable Babies Service] being a targeted service which required evidence that a child was at higher risk in order to allocate any resource, being primarily a preventative service aimed at leading on practices that reduced the risk of sudden infant mortality with higher risk children. If the risk factors had been collated and described in a referral to VBS it would probably have resulted in VBS becoming involved* (pp46–7). This suggests that a problem arose and a service was not provided because the referral information from CSC did not meet the requirements of the VBS, possibly because the information provided was not focused on what the health service would consider to be particularly concerning. Again, this is another example of the particular focus of professionals due to working within a Role Culture.

The problem, returning to Glasby (2012), is that the service users and carers that health and social care professionals tend to encounter have *complex, cross-cutting needs, typically* requiring a more coherent and 'joined-up' response from a range of agencies (p73). Perhaps it is therefore time to reconsider the way in which professional courses are taught, so that professionals are joined-up themselves in their holistic views of people, rather than the emphasis being on individual practitioners trying to co-ordinate their different perspectives together. As Glasby (2012) suggests, the faulty assumption is that health and social care can be distinguished.

Activity 20.2

After having read this chapter, how much knowledge on organisational culture do you think you need in order to be an effective social worker? In which areas do you think it is particularly important, if any? What has changed in your thinking?

Chapter Summary

This chapter has set out an understanding of the theoretical perspective of Charles Handy regarding organisational cultures. These four cultures (Power, Role, Task and Person) have all been considered and used to help understand partnership working in social work practice and, indeed, the significant challenges that it faces.

Further Reading

Glasby, J (2012) Understanding Health and Social Care (2nd edition). Bristol: Policy Press.

Hughes, M and Wearing, M (2013) Organisations and Management in Social Work. London: SAGE Publications.

Conclusion

Lesley Deacon and Stephen J Macdonald

This book has offered a unique way of bringing together a number of different theoretical approaches that influence social work practice today. It should be used as an introduction for social work students as well as a prompt and reference book for social work practitioners.

Key theoretical ideas and ideologies have been presented across the disciplines of psychology, sociology, moral philosophies, political theories and organisational theories. Together, these constitute what should be understood as social work theory as by applying these theories to practice the theoretical perspectives have evolved in a paradigm shift. So, for example, rather than being psychological or sociological they become social work theories. The range of theories, and the depth to which they have been considered, have been written to recognise the complexities of the original theories, while aimed at introducing key concepts. There is no substitute, however, for further reading and it is anticipated that the reader now has the building blocks of knowledge in order to understand social work theory in a more confident manner while reflecting its complexity.

As social work practitioners we are constantly confronted with such complex situations that are often difficult to understand or respond to. Theory, which is underpinned by research, allows us to address these – to give us different ways to conceptualise the situation. Without theory practitioners may just refer to policy, which is politically influenced and constantly in flux. As demonstrated in the chapters on Moral Philosophies, the implementation of policy can in fact lead to discriminatory practice if not fully understood. Theory gives us a bedrock from which we can refer back to, as it developed over a considerable period of time and is rooted within evidence-based research.

As social work has developed there has been a significant focus on multi-agency working and these different professions work within different theoretical frameworks. This book can help students and social work practitioners to understand that differing focus through their acquired knowledge of different theoretical paradigms. For example, the psychology chapters demonstrate a particular focus for psychologists on individual agency. This is also evident in the chapters on Organisational Theories.

As suggested, this is a book for practice and not just university. It should be viewed as a Toolkit to refer back to, to remind social work practitioners about the importance of embedding different theoretical perspectives within their practice. The importance is for students and social work practitioners to become more confident in the knowledge they have so that considering different theoretical perspectives within a practice situation becomes more commonplace. This knowledge needs to become a *habit* as theoretical understanding becomes so entrenched in the knowledge of the practitioner.

The use of the SCR of Child Z has been a very carefully considered addition. One of the significant difficulties often identified by social work students has been the ability to apply different theories into practice – to be able to move from the abstract into the real. By using aspects of a real social work situation it is hoped that this will have helped the reader to understand how to think theoretically in practice. While the examples of application in each chapter are relatively simplistic they do demonstrate the beginnings of theoretical application. Again, the intention is to provide the reader with the building blocks of knowledge in the application of theory in social work practice.

As a final point, we would like to say something directly to students and social work practitioners. You need to not be afraid of theory and instead you need to embrace it as a natural part of your social work practice. Do not think of theories as abstract concepts but as different lenses through which to view human interaction and social situations that you encounter in practice. You should not think that you do not need to pick up a textbook again just because you have finished your degree; in fact, refreshing knowledge and keeping up to date with current changes through research is absolutely imperative in order to ensure best practice and fairness for service users and carers.

References

Akhtar, F (2012) *Mastering Social Work Values and Ethics*. London: Jessica Kingsley Publishers.

Aldgate, J, Healy, L, Malcolm, B, Pine, B, Rose, W and Seden, J (2007) *Enhancing Social Work Management*. London: Jessica Kingsley Publishers.

Anscombe, GEM (1958) Modern moral philosophy. *Journal of Philosophy*, 33 (124).

Archer, MS (2000) *Being Human: The Problem of Agency*. Cambridge: Cambridge University Press.

Archer, MS (2003) *Structure, Agency and the Internal Conversation*. Cambridge: Cambridge University Press.

Bailey, M and Brake, R (1975) *Radical Social Work*. London: Hodder and Stoughton.

Bailey, M and Brake, R (eds) (1980) 'Contributions to a Radical Practice in Social Work' in M Brake and R Bailey, *Radical Social Work Practice*. London: Edward Arnold.

Bandura, A (1977) *Social Learning Theory*. Englewood Cliffs, NJ: Prentice Hall.

Bandura, A (1986) *Social Foundations of Thought and Action: A Social Cognitive Theory*. Englewood Cliffs, NJ: Prentice-Hall.

Bandura, A, Ross, D and Ross, SA (1961) Transmission of aggression through the imitation of aggressive models. *Journal of Abnormal and Social Psychology*, 63: 575–82.

Banks, S (2004) *Ethics, Accountability and the Social Professions*. Basingstoke: Palgrave Macmillan.

Banks, S (2006) *Ethics and Values in Social Work* (3rd edition). Basingstoke: Palgrave Macmillan.

Banks, S (2012) *Ethics and Values in Social Work* (4th edition). Basingstoke: Palgrave Macmillan.

Banks, S and Gallagher, A (2009) *Ethics in Professional Life*. Basingstoke: Palgrave Macmillan.

Bartoli, A (2013) *Anti-Racism in Social Work Practice*. St Albans: Critical Publishing.

BASW (2012) *The Code of Ethics for Social Work: A Statement of Principles*. London: BASW.

Bauer A, Wistow, G, Dixon, J and Knapp, M (2015) Investing in advocacy for **parents** with learning disabilities: What is the economic argument?' *British Journal of Learning Disabilities*, 43(1): 66–74.

Baujard, A (2010) Collective and individual interest in Bentham's Felicific Calculus. *European Journal of the History of Economic Thought*, 17(4): 607–34.

Beauman, KB (1996) *Women and the Settlement Movement*. London: Radcliffe Press.

Beckett, C and Maynard, A (2013) *Values and Ethics in Social Work*. London: SAGE Publications.

Beckett, C and Taylor, H (2010) *Human Growth and Development*. London: SAGE Publications.

Bell, M, Shaw, I, Sinclair, I, Sloper, P and Rafferty, J (2007) The Integrated Children's System: An Evaluation of the Practice, Process and Consequences of the ICS in Councils with

Social Services Responsibilities. Report for the Department for Education and Skills, Welsh Assembly Government.

Bensons, HH (1997) 'Socrates and the Beginnings of Moral Philosophy' in CCW Taylor (ed.), *From the Beginning to Plato*. London: Routledge.

Bentham, J 1988 [1789] *The Principles of Morals and Legislation*. New York: Prometheus Books.

Berger, PL, and Luckmann, T (1967) *The social construction of reality: a treatise in the sociology of knowledge*. Garden City, N.Y.: Doubleday.

Besthorn, FH (2013) 'Ecological Approach' in Gray, M and Webb, SA (2013) *Social Work Theories and Methods* (2nd edition). London: Sage.

Biestek, F (1957) *The Casework Principle*. Chicago: Loyola Press.

Biestek, FP (1961) *The Casework Relationship*. London: Allen and Unwin.

Bilton, T, Bonnett, K and Jones, P (2002) *Introductory Sociology* (4th edition). London: Palgrave Macmillan.

Bourdieu, P and Wacquant, LJD (1992) *An Invitation to Reflexive Sociology*. Chicago: The University of Chicago Press.

Bowlby, J (1965) *Childcare and the Growth of Love* (2nd edition). Harmondsworth: Pelican Books.

Bowlby, J (1969) *Attachment and Loss, Vol. I: Attachment*. New York: Basic Books.

Bowles, W, Collingbridge, M, Curry, S. and Valentine, B. (2006) *Ethical Practice in Social Work: An Applied Approach*. Milton Keynes: OUP.

Brake, M and Bailey, R (eds) (1980) *Radical Social Work and Practice*. London: Edward Arnold.

Bronfenbrenner, U (1979) *The Ecology of Human Development: Experiments by Nature and Design*. Cambridge: MA. Available online at: https://en.wikipedia.org/wiki/Harvard_University_Press"Harvard University Press.

Bruce Douglass, R (2012) John Rawls and the revival of political philosophy: Where does he leave us? *Theoria: A Journal of Social & Political Theory*, December.

Burke, B and Harrison, P (2002) 'Anti-Oppressive Practice' in R Adams, L Dominelli and M Payne (eds) *Social Work: Themes, Issues and Critical Debates* (2nd edition). Basingstoke: Palgrave.

Burkitt, I (2012) Emotional reflexivity: Feeling emotion and imagination in reflexive dialogues. *Sociology*, 46(3): 458–72.

Burns, L and Dallos, R (2014) Guide to Applying Systemic Practice in Social Work. Guides. Community Care Inform [online] http://www.ccinform.co.uk/guides/guide-applying-systemic-practice-social-work/ (accessed 22 July 2016)

Burns, JH and Hart, LHA (1996) *The Collected Works of Jeremy Bentham: An Introduction to the Principles and Morals of Legislation*. Oxford: Oxford University Press.

Burns, L and Dallos, R (2014) *Guide to applying systemic practice in social work*. Community Care Inform.

Burr, V (2003) *Social Constructionism* (2nd edition). Hove: Routledge.

Burr, V (2015) *Social Constructionism* (3rd edition). Hove: Routledge.

Butler, J (1990) *Gender Trouble: Feminism and the Subversion of Identity*. New York: Routledge.

Calhoun, C, Gerteis, J, Moody, J, Pfaff, S, and Virk, I, (eds) (2007) *Classical Sociological Theory* (2nd edition). Oxford: Blackwell Publishing.

Callaghan, J and Lazard, L (2011) *Social Psychology*. Exeter: Learning Matters.

Cameron, C (2011) Not our problem: Impairment as difference, disability as role. *Journal of Inclusive Practice in Further and Higher Education*, 3 (2): 10–25.

Carson, D and Bain, A (2008) *Professional Risk and Working with People: Decision-Making in Health, Social Care and Criminal Justice*. London: Jessica Kingsley Publishers.

Children Act 1989. London: HMSO.

Chow, AYM, Lam, DOB, Leung, DSM, Wong, DFK and Chan, BFP (2011) Promoting reflexivity among social work students: The development and evaluation of a programme. *Social Work Education*, 30(2): 141–56.

Clifford, D (2014) Limitations of virtue ethics in the social professions. *Ethics and Social Welfare*, 8(1): 2 –19.

Clifford, D and Burke, D (2009) *Anti-Oppressive Ethics and Values in Social Work*. Basingstoke: Palgrave Macmillan.

Cole, GA and Kelly, P (2011) *Management Theory and Practice*. Andover: Cengage Learning.

Collingwood, P, Emond, R and Woodward, R (2008) The Theory Circle: A tool for learning and practice. *Social Work Education*, 27(1): 70–83.

Connell, R (2009) *Gender: In World Perspective*. Cambridge: Polity Press.

Corker, M (1999) Differences, conflations and foundations: The limits to 'accurate' theoretical representation of disabled people's experience? *Disability and Society*, 14(5): 627–42.

Corker, M and French, S (1999) *Disability Discourse*. Buckingham: Open University Press.

Crawford, K and Walker, J (2010) *Social Work and Human Development* (3rd edition). Exeter: Learning Matters.

Crenshaw, K (1989) 'Demarginalizing the Intersection of Race and Sex: A Black Feminist Critique of Antidiscrimination Doctrine, Feminist Theory and Antiracist Politics' in *University of Chicago Legal Forum*, Vol 1.

Crow, L (1996) 'Including all of our Lives: Renewing the Social Model of Disability' in C Barnes and G Mercer (eds) *Exploring the Divide* (pp55–72). Leeds: The Disability Press.

CWDC (2009) *The Common Assessment Framework for Children and Young People: A Guide for Practitioners*. Leeds: CWDC.

D'Cruz, H, Gillingham, P and Melendez, S (2007) Reflexivity, its meanings and relevance for social work: A critical review of the literature. *British Journal of Social Work*, 37: 73–90.

Davies, L (2012) Lone parents: Unemployed or otherwise engaged? *People, Place and Policy Online*, 6(1): 16–28.

Deacon, L (2015) *Children's Social Care Services' Response to Children who display Sexually Harmful Behaviour.* PhD, Durham University. http://etheses.dur.ac.uk/10969/

Department for Education (2014) *Knowledge and Skills Statement for Approved Child and Family Practitioners.* Available online at: www.gov.uk/government/uploads/system/uploads/attachment_data/file/524743/Knowledge_and_skills_statement_for_approved_child_and_family_practitioners.pdf

Department for Education (2015) SFR 41/2015: *Characteristics of Children in Need: 2014 to 2015,* Crown Copyright.

Department of Health (1999) *Patient and Public Involvement in the NHS.* London: DoH.

Department of Health (2000) *Framework for the Assessment of Children in Need and their Families.* London: TSO.

Department of Health (2000a) *The NHS Plan: A Plan for Investment, A Plan for Reform.* London: DoH.

Department of Health (2000b) *A Quality Strategy for Social Care.* London: DoH.

Department of Health (2010) *A Vision for Adult Social Care: Capable Communities and Active Citizens.* London: DoH.

Department of Health (2015) *Knowledge and Skills Statement for Social Workers in Adult Services.* Available online at: www.gov.uk/government/uploads/system/uploads/attachment_data/file/411957/KSS.pdf

Dominelli, L (1988) *Anti-Racist Social Work.* Basingstoke: Palgrave Macmillan.

Dominelli, L (2002) *Anti-Oppressive Social Work Theory and Practice.* Basingstoke: Palgrave Macmillan.

Dominelli, L (2005) 'Social Work Research: Contested Knowledge for Practice' in R Adams, L Dominelli and M Payne, *Social Work Futures: Crossing Boundaries, Transforming Practice.* Basingstoke: Palgrave Macmillan.

Donaldson, LP and Mayer, LM (2014) Justice as a core virtue for social work practice. *Social Work and Christianity,* 41(2/3): 207–31.

Donovan, C and Griffiths, S (2013) Domestic violence and voluntary perpetrator programmes: Engaging men in the pre-commencement phase. *British Journal of Social Work,* 1–17.

Dracopoulou, S (2015) 'Major Trends in Applied Ethics, Including Ethics of Social Work' in L Bell and T Hafford-Letchfield, *Ethics, Values and Social Work Practice.* Maidenhead: Open University Press.

Dunk-West, P (2014) 'Social Work Identity, Power and Self-hood: A Re-imagining' in C Cocker and T Hafford-Letchfield, *Rethinking Anti-Discriminatory & Anti-Oppressive Theories for Social Work Practice.* Basingstoke: Palgrave Macmillan.

Dyke, C (2016) *Writing Analytical Assessments.* Northwich: Critical Publishing Ltd.

Elder-Vass, D (2012) *The Construction of Social Reality.* Cambridge: Cambridge University Press.

Engel, G (1977) The need for a new medical model: a challenge to biomedicine. *Science,* 196: 129–36.

Erikson, EH (1964). *Insight and Responsibility.* New York: Norton.

Erikson, EH (1995 [1950]) *Childhood and Society.* London: Vintage Books.

Evans, D and Kearney, J (1996) *Working in Social Care: a systemic approach*. Aldershot: Ashgate Publishing Limited.

Featherstone, B (2009) *Contemporary Fathering: Theory, Policy and Practice*. Bristol: University of Bristol Press.

Featherstone, B (2010) 'Ethics of Care' in M Gray and SA Webb, *Ethics and Value Perspectives in Social Work*. Basingstoke: Palgrave Macmillan.

Featherstone, B, Broadhurst, K and Holt, K (2012) Thinking systematically – thinking politically: Building strong partnerships with children and families in the context of rising inequality. *British Journal of Social Work*, 42: 618–33.

Ferguson, I and Woodward, R (2009) *Radical Social Work in Practice: Making a Difference*. Bristol: Policy Press.

Fernando, S (2010) *Mental Health, Race and Culture* (3rd edition). Basingstoke: Palgrave Macmillan.

Fook, J (2000) 'Deconstructing and reconstructing professional expertise', in Fawcett, B, Featherstone, B, Fook, J and Rossiter, A (eds.), *Practice and Research in Social Work: Postmodern Feminist Perspectives*. London: Routledge.

Fook, J (2002) *Social Work: Critical Theory and Practice*. London: SAGE Publications.

Fook, J, Ryan, M and Hawkins, L (1996) 'Expertise in social work practice: An exploratory study', *Canadian Social Work Review*.

Fook, J, Ryan, M and Hawkins, L (1997) 'Towards a theory of social work expertise', *British Journal of Social Work* 27(2): 399–417.

Freud, A (1916) *General Introduction to Psychoanalysis*. London: Sheba Blake Publishers.

Freud, A (1936) *The Ego and the Mechanisms of Defence*. London: Karnac Books.

Freud, S (1953) 'Three Essays on the Theory of Sexuality' in J Strachey (Ed. and Trans.) *The Standard Edition of the Complete Psychological Works of Sigmund Freud* (Vol. 7, pp125–245). London: Hogarth Press. (Original work published 1905).

Freud, S (1961) 'The Ego and the Id' in J Strachey (Ed. and Trans.) *The Standard Edition of the Complete Psychological Works of Sigmund Freud* (Vol. 19, pp3–66). London: Hogarth Press. (Original work published 1923).

Galvani, S, Dance, C and Hutchinson, A (2013) Substance use training experiences and needs: Findings from a national survey of social care professionals in England. *Social Work Education*, 32(7): 888–905.

Gazeley, I, Newell, A, Reynolds, K and Searle, R (2014) The poor and the poorest, fifty years on. *IZA Discussion Paper Series*, 7909.

Gergen, K (1999) *An Invitation to Social Construction*. London: Sage.

Germain, C (1979) *Social work Practice; People and Environments*. New York: Columbia University Press.

Gibbs, J (2009) Changing the cultural story in child protection: Learning from the insiders' experience. *Child and Family Social Work*, 14(3): 289–99.

Giddens, A (1991) *Modernity and Self-identity: Self and Society in the Late Modern Age,* cited in I Burkitt (2012) Emotional reflexivity: Emotion and imagination in reflexive dialogues. *Sociology,* 46(3): 458–72.

Gilligan, C (1982) *In a Different Voice.* Cambridge, MA: Harvard University Press.

Gitterman, A and Germain, CB (1996) *The Life Model of Social Work Practice; Advances in Theory and Practice* (2nd edition). New York: Columbia University Press.

Gitterman, A and Germain, CB (2008) *The Life Model of Social Work Practice: Advances in Theory and Practice* (3rd edition). New York: Columbia University Press.

Gitterman, A and Heller, N (2011) Integrating social work perspectives and models with concepts, methods and skills with other professions' specialized approaches. *Clinical Social Work Journal,* 39 (2): 204–11.

Glasby, J (2007) *Understanding Health and Social Care.* Bristol: Policy Press.

Glasby, J (2012) *Understanding Health and Social Care.* Second edition. Bristol: Policy Press.

Goldstein, H (1973) *Social Work Practice: a Unitary Approach.* Columbia: University of South Carolina Press.

Gouldner, A (1970) *The Coming Crisis of Western Sociology.* New York: Basic Books, Inc.

Gray, I (2010) 'Managing Change and Developing the Team and the Organisation; with a contribution from Liz (person who uses service)' in I Gray, I, R Field, and K Brown, *Effective Leadership, Management and Supervision in Health and Social Care.* Exeter: Learning Matters.

Gray, M (2010) Moral sources and emergent ethical theories in social work. *British Journal of Social Work,* 40: 1794 –811.

Gray, M and Webb, SA (2009) *Social Work Theories and Methods.* London: Sage.

Gray, M and Webb, SA (2010) 'Introduction: Ethics and Value Perspectives in Social Work' in M Gray and SA Webb, *Ethics and Value Perspectives in Social Work.* Basingstoke: Palgrave Macmillan.

Gray, M and Webb, SA (2013) 'Introduction' in M Gray and SA Webb, *Social Work Theories and Methods* (2nd edition). London: SAGE Publications.

Griffiths, R (1988) *Community Care: Agenda for Action.* London: HMSO.

Gross, R (2015) *Psychology: The Science of Mind and Behaviour* (7th edition). London: Hodder Education.

Gyngell, C (2015) 'The case for genetically engineered babies'. *Guardian.*

Hafford-Letchfield, T (2009) *Management and Organisations in Social Work.* Exeter: Learning Matters.

Handy, C (1976) *Understanding Organizations.* London: Penguin.

Haslanger, S (2016) What is a social (structural) explanation? *Philosophical Studies,* 173(1): 113–30.

Healey, K (2005) *Social Work Theories in Context Creating Frameworks for Practice.* Basingstoke: Palgrave Macmillan.

Health and Care Professions Council (HCPC) (2012) *Standards of Proficiency – Social Workers in England.* London: HCPC.

Health and Care Professions Council (HCPC) (2016) *Standards of Conduct, Performance and Ethics.* London: HCPC.

Heffernan, K (2006) Social work, new public management and the language of the 'service user'. *British Journal of Social Work,* 36(1): 139–47.

Hester, M (2011) The three planet model: Towards an understanding of contradictions in approaches to women and children's safety in contexts of domestic violence. *British Journal of Social Work,* pp837–53.

Hill Jr, TE (2005) Assessing moral rules: Utilitarian and Kantian perspectives. *Philosophical Issues,* 15: 158–78.

HMG (2015) *Working Together to Safeguard Children.*

Hollis, F (1977) 'Social casework: the psychosocial approach', in JB Turner (ed.) *Encyclopaedia of Social Work* (17th edition). Washington, DC:NASW.

Horner, N. (2013) *What is Social Work?* Exeter: Learning Matters.

Horwath, J. (2007) The missing assessment domain: Practitioner subjectivity when identifying and referring child neglect. *British Journal of Social Work,* 37: 1285–303.

Howe, D (2009) *A Brief Introduction to Social Work Theory.* Basingstoke: Palgrave Macmillan.

Howe, D (2011) *Attachment Across the Lifecourse: A Brief Introduction.* London: Palgrave.

Hughes, M and Wearing, M (2013) *Organisations and Management in Social Work.* London: SAGE Publications.

Hutchison, ED and Charlesworth, LW 'Theoretical Perspectives on Human Behavior' (2003) in Hutchison, ED (ed.) *Essentials of Human Behavior: Integrating Person, Environment and the life Course. Thousand Oaks: Sage, 34-69.*

Ixer, G (1999) There's no such thing as reflection. *British Journal of Social Work,* 29(4): 513–27.

Jackson, S and Scott, S (2010) *Theorising Sexuality.* Milton Keynes: Open University Press.

Jones, P (2002) *Introducing Social Theory.* Cambridge: Polity Press.

Jung, CG (1921/1971) *Psychological Types: Collected works of C. G. Jung, volume 6.* Bollingen Series XX. Princeton, NJ: Princeton University Press.

Kaminitz, SC (2014) JS Mill and the value of utility. *History of Political Economy,* 46(2): 231–46.

Kandel, DB, Yamaguchi, K and Klein, LC (2006) Testing the gateway hypothesis. *Addiction,* 101(4): 470–2.

Kant, I (1785) *Fundamental Principles of the Metaphysics of Morals* (Trans. T.K. Abbott).

Kant, I (1800) *The Metaphysics of Morals.* (Trans. M. Gregor) Cambridge: Cambridge University Press.

Karban, K (2011) *Social Work and Mental Health.* Cambridge: Polity Press.

Keddell, E (2014) 'Theorizing the Signs of Safety Approach: positioning codes and power'. *Children and Youth Services Review* 47(1):70-7.

King, S and Timmins, G (2001) *Making Sense of the Industrial Revolution: English Economy and Society 1700–1850.* Manchester: Manchester University Press.

Klein, M (1932) *The Psycho-analysis of Children.* London: Hogarth Press.

Knott, C and Scragg, T (2013) *Reflective Practice in Social Work.* Exeter: Learning Matters.

Kohlberg, L (1963) The development of children's orientations toward a moral order. I. Sequence in the development of moral thought. *Vita Humana,* 6 (1): 11–33.

Koprowska, J (2014) *Communication and Interpersonal Skills in Social Work.* (4th edition). London: Sage/Learning Matters.

Lacan, Jacques (1992) *The Seminar of Jacques Lacan, Book VII: The Ethics of Psychoanalysis* (trans. Dennis Porter). New York: Norton.

Lam, CM, Wong, H and Leung, TTF (2007) An unfinished reflexive journey: Social work students' reflection on their placement experiences. *British Journal of Social Work,* 37: 91–105.

Langan, M (1985) 'The Unitary Approach: A Feminist Critique' in Brook, E and Davis, A (eds) *Women, the Family and Social Work.* London: Tavistock.

Langam, M (1992) 'Women and Social Work in the 1990s' in M Langam and L Day (eds) *Women, Oppression and Social Work. Issues in Anti-Discriminatory Practice.* London: Routledge.

Latting, J (1995) Postmodern Feminist Theory and Social Work: A Deconstruction. *Social Work,* 40(6): 831–3.

Lavalette, M (ed.) (2011) *Radical Social Work Today: Social Work at the Crossroads.* Bristol: Polity Press.

Lieb, R (2015) 'Epidemiological Perspectives on Comorbidity between Substance Use Disorders and Other Mental Disorders' in G Dom and F Moggi (eds) *Co-ocurring Addictive and Psychiatric Disorders: A Practice-based Handbook from a European Perspective.* New York: Springer.

Lovell, RJ (2015) 'Nine Reasons to Become a Social Worker in 2015', *the Guardian,* supported by Skills for Care.

Marx, K and Engels, F (2004[1848]) *The Communist Manifesto* (A. Blunden, English Edition). Marxists Internet Archive (marxists.org).

Maslow, AH (1943) A theory of human motivation. *Psychological Review, 50(4):* 370–96.

Maslow, AH (1970) *Motivation and Personality.* New York: Harper & Row.

McAuliffe, D (2010) in M Gray and SA Webb, *Ethics and Value Perspectives in Social Work.* Basingstoke: Palgrave Macmillan.

McKeown, K (2000) *A Guide to What Works in Family Support Services for Vulnerable Families.* Dublin: Department for Health and Children.

Mead, GH (1934) *Mind, Self and Society.* London: University of Chicago Press.

Meyer, CH *Assessment in Social Work Practice.* New York: Columbia University Press.

Mill, JS (1863) *Utilitarianism.* London: Parker, Son and Bourn.

(Public domain text: http://www.utilitarianism.com/mill1.htm)

Mill, JS (1972) *Three Essays: Utilitarianism, On Liberty, and Considerations on Representative Government.* London: Dent.

Miller, GA (1956) The magical number seven, plus or minus two: Some limits on our capacity for processing information. *Psychological Review, 63* (2): 81–97.

Morley, C and Macfarlane, S (2012) The nexus between feminism and postmodernism: Still a central concern for critical social work. *British Journal of Social Work, 42:* 687–705.

Morrison, T (2010) in J. Horwath (ed.) *The Child's World: The Comprehensive Guide to Assessing Children in Need* (2nd edition). London: Jessica Kingsley Publishers.

Munro, E (2011) *The Munro Review of Child Protection – Final Report: A Child-centred System.* London: DfES.

Myers, JEB (2005) *Myers on Child, Domestic and Elder Abuse Cases.* New York: Aspen Publishers.

Nevid, JS (2012) *Essentials of Psychology: Concepts and Applications.* Canada: Cengage.

Newman, BM and Newman PR (2016) *Theories of Human Development.* New York: Psychology Press.

Nicolson, P (2014) *A Critical Approach to Human Growth and Development.* Basingstoke: Palgrave Macmillan.

Nicolson, P and Bayne, R (2014) *Psychology for Social Work Theory and Practice.* Basingstoke: Palgrave Macmillan.

Nicolson, P, Bayne, R and Owen, J (2006) *Applied Psychology for Social Workers.* Basingstoke: Palgrave Macmillan.

O'Sullivan, T (2011) *Decision Making in Social Work.* Basingstoke: Palgrave Macmillan.

Oakley, A (1993) [1972] *Sex, Gender and Society.* Aldershot: Arena.

Okitikpi, T and Aymer, C (2010) *Key Concepts in Anti-Discriminatory Social Work.* London: SAGE Publications.

Oko, J (2011) *Understanding and Using Theory in Social Work.* Exeter: Learning Matters.

Oliver, M (1993) *What's So Wonderful About Walking?* Disability Achieves: Leeds.

Oliver, M (1996) *Understanding Disability from Theory to Practice.* Basingstoke: Palgrave.

Parrish, M (2014) *Social Work Perspectives on Human Behaviour.* Maidenhead: McGraw-Hill.

Parrott, L (2014) *Values and Ethics in Social Work Practice.* London: Learning Matters.

Parsons, T (1961) 'An Outline of the Social System' in Calhoun, C, Gerteis, J, Moody, J, Pfaff, S and Virk, I (eds) (2007) *Classical Sociological Theory* (2nd edition). Oxford: Blackwell Publishing.

Parton, N (1997) *Child Protection and Family Support: Tensions, Contradictions and Possibilities.* London: Routledge.

Parton, N (2003) Rethinking Professional Practice: The contributions of Social Constructionism and the Feminist 'Ethics of Care'. *British Journal of Social Work.* 33:1-16.

Parton, N (2011) 'Child Protection and Safeguarding in England: Changing and Competing Conceptions of Risk and their Implications for Social Work'. *British Journal of Social Work.* 41(5):854-73.

Parton, N and O'Byrne, P (2000) *Constructive Social Work: Towards New Practice.* Basingstoke: Macmillan Press Ltd.

Pavlov, IP (1910) *The Work of the Digestive Glands*. Exeter: Charles Griffin and Company.

Payne, M (2002) 'Social Work Theories and Reflective Practice' in R Adams, L Dominelli and M Payne (eds) *Social Work: Themes, Issues and Critical Debates* (2nd edition). Basingstoke: Palgrave Macmillan.

Payne, M (2005) 'Social Work Processes' in R Adams, L Dominelli and M Payne, *Social Work Futures: Crossing Boundaries, Transforming Practice.* Basingstoke: Palgrave Macmillan.

Payne, M (2014) *Modern Social Work Theory* (4th edition). Basingstoke: Palgrave Macmillan.

Petersen, AC and Olsson, JI (2015) 'Calling Evidence-based Practice into Question: Acknowledging Phronetic Knowledge in Social Work'. *British Journal of Social Work*. 45(5):1581-97.

Phillips, R and Cree, V (2014) What does the 'fourth wave' mean for teaching feminism in twenty-first century social work? *Social Work Education*, 33(7): 930–43.

Piaget, J (1957) *Construction of Reality in the Child*. London: Routledge & Kegan Paul.

Piaget, J (1958) The growth of logical thinking from childhood to adolescence. *AMC*, 10, 12.

Piaget, J and Cook, MT (1952) *The Origins of Intelligence in Children*. New York, NY: International University Press.

Pincus, A and Minahan, A (1973) *Social Work Practice: Model and Method*. Itarca, Illionois: F.E. Peacock.

Pullen-Sansfacon, A (2010) Virtue ethics for social work: A new pedagogy for practical reasoning. *Social Work Education*, 29(4): 402–15.

Rahman, M and Jackson, S (2010) *Gender and Sexuality*. Bristol: Polity Press.

Rawls, J (1971) *A Theory of Justice*. Cambridge, MA: Harvard University Press.

Rawls, J (1985) Political liberalism. *Journal of Philosophy*, September.

Regier, DA, Farmer, ME, Rae, DS, Locke, BZ, Keith, SJ, Judd, LL and Goodwin, FK (1990) Comorbidity of mental disorders with alcohol and other drug abuse. Results from the Epidemiologic Catchment Area (ECA) Study. *JAMA*. 21; 264(19): 2511-30.

Robson, D (2014) Moral regret in mental health social work. *Ethics and Social Welfare*, 8(1): 86–92.

Rogers, C (1951) *Client-centred Therapy: Its Current Practice, Implications and Theory*. London: Constable.

Rogers, C (1959) 'A Theory of Therapy, Personality and Interpersonal Relationships as Developed in the Client-centered Framework' in S Koch (ed.), *Psychology: A study of a science. Vol. 3: Formulations of the person and the social context*. New York: McGraw Hill.

Rogers, CR (1961) *On Becoming a Person: A Psychotherapist's View of Psychotherapy*. Boston, MA: Houghton Mifflin.

Rojek, C, Peacock, G and Collins, S (1988) *Social Work and Received Ideas*. London: Routledge.

Rose, I and Hanssen, D (2010) The feminist perspective and social work education. *The Journal of Baccalaureate Social Work*, 15(1): 1–13.

Rosen, F (1996) 'Introduction' in JH Burns and LHA Hart, *The Collected Works of Jeremy Bentham: An Introduction to the Principles and Morals of Legislation*. Oxford: Oxford University Press.

Rosenthal, DA and Keys, D (2005) Young people, drug use and family conflict: Pathways into homelessness. *Journal of Adolescence,* 28 (0): 185–99.

Ross, S and Bilson, A (1989) *Social Work Management and Practice: Systems Principles,* London: Jessica Kingsley.

Salkind, NJ (2004) *An Introduction to Theories of Human Development.* London: SAGE Publications.

Schön, DA (1983) *The Reflective Practitioner: How Professionals Think in Action.* New York: Basic Books.

SCIE (2008) *Workforce Development: The Learning, Teaching and Assessment of Partnership Work in Social Work Education.* London: SCIE.

SCIE (2012) *SCIE Guide 1: Managing Practice.* London: SCIE.

Secades-Villa, R, Garcia-Rodriguez, O, Jin, CJ and Wang, S (2015) Probability predictors of the cannabis gateway effect: A national study. *International Journal of Drug Policy,* 26(2): 135–42.

Semple, D, Smyth, R, Burns, J, Darjee, R and McIntosh, A (2013) *Oxford Handbook of Psychiatry* (2nd editon). Oxford: Oxford University Press.

Shafritz, JM, Ott, J and Yang, YS (2015) *Classics of Organizational Theory.* Andover: Cengage Learning.
Shakespeare, T (2013). *Disability Rights and Wrongs* (2nd edition). London: Routledge.

Shakespeare, T (2015) *Disability Research Today.* Routledge: London.

Shakespeare, T, Watson, N and Abu Alghaib, O (2016) Blaming the victim, all over again: Waddell and Aylward's biopsychosocial (BPS) model of disability. *Critical Social Policy,* 36 (4): 1–20.

Shakespeare, T and Watson, N (2001) 'The Social Model of Disability: An Outdated Ideology?' in SN Barnartt and BM Altman (eds) *Exploring Theories and Expanding Methodologies: Where We Are and Where We Need To Go* (pp9–28). London: JAI.

Sheppard, M (1998) Practice validity, reflexivity and knowledge for social work. *British Journal of Social Work,* 28: 763–81.

Sheppard, M (2006) *Social Work and Social Exclusion: The Idea of Practice.* Aldershot: Ashgate Publishing Limited.

Skinner, BF (1938) *The Behavior of Organisms: An Experimental Analysis.* New York: Appleton-Century.

Skinner, BF (1948) 'Superstition' in the pigeon. *Journal of Experimental Psychology, 38:* 168–72.

Skinner, BF (1953) *Science and Human Behavior.* New York: Simon and Schuster.

Skinner, BF (1985) Cognitive science and behaviourism. *British Journal of Psychology,* 76: 291–301.

Smith, R (2008) *Social Work and Power.* Basingstoke: Palgrave Macmillan.

Solas, J (2008) Social work and social justice: What are we fighting for? *Australian Social Work,* 61(2): 124–36.

Statman, D (1997) *Virtue Ethics.* Georgetown: Georgetown University Press.

Swain, J and French, S (2000). Towards an Affirmation Model. *Disability and Society* 15(4): 569-82.

Taylor, C and White, S (2000) *Practising Reflexivity in Health and Welfare: Making Knowledge.* Buckingham: Open University Press.

Taylor, H, Stuttaford, M, Broad, B and Vostanis, P (2006) Why a 'roof' is not enough: The characteristics of young homeless people referred to a designated mental health service. *Journal of Mental Health,* 15(4): 491–501.

Teater, B (2010) *An Introduction to Applying Social Work Theories and Methods.* Maidenhead: Open University Press.

Teater, B (2014) *Applying Social Work Theories and Methods* (2nd edition). Maidenhead: Open University Press McGraw-Hill Education.

Thomas, C (2007) *Sociologies of Disability and Illness.* Basingstoke: Palgrave Macmillan.

Thompson, N (2006) *Anti-discriminatory Practice* (4th edition). Basingstoke: Palgrave Macmillan.

Thompson, N (2010) *Theorising Social Work Practice.* Basingstoke: Palgrave Macmillan.

Thompson, N (2011) *Promoting Equality: Working with Diversity and Difference.* Basingstoke: Palgrave Macmillan.

Thompson, N (2012)) *Anti-discriminatory Practice* (5th edition). Basingstoke: Palgrave Macmillan.

Thompson, N (2015) *Understanding Social Work: Preparing for Practice.* Basingstoke: Palgrave Macmillan.

Townsend, P and Abel-Smith, B (1966) *The Poor and the Poorest.* Occasional Papers in Social Administration. London: Bedford Square Press.

Trevithick, P (2012) *Social Work Skills and Knowledge: A Practice Handbook.* (3rd edition). Maidenhead: Open University.

Tronto, J (1993) *Moral Boundaries: A Political Argument for an Ethics of Care.* New York: Routledge.

Tuffrey, B (2010) *The Human Cost: How the Lack of Affordable Housing Impacts on All Aspects of Life.* London: Shelter.

Walby, S (1997) *Gender Transformations.* London: Routledge.

Walby, S (2007) Complexity theory, systems theory, and multiple intersecting social inequalities. *Philosophy of the Social Sciences,* 37: 449–70.

Warwick-Booth, L (2013) *Social Inequality.* London: SAGE Publications.

Wastell, D and White, S (2014) Making sense of complex electronic records: Socio-technical design in social care. *Applied Ergonomics,* 45(2): 143–9.

Watson, JB (1913) Psychology as the behaviorist views it. *Psychological Review, 20:* 158–77.

Watson, JB (1924) *Behaviorism.* New York: People's Institute Publishing Company.

Watson, JB and Rayner, R (1920) Conditioned Emotional Reactions. *Journal of Experimental Psychology, 3(1):* 1–14.

Webb, S (2010) 'Virtue Ethics' in M Gray and SA Webb, *Ethics and Value Perspectives in Social Work.* Basingstoke: Palgrave Macmillan.

Weinbach, R (2008) *The Social Worker as Manager: A Practical Guide to Success* (5th edition). Boston, MA: Pearson.

White, P (ed) (2005) *Biopsychosocial Medicine.* Oxford: Oxford University Press.

Whitham, G (2012) *Challenging 12 Myths and Stereotypes about Low Income Families and Social Security Spending.* London: Save the Children.

Whiting, R (2010) 'Christianity and Ethics' in M Gray and SA Webb (eds) *Ethics and Value Perspectives in Social Work.* Basingstoke: Palgrave Macmillan.

Wilkins, G and Boahen, D (2013) *Critical Analysis Skills for Social Workers.* Maidenhead: Open University Press McGraw-Hill Education.

Woolfall, K and Sumnall, H (2010) Evaluating interventions for children of substance using parents: A review of outcome measures. *Addiction Research and Theory,* June 2010; 18(3): 326–43.

Wright Mills, C (1959) *The Sociological Imagination.* New York: Oxford University Press Inc.

Websites

Manchester Safeguarding Children's Board, Child Z, September 2013 http://www.manchester scb.org.uk/prof-scr.asp

Downloaded and used throughout the book as a case example.

Regus website – regus.co.uk – accessed 15 June 2016. Regus arranges for office spaces at Doxford International Business Park to be rented out.

Reed website – reed.co.uk – accessed 15 June 2016. Reed is a recruitment company.

International Federation of Social Workers (2014) *Definition*

http://ifsw.org/ (accessed 2 March 2016)

International Federation of Social Workers (IFSW) *Ethical Principles*

http://ifsw.org/policies/statement-of-ethical-principles/ (accessed 12 July 2016)

NHS website http://www.nhs.uk/conditions/pregnancy-and-baby/pages/smoking-pregnant.aspx (accessed 26 May 2016)

NHS Birth to Five website http://www.nhs.uk/Tools/Pages/birthtofive.aspx (accessed 18 July 2016)

ONS data http://www.ons.gov.uk/peoplepopulationandcommunity/birthsdeathsandmarriages/livebirths/bulletins/livebirthsinenglandandwalesbycharacteristicsofmother1/2014-10-16 (accessed 18 July 2016)

'*Reflexive, adj. and n.*'. Online: http://www.oed.com/view/Entry/160948 (accessed 8 May 2016)

Index